Pragmatism and the Pro

EDITED BY BILL E. LAWSON
AND DONALD F. KOCH

Pragmatism and the Problem of Race

INDIANA UNIVERSITY PRESS
Bloomington and Indianapolis

Publication of this book is made possible in part with the assistance of a Challenge Grant from the National Endowment for the Humanities, a federal agency that supports research, education, and public programming in the humanities.

This book is a publication of

Indiana University Press
601 North Morton Street
Bloomington, IN 47404-3797 USA

http://iupress.indiana.edu

Telephone orders 800-842-6796
Fax orders 812-855-7931
Orders by e-mail iuporder@indiana.edu

The paper used in this publication meets the minimum requirements of American National Standard for Information Sciences—Permanence of Paper for Printed Library Materials, ANSI Z39.48-1984.

Manufactured in the United States of America

Library of Congress Cataloging-in-Publication Data

Pragmatism and the problem of race / edited by Bill E. Lawson and Donald F. Koch.
    p. cm.
Includes bibliographical references and index.
ISBN 0-253-34361-5 (alk. paper) — ISBN 0-253-21647-8 (pbk. : alk. paper)
  1. Pragmatism. 2. Racism—United States. 3. United States—Race relations. I. Lawson, Bill E., date II. Koch, Donald F., date.
  B832.P7565 2004
  305.8′00973—dc22

                                   2003015566

1 2 3 4 5 09 08 07 06 05 04

To Renée and William

To Barb, Leah, and Will

Contents

Preface

The idea for this volume originated in serious, mutually enriching conversation. We would walk and talk about jazz, philosophy, our families, ethical theory, and race. During these open and frank discussions we gradually developed the hypothesis that pragmatists should discuss racial questions. We continued discussion during the editing process. Each submitted paper forced us to grapple with concerns raised about the enduring problem of race raised by the contributor. We had to communicate.

Communication as we conceive of it is not an adversarial event wherein participants defend "positions" on contested "issues" such as affirmative action. It requires constructive engagement which addresses genuine difficulties and searches for the solution to them. The two of us, black and white persons, have time and time again been called upon to work together morally: to develop a working relationship and take on the task of shaping the contents of this volume. Our experience together has been and will continue to be a source of mutual enrichment.

We hope that the essays in this volume will initiate ongoing discussion of the problems of race by pragmatists as well as others and the search for resolutions to them. The proposed resolutions must emerge from our shared understanding of the ever-evolving American experience. They must be so rooted, or they accomplish nothing.

Unless otherwise indicated, references to Dewey are to the standard edition of his works, edited by Jo Ann Boydston (Carbondale: Southern Illinois University Press, 1969–93), designated as *The Early Works, 1882–1898* (EW), *The Middle Works, 1899–1924* (MW), and *The Later Works, 1925–1953* (LW).

Pragmatism and the Problem of Race

Introduction

Bill E. Lawson and Donald F. Koch

The Origin and Character of Pragmatism

The idea for a volume connecting pragmatism and the problem of race arises from two widely accepted premises. Pragmatism is a philosophical movement which originated within the American experience. It attempts to respond to difficulties which arise within that experience. The "race problem" generated by slavery and its aftermath was, and still is, a uniquely American problem. How then should pragmatists respond to and contribute to the resolution of one of our greatest and perhaps most enduring American problem?

The movement of thought designated by the term "pragmatism" is currently undergoing a significant revival. Originally developed by Charles S. Peirce, William James, John Dewey, and George Herbert Mead in the late nineteenth century and first half of the twentieth century, its central feature is the belief that ideas are connected with action, theory with practice. This expectation that we should "tackle difficulties," "get things done," is characteristically American, and it is not surprising that pragmatism is commonly regarded as the most significant American contribution to philosophy.

Yet contemporary pragmatists must ask themselves whether they are content to restate the *old* ideas of the founders of the movement or use these ideas to work out a *reconstruction* of pragmatism to deal with contemporary problems and issues. The question takes on added poignancy in view of the fact that pragmatists were not major contributors to what we might call the "practical philosophy movement" that began about thirty-five years ago. Where were they during the civil rights protests, the demonstrations against the Vietnam war, the period of Black Power and Black Nationalism, the rise of feminism, and the developing public interest in problems centering around health care and the practice of medicine? The search for an explanation for the relative silence of the pragmatists with regard to these matters digresses from the subject matter of this anthology. But their failure to participate in the practical philosophy movement entails that if they are to deal with current problems of race they must find a way to utilize the aforementioned old ideas which were generated during a time when racial segregation and racism were taken for granted and reconstruct them to deal with contemporary problems of race.[1] We cannot carry out this reconstruction here, but we can set forth the hypothesis that there is one basic essential element in the old pragmatism which must be carried over to any reconstructed pragmatism. This is the new account of inquiry developed by the founders.

One of the central tenets of classic pragmatism is that it calls into question the traditional account of the connection between thought and action. This account takes it for granted that philosophers must *first* formulate, explain, and justify some fundamental ideas and principles. If they are successful, every rational person must then acknowledge these fundamental ideas and principles and apply them to specific situations. *Then* rational persons must act accordingly. So, for example, if it is morally reasonable to respect other persons and not treat them as means to your own special ends, this fundamental moral idea leads us to the conclusion that slavery and racial prejudice are wrong. All rational persons must act to get rid of these practices.

In other words, the traditional standpoint asserts that inquiry begins with a search for knowledge. Action comes after knowledge is attained. The founders of pragmatism challenged this account by introducing the hypothesis that thinking and doing are aspects of, phases within, a single human activity introduced *because of* and *in response to* experienced trouble. With Peirce, anomalies are discovered in currently acceptable scientific explanations or as widely accepted scientific explanations suggest new problems, which in turn lead inquirers to pursue new discoveries. Peirce's account of the general process of inquiry as initiated by doubt in the form of irritation about some unsatisfactory state of affairs and ending in a satisfactory state has been found to have broad application. James focuses upon the trouble experienced by an individual engaged in the search for a better life, and his great book *Psychology* (1890) set forth an account of ongoing consciousness seeking to restore normal functioning in dealing with the vicissitudes of life. For Dewey, consciousness becomes experience and troubles of life become problematic situations which function as the generic element in the initiation of an inquiry.

In sum, pragmatism introduces the radical hypothesis that thought is a phase within *active, working* human experience. Inquirers do not "step outside" that experience to cognize true ideas and then somehow "go back into experience" to act upon these ideas because they are true. Inquiry arises within experience as an attempt to work out a response to some difficulty within experience. This new conception of the role of intelligence leads us to rethink and presumably reconstruct the traditional account of the relation of thought to action. Thought is not preparatory to action but a function within action which seeks out an intelligent response to a difficulty encountered or anticipated.

So inquirers with a pragmatic bent are called upon to deal with actual difficulties, whether encountered or anticipated to occur in the future. With regard to concerns about race, they must, as our previous discussion implies, seek out a potentially successful response to a difficulty in the form of a proposal or hypothesis for action. They will be concerned about working out what is involved in successful doing rather than with telling others what to do and leaving them to do it on their own.

In his essay "The Sentiment of Rationality," James speaks of the human need to philosophize, to search for "universality or extensiveness" as a "passion for simplification," and contrasts it with the alternative and equally strong "passion for distinguishing . . . the impulse to be *acquainted* with the parts rather than to comprehend the whole."[2] James's comment about this division within human personality suggests the two-part division of the essays in this volume. Essays in Part I raise the question whether the general ideas associated with classic pragmatism can be utilized and reworked to deal with contemporary problem of race. Those in Part II deal with specific questions and concerns.

Part I. Pragmatism as a General Approach to the Problem of Race

The writings of the founders of pragmatism do not reveal much interest in racial questions. This omission reflects an older consensus account of American history and culture in which problems of race are not given prominence. In *The American Evasion of Philosophy: A Genealogy of Pragmatism,* Cornel West asserts that "American pragmatism emerges with profound insights and myopic blindnesses, enabling strengths and debilitating weaknesses, all resulting from distinctive features of American civilization." Among the latter are its origin in "a slave-based economy" and its "collective self-definition as homogeneously Anglo-American. . . ." Although "American pragmatism is a diverse and heterogeneous tradition . . . [its] rebelliousness . . . is severely restricted by an ethnocentrism and a patriotism cognizant of the exclusion of peoples of color." He concludes that

> The pragmatist's preoccupation with power, provocation, and personality . . . signifies an intellectual calling to administer to a confused populace caught in the whirlwinds of societal crisis, the cross fires of ideological polemics, and the storms of class, racial, and gender conflicts. This deep intellectual vocation, quite different from our sense of the emasculation of the academic profession, impels the major American pragmatists to be organic intellectuals of some sort; that is, participants in the life of the mind who revel in ideas and related ideas to action by means of creating, constituting, or consolidating constituencies for moral aims and political purposes.[3]

These passages set forth a formidable challenge. Myopia and neglect with regard to past and present racial difficulties are no longer acceptable. In effect, West is demanding that all who claim to be pragmatic recognize the need to extend their inquiries to include consideration of concern about race. Moreover, this quest must be "organic" in the sense that ideas are connected with the organization of constituencies for action.

Yet this project is complicated by still another difficulty: a contemporary culture of academic inquiry which shuts itself off from practical tasks. Commenting on recent academic thought, West asserts that "the time is now past for empty academic theoreticism, professional antitheoreticism, and complacent 'radical' antiprofessionalism."[4] His proposed solution is a "prophetic pragmatism [which] purports to be not only an oppositional cultural criticism but also a material force for individuality and democracy . . . a practice that has some potency and effect or makes a difference in the world."[5] What would a form of pragmatism which attempts to meet this demand be like?

In Part I Michael Eldridge shows that race issues were not one of Dewey's major concerns but that his general approach to social and political thinking can be applied to race problems. In the second chapter Gregory F. Pappas utilizes Dewey's approach to the doing away with racial prejudice to open up a discussion of the value and limitations of philosophers in dealing with specific situations. Donald F. Koch points to the importance of work in contemporary society and shows how Dewey's theory of inquiry directs us to the hypothesis that the key to better race relations is doing away with educational segregation. In Chapter 4 John R. Shook develops Dewey's general account of democracy and theory of education to defend public education as a central element in equal opportunity education. D. Micah Hester shows how the use of Mead's social self sheds new light on the way to deal with the problems of race, and Eddie S. Glaude, Jr., gives a fascinating exposition of Dewey's philosophy in order to raise the question whether Dewey's account of democracy is compatible with the tragedy of the African American experience.

Part II. Pragmatism and Means

Racial difficulties are temporal, contingent in time and space. Current racial problems reflect the complexity of contemporary social life. Apparently there is a bundle of race problems rather than a single race problem. Our situation contrasts with the period of protests culminating in the Civil Rights Acts of 1964 and 1965. Protest at that time was an endeavor by some people to get other people to take their side with regard to a given demand: the elimination of legal segregation. Protesters engaged in nonviolent public activities which called out government-sanctioned resistance. The brutality of this resistance brought out additional protesters and eventually created a nationwide national forum which directed public attention to the problem and led to the passage of the Civil Rights Acts.

From our latter-day vantage point, the reforms promulgated during the civil rights era were a successful attempt to correct segregation and overt discrimination as significant defects in American life and culture. The function of protest was to make these defects stand out like a sore thumb for all to see. Changes were made. But what are the current problems of race? How shall we identify them and deal with them? The essays in Part II concern a variety of different problems and the search for means to deal with them. In distinction from the essays in Part I, they are less involved with the general conception of pragmatism and more involved in dealing with actual problematic situations.

Here it is helpful to briefly discuss one of the more neglected aspects of Dewey's approach to inquiry: his standpoint that questions about moral ends cannot be separated from questions about means.[6] Discussion of this point begins with the central place of "the problematic" in the initiation and conduct of an inquiry:

> It [the problematic] covers the features that are designated by such adjectives as confusing, perplexing, disturbed, unsettled, indecisive; and by such nouns as jars, hitches, breaks, blocks—in short, all incidents occasioning an interruption of the smooth, straightforward course of behavior and that deflect it into a kind of behavior constituting inquiry.[7]

Taken as a directive to concrete action, this very general account of the conditions for the initiation of inquiry is not very helpful. But take it as an instrument which leads us to more specific elements in a successful inquiry, and the account acquires greater significance.

First, reference to the problematic notifies us that further inquiry must involve means. As already stated, inquiry occurs within experience, that is, as a response to existential conditions designated by the term "problematic." From this standpoint, proposed specific ideals do not exist somewhere outside the flow of experience. Working ideals, or ideals that work, must utilize and transform available resources.

Take as illustration the ideal of integrating public schools and the proposal of busing as means to deal with it. Busing utilizes available resources, that is, resources already familiar and available to the public schools. But difficulties encountered with busing as means to integration lead us to seek out other means, or perhaps even to modify or give up on the ideal of integration as a social policy. Resort to these considerations will not be acceptable to those who seek to sustain integration as a fixed, unalterable ideal. The pragmatic inquirer, by contrast, is driven back to the occurrence of the demand for integration as response to a problematic situation. He or she must start anew in the search for the means required for the response to be successful.

This conclusion leads us to a second point about the role of means in an inquiry: that the search for means involves distinguishing between the occurrence of a difficulty and the location and definition of the problem.[8] In other words, means are not just "lying around somewhere" like snow shovels to be picked up when the driveway needs to be cleared. We can, of course, take it for granted that the snow shovel is the location of the difficulty about how to remove snow. By contrast, we are not so sure whether busing locates the difficulty of achieving integration. The challenge of inquiry is to locate this difficulty and deal with it.

These general remarks serve to introduce the essays in Part II of this volume. They share the search for means to deal with the difficulties they discuss. They are attempts to begin with experience, and to locate the problem and the proposed solution. From this standpoint they enlarge upon the pragmatic enterprise of developing specific political technologies to deal with specific problems. In his book *Transforming Experience: John Dewey's Cultural Instrumentalism* (1998), Michael Eldridge discusses the successful project of lawyer and community activist Randy Shaw, who organized residents of the San Francisco tenderloin area to revitalize their neighborhood in response to encroachment from hotel developers who sought to destroy their homes and totally rebuild the area.[9] Shaw did not need to invoke or discuss Dewey to be successful. This observation reminds us that if pragmatic instrumentalism as a general theory is to retain cogency and respect, it must employ specific suggestions and proposals set forth by inquirers who focus upon the solution to specific difficulties. These specific inquiries, if successful, can serve as illustrations of the pragmatic method in action.

In the first essay in Part II, Bill E. Lawson reminds us that Booker T. Washington's practical approach to education did a good deal to improve the lot of Negroes during the early Jim Crow era. The essay sheds new light on the disputed question as to how far so-called moral ideals are to be bent or even sacrificed in the pursuit of practical results. David E. McClean and Paul C. Taylor take opposite sides on the practical value of conserving the notion of race. McClean argues that if the notion of race is associated with trouble and exacerbates it, we should abandon it. Taylor, by contrast, shows a number of areas where we should retain the conception. Alfred E. Prettyman identifies the "civil smother" as a general tactic used to thwart the aspirations of African Americans, and he seeks ways to overcome it. Scott L. Pratt utilizes the ideas of W. E. B. Du Bois to propose the introduction of racial studies into all areas of the college curriculum, and Judith M. Green concludes the volume by introducing the novel idea of hospitality in building community.

In Dewey's 1901 Lectures on Social Ethics there is a remarkable discussion of the evolution of social consciousness from primitive societies to the present complex society. Change is initiated when relatively fixed ends and the habits which reflect them encounter a social crisis. As time goes on social life becomes more complicated and the demand for change is more frequent:

> The reconstruction from one end to another becomes more and more complicated, and consequently the habits and ends become more overt and complicated, and require more conscious adjustment until, at present, the crisis becomes the rule. In other words, our ends and habits are only relatively fixed. . . . all our ends, in the particular content which they present to us, are relatively a matter of circumstances, of conditions. . . . we need always to be on the lookout . . . for further statements of ends which would really answer to what we want better than does the statement we now have.[10]

If we are to regard Dewey's references to ends as references to "working ends" or "ends in action," his last assertion constitutes the promise of pragmatism. The call for the evolution of newly proposed working ends and the search for new means to make these ends a working, functioning aspect of our shared experience are a unique feature of pragmatism. It is up to future inquirers to carry out this quest for the "better" as it relates to the problems of race.

NOTES

1. Some more recent books which connect pragmatism with specific questions and issues are *Pragmatism in Law and Society,* ed. Michael Brint and William Weaver (Boulder: Westview Press, 1991); Charlene Haddock Seigfried, *Pragmatism and Feminism* (Chicago: University of Chicago Press, 1995); *The Revival of Pragmatism: New Essays on Social Thought, Law, and Culture,* ed. Morris Dickstein (Durham: Duke University Press, 1998); *Environmental Pragmatism: Environmental Philosophies,* ed. Andrew Light and Erick Katz (New York: Routledge, 1998); and *Pragmatic Bioethics,* ed. Glenn McGee (Nashville: Vanderbilt University Press, 1999). Three general works dealing with social reconstruction are James Campbell, *The Community Reconstructs: The Meaning of Pragmatic Social Thought* (Urbana: University of Illinois Press, 1992); Michael Eldridge, *Transforming Experience: John Dewey's Cultural Instrumentalism* (Nashville: Vanderbilt University Press, 1998); and Larry A. Hickman, *Philosophical Tools for Technological Culture* (Bloomington: Indiana University Press, 2001).
2. William James, "The Sentiment of Rationality," in *The Will to Belief and Other Essays in Practical Philosophy* (Cambridge, Mass.: Harvard University Press, 1979), p. 59.
3. Cornel West, *The American Evasion of Philosophy: A Genealogy of Pragmatism* (Madison: University of Wisconsin Press, 1989), pp. 5–6.
4. Ibid, p. 210.
5. Ibid, p. 232.
6. See *Theory of Valuation,* chap. VI, "The Continuum of Ends-Means" (1939, LW 13:226–36).
7. "Dewey's Reply to Albert G. A. Balz" (1949, LW 16:282). Dewey asserts that the concept of the problematic is central to his theory of inquiry. See *Logic: The Theory of Inquiry* (1937, LW 12:3).
8. For this distinction, see *How We Think* (1910, MW 6:236–37).
9. Michael Eldridge, *Transforming Experience: John Dewey's Cultural Instrumentalism* (Nashville: Vanderbilt University Press, 1998), pp. 113–23.
10. John Dewey, *Lectures on Ethics: 1900–1901,* ed. Donald F. Koch (Carbondale: Southern Illinois University Press, 1991), pp. 284–85.

Part One.

Pragmatism as a General Approach to the Problem of Race

1 Dewey on Race and Social Change

Michael Eldridge

One committed to a multicultural society will find some help in John Dewey's direct statements on race; he or she will, however, find greater assistance in Dewey's more general social and political thinking and overall philosophical approach. I begin with a brief consideration of Dewey's values. Then I turn to Dewey's discussions of race, including his address to the National Negro Conference (1909), his comments to a Chinese audience (1919–21), and his address to the NAACP (1932), as well as relevant material from *The Correspondence of John Dewey.* Finally, I will argue that Dewey's approach to social change is broader than the deliberative-experimental-educational model that is often ascribed to him.[1] A Deweyan can, if the situation requires, employ a coercive strategy. Yet he or she will press in the direction of deliberation, experimentation, and education.

Ordered Richness

Given pragmatism's nonfoundational commitment, one is reluctant to speak of basic values in Dewey. Yet there are some that are pervasive and even play an ordering role in Dewey. That to which I called attention in *Transforming Experience: John Dewey's Cultural Instrumentalism*[2] and want to single out here is the phrase "ordered richness," which was used by Dewey in his contribution to a conference celebrating his eightieth birthday: "Creative Democracy—The Task before Us" (LW 14:229). I do so not because I think it is foundational or more basic than others, such as growth or sustainable development, but because it is central and relevant to the issues addressed by this essay.

The idea is that there needs to be sufficient social structure to enable individuals to flourish. Moreover, the diversity that occurs can be used, if a society so orders itself, to enhance the common life. So it is not just a matter of letting individuals do their own thing. Rather, an appropriately structured society will simultaneously enhance individuality and community. This valuing of individuality, given Dewey's understanding of persons as *social* individuals, will also recognize, if not embrace, their ethnicity and other forms of cultural identity. This, of course, will not be an uncritical acceptance of either individuality or group identity, but ordered richness will encourage the diversity that is intrinsic to both individuality and multiculturalism. It will do so, as I have said, for the sake of the individual members of the society and for the society as a whole.

An advocate of multiculturalism is right, therefore, to look to Dewey for intellectual guidance. Given his overall commitments, social and political involvements, and prominence as a philosopher in the first half of the twentieth century, he seems a likely resource for those of us concerned about the role that race plays in our culture.

Dewey on Race

Dewey was considered an ally by African Americans and was honored by the NAACP, an organization he helped to found. Roy Wilkins, as acting secretary of the NAACP, telegrammed the organization's best wishes for Dewey's ninetieth birthday, recalling his "immeasurable contribution to the struggle against racial discrimination as a signer of the original Lincoln Day call which forty years ago marked the birth of the NAACP" [(1949.10.19 (11410)].[3] Then, fewer than three years later, in 1952, upon Dewey's death, Walter White, the NAACP secretary at the time, telegrammed Mrs. Roberta Dewey: "We are profoundly grieved at the passing of your distinguished husband. We are proud that he was one of the founders of the National Association for the Advancement of Colored People and as you know unremittingly and uncompromisingly a supporter of the fight for full citizanship [sic] rights for the American Negro. We shall miss his wise and kindly counsel but we are grateful that he was spared enough years of life to advance so measurably the thinking of mankind" [1952.06.02 (15984)].

One would not expect these celebratory messages to be a balanced reflection of Dewey's attitudes toward or efforts on behalf of African Americans. To approach that we need to look elsewhere in the correspondence and in his published statements. This will reveal a man who was less than what some expect of America's most prominent philosopher—and public philosopher at that—in the first part of the twentieth century and whose work is now receiving renewed interest.

I would like to review the less-than-admirable material first, then his published work, which some find of mixed value, and finally I will mention a political involvement that fully meets our expectations.

Dewey at one point in the two decades (1919–39) of correspondence that I surveyed—in preparing the introduction for the second volume of the CD-ROM edition—used the phrase "nigger in the woodpile" [1931.02.25 (04285)]. His adopted son, Sabino, while in Hawaii, refers to his employment as a "white mans job" [1919.06.13 (03908)]. And one of Dewey's sons-in-law refers to a woman who kept a boarding house where his wife Jane was staying as "real white-folks" [1926.12.05 (04048)]. This usage I regard as casually racist and reflective of pre-1960s white America.

The correspondence also reveals that Dewey was not always as attentive to the concerns of African Americans as one might like. In 1931 and 1932 W. E. B. Du Bois, a political ally, wrote Dewey repeatedly about contributing a short piece for *Crisis,* the magazine which he edited. Initially he wanted something on Negro education for an issue on that theme. Later he asked for a brief statement on "the political situation" of "the colored people" in New York City [1931.05.15 (07496), 1931.06.22 (07497), 1931.08.06 (07498), 1932.01.12 (07500), 1932.01.22 (07499)]. According to my UNC Charlotte colleague Steve Fishman, who searched the issues of *Crisis* during this period, nothing of Dewey's was ever published in the journal. By itself this could reflect nothing more than the fact that Dewey was a busy man who could not respond to all of the many requests that were made of him. But it could also indicate that writing something for an African American audience was not a high priority.

Finally there is this revealing incident. In 1937 Dewey taught a course at the University of Cincinnati. At the end of his stay he agreed to meet with a group of African American educators. Here is an excerpt from a letter he wrote to Roberta Grant, who was to become his second wife:

> My darling Robin . . . Went with the negro school principal to his house—like any "middle class" home in a good locality—didn't look like a segregated black district. About 25 at the conference—must have been some local teachers besides those in the class. After the conference I ate 4 kinds of sandwiches & I don't know how many kinds of cookies & cakes. . . . Find myself more easily comfortably at home in a group like that this morning than in lots of others. [1937.06.17 (06654)]

Although Dewey was comfortable with the group, it appears that this sort of encounter with African Americans was an unfamiliar experience for him. That it was unfamiliar is given credence when we realize the paucity of references to African Americans in the correspondence. Dewey, of course, had contact with African Americans, but these were in white-controlled venues or nonintimate settings, such as an NAACP convention.

Dewey was much more involved with Jews than with African Americans. Many of his students were Jewish, as was Roberta. At least in one instance he was quick to take offense at a friend's anti-Semitic statements: "Your antisemitism made my blood run cold—aside from the intrinsic merits of the question— if any—under present circumstances the attitude you express if widely shared is the forerunner of Nazi business & a regime of general hate & distrust. There are all kinds of Jews just as there all kinds of Yankees, negroes, Catholics &— probably—methodists—I cant understand why you should damn the Jews collectively because of the obnoxiousness of some" [1939.02.25 (06786)]. I found no similarly impassioned statement about any other racial group.

Dewey was active at times in behalf of African Americans. A notable case was that of Odell Walker, an African American sharecropper, who, despite his plea of self-defense, was convicted of killing his white landlord in 1940 and executed in 1942. Dewey wrote a lengthy letter to the *New York Times* in Walker's behalf (LW 15:356–58; 550–51). This sort of involvement is what one might have expected of America's foremost public philosopher, but it is revealing that of Dewey's many public interventions in behalf of various victims this is the only one that I found involving race.[4]

Of course, there are brief statements in the correspondence and his published work in which he declares his opposition to lynchings and cites racism as a problem. For instance, in *Freedom and Culture* he wrote, "Certainly racial prejudice against Negroes, Catholics, and Jews is no new thing in our life. Its presence among us is an intrinsic weakness and a handle for the accusation that we do not act differently from Nazi Germany" (LW 13:153; see also his letter to Arthur Dunn: 1923.02.12 [02749]).

Turning now to his fuller published statements on race, there are three notable ones. The last, his address to the NAACP in 1932, has been singled out by Charlene Haddock Seigfried as a clear example of his failure *in this address* to recognize the fundamental reality of racism as a problem for African Americans, choosing instead to find the basis of racial prejudice in economic factors. She writes, "What is needed to complete his analyses and proposals is a more penetrating account of the sources of inherited prejudice and motivations for beliefs ranging from indifference, to distrust, derision, and violent antipathy toward select groups of people."[5] She also finds that Dewey was overly reliant on deliberative methods of conflict resolution. Although he would at times concede the need for coercive action, his commitment to nonviolence is such that he does not develop a sufficiently full and nuanced theory of social action (199). In Dewey the emphasis is almost always upon deliberation and experimentation.[6]

Before I respond to these concerns there are two other Deweyan statements that we need to take note of. The first is his address to the National Negro Conference in 1909, in which he argued that an individual's acquired characteristics are not transmitted. Hence "each generation biologically commences over again very much on the level of the individuals of the past generation, or a few generations gone by. In other words, there is no 'inferior race,' and the members of a race so-called should each have the same opportunities of social environment and personality as those of a more favored race" (MW 4:157). Dewey, of course, thinks that a society's acquired characteristics can be transmitted. This is precisely what a culture does. Hence he is careful to say that it is an *individual's* acquired characteristics that are not transmitted. Also of interest is the phrase "race so-called." Dewey does not think that race is a biological fact; it is a culturally conditioned term.[7]

This Dewey says explicitly in a paper on racial prejudice that he read to the Chinese Social and Political Science Association on his visit to China in 1919–21. His effort is a "scientific" one in that he attempts to identify the causes of racial prejudice rather than deal with it by "vigorous condemnation and by preaching to people about how evil they are." Dewey shares the hope that people will be emancipated from prejudice, but he thinks those liberals who treat racial prejudice as simply a moral evil are employing the wrong means. Just as progress was made in treating physical disease "by discovering the conditions which produce it," so progress in destroying this cultural ailment will be made when society is able to "remove the causes that produce it" (MW 13:242).

The causes, he discovers, are several—hostility and fear of that which is strange, taking accidental physical and cultural differences as fundamentally important, and underestimating the significant roles played by certain complex economic and political factors. These causes are not fully appreciated by most people because they take race to be a natural, fixed category, rather than the name we give to these very real causes. Here is his own summary of his findings:

> The basis of race prejudice is instinctive dislike and dread of what is strange. This prejudice is converted into discrimination and friction by accidental physical features, and by cultural differences of language and religion, and, especially at the present time, by an intermixture of political and economic forces. The result is the present concept of race and of fixed racial difference and race friction. Scientifically, the concept of race is largely a fiction.

But this does not mean that race is explained away or to be ignored, for "as designating a whole group of actual phenomena it is a practical reality" (MW 13:251).

This is a more sophisticated account than what we find in the NAACP address just over ten years later. He does not emphasize the economic over other factors, and he acknowledges the "practical reality" of race. I do not think Dewey changed his mind. Rather, as Seigfried notes, he was keenly aware of the "severe economic crisis" of the 1930s, leading him to emphasize the connection between economics and racial prejudice. But this later address should not be read as Dewey's definitive view on race. It is, as with much of Dewey's writing, situational. To get a fuller view we need to read it alongside these earlier statements. When we do, we realize that Seigfried's "blindness to the virulence of racial prejudice" claim,[8] while appropriate to the NAACP address, is too strong if taken to characterize Dewey's view on the whole.

But it is surprising, particularly to those of who have lived through the last half of the twentieth century, to find Dewey addressing an African American audience and urging that their primary problem is economic.

Given the pervasive, deep problem of racism in American history, Dewey could have and perhaps should have said and written more. It was but one of many issues that he addressed. And he did so, for the most part, without much passion, choosing to coolly analyze the situation. In the earlier addresses he was explicitly scientific; in the NAACP address he emphasized economic factors. Although he was not without empathy, he was certainly analytical in his approach. Even if we limit Seigfried's judgment about his blindness to the NAACP address, we still must judge Dewey to have been not sufficiently alert to "the virulence of racial prejudice."

Dewey on Social Change

We would not have made the progress that we have made in racial matters if a dispassionate, intellectual approach had been the only one employed. Seigfried is right to question the effectiveness of a resolutely deliberative and experimental strategy. As Dewey himself said in the China paper, "man is naturally or primarily an irrational creature" (MW 13:247). We cannot hope to deal effectively with racism with only a cognitive approach. Fortunately Dewey's proposal is more sophisticated than that, thus escaping to some extent the force of Seigfried's criticism.

In *Transforming Experience* I argued that a Deweyan was not limited to deliberative and experimental methods of social-political action. I examined three cases of Deweyan involvements in which he either took or recognized the value of coercive action. The key for my broadened understanding was a story that Charles Frankel told about Dewey that I must repeat here in order to make my point. After retelling the story I will show how Dewey's actual social change efforts went beyond a strictly deliberative and experimental approach.

In 1939 the American Philosophical Association honored Dewey's eightieth year with a dinner at their annual meeting. In introducing him, his longtime Columbia University colleague William Pepperell Montague praised him for "practicalizing intelligence." Dewey, however, did not accept the compliment. Charles Frankel, a graduate student at Columbia at the time, recalls, "Dewey replied quietly but firmly that Montague was taking a narrow, inbred view—a philosopher's trade-union view, he implied—of what he, Dewey, had tried to accomplish. His effort had not been to practicalize intelligence but to intellectualize practice."[9] I take this to mean that we are to make our practices, our ongoing activities, more intelligent. We act in habitual ways, but sometimes our customary ways of acting cease to be effective ways of meeting our needs. Thus we, when we sense a discrepancy between our interests and our satisfactions, should examine our practices, asking if there is a good fit between ends and means. If not, we rethink what we are doing to make it more intelligent. Hence Dewey's repeated calls for deliberation and experimentation.

But Dewey recognized that the conditions are not always right for one to rely solely on discussion, analysis of the appropriate ends and means, and careful experimentation. In 1918 he short-circuited the public discussion phase of the ideal process and went directly to the White House in order to block a convention of Poles in Detroit that he thought would be undemocratic. The next year, while in China, he understood the significance of the politically radical May Fourth movement and urged both a new politics and a new culture for China. In 1933 he was willing to suspend some Communist members of the New York teachers union for being disruptive to the union's activities.[10]

The issue is not simply which means to use. Means must always be considered in relation to the ends sought. Dewey thinks it is unintelligent to employ a means that will be counterproductive. One selects a means that will, in one's judgment, bring about the desired end. The trouble with coercive tactics, generally speaking, is that they run the risk of being not only harmful but wasteful. In the 1916 essay "Force, Violence and Law," he argued that force should be used "efficiently" and "economically," for the "objection to violence is not that it involves the use of force, but that it is a waste of force, that it uses force idly or destructively" (MW 10:212).

Yet it is the case that Dewey generally recommended more educational strategies than ones relying on coercion. There are two reasons for this. One, a deliberation-experimentation-education model was not the first thought of most people. Most people are inclined to use more direct means. Two, the deliberation-experimentation-education model has a greater chance of success over the long run. If people become convinced through an explicitly educational process, they will more likely stay the course of the needed change.

This is seen, according to Joseph Ratner and Robert Westbrook, in Dewey's support of the proposal to outlaw war in the 1920s. Without getting into the details of this now obscure campaign, let me cite Dewey's rationale for popular participation: "Other schemes for peace, excepting the purely educational and moral ones, have relied upon the initiative of rulers, politicians or statesmen, as has been the case, for example, in the constitution of the League of Nations." The Outlawry of War campaign, however, "is a movement for peace which starts from the peoples themselves, which expresses their will, and demands that the legislators and politicians and the diplomats give effect to the popular will for peace. It has the advantages of the popular education movement, but unlike the other educational movements for peace it has a definite, simple, practical legislative goal" (MW 15:100). In other words, means and ends are reciprocal. Popular participation, which was to be mobilized by extensive educational efforts, is necessary for the end sought—a process whereby war would be outlawed. Ratner explained that the means employed in the campaign—popular ratification of the plan—would establish a World Court whose decisions would reinforce the means—popular support. Thus a basic social-political change would be brought about.[11]

The point here is not the merits of the Outlawry of War campaign. What is at issue is Dewey's basic proposal regarding social change. I think that even more fundamental than his often preferred educational strategy was his commitment to intelligent action. He was willing to use more radical and more coercive means at times. The test for him was not how conventional or radical or peaceful or educational or forceful a strategy was. Rather, would the proposed plan actually bring out the consequences desired? He was keenly aware of the undesirable consequences of more direct uses of force and often counseled greater deliberation and experimentation than what most people thought feasible. But he did not rule out in principle the use of force. I will term this his permissible strategy, distinguishing it from his preferred educational one.

Because Dewey is not the one-note social strategist that some take him to be, he escapes the charge that he has difficulty standing against his society. He is not so thoroughly pragmatic, in the more popular, opportunistic, sense of this term, that he must always stay close to the popular will. By permitting any intelligent action, even a coercive or radical one, he liberates the philosophical pragmatist from the straitjacket of conventionalism.

I also found in writing *Transforming Experience* that Dewey acknowledged, in response to a criticism of his younger Columbia colleague John Herman Randall, Jr., that he lacked a "political technology." Citing several pleas for greater use of social intelligence in Dewey's *Liberalism and Social Action* (LW 11), Randall expressed agreement with Dewey's analysis that our present institutions needed to be reformed. But he found Dewey's proposal to be deficient in terms of the requisite political skills:

> Instead of many fine generalities about the "method of coöperative intelligence," Dewey might well direct attention to this cruical problem of extending our political skill. For political skill can itself be taken as a technological problem to which inquiry can hope to bring an answer. . . . Thus by rights Dewey's philosophy should culminate in the earnest consideration of the social techniques for reorganizing beliefs and behavior—techniques very different from those dealing with natural materials. It should issue in a social engineering, in an applied science of political education—and not merely in the hope that someday we may develop one.[12]

Dewey agreed, expressing "full agreement with what Dr. Randall says in his paper about the importance of developing the skills that, if they were produced, would constitute political technology. The fact—which he points out—that I have myself done little or nothing in this direction does not detract from my recognition that in the concrete the invention of such a technology is the heart of the problem of intelligent action in political matters.[13]

In *Transforming Experience* I took this to mean full agreement and an admission of a deficiency in Dewey's philosophy, and I offered some corrective suggestions. I still like my suggestions, but now I am cognizant that Dewey's response is cagier than what I then realized. He does not say he should have developed a political technology. Rather, he says Randall is right to call attention to the need for such, and he has not done it. This leaves open the possibility that the invention of such a technology can be left to others. There is no expectation that a social philosopher must offer a complete theory of social change, one that includes a manual for effective social change.

Having broadened our understanding of Dewey's social change proposal, there is a matter that I want to address more directly than I have thus far. It is a mistake to reduce Dewey's approach to education, but it is also a mistake to undervalue the deliberative-experimental-educational model. One employs force reluctantly, and, when one does so, he or she uses it as a part of a broader effort to educate the affected parties. There are times when one must physically restrain someone, but it is far better to bring about the needed change with the affected person's consent. This will admittedly slow the desired progress of the social change, but it will, Dewey thought, lead to a more sustainable change, as we saw with his advocacy of the Outlawry of War proposal.

But it is more than this. Dewey was faulted for not having a political technology, but this assumes that he should have been a more systematic and comprehensive thinker than he actually was. In emphasizing the role of public deliberation of problems and suggested solutions, Dewey relieves himself of having to have all the answers. He clears a space for many voices, some of whom will be experts in various relevant areas. He does not have to have a political technology if there are political thinkers who are participating in the public discussion. Recall his famous statement: "Philosophy recovers itself when it ceases to be a device for dealing with problems of philosophers and becomes a method, cultivated by philosophers, for dealing with the problems of men" (MW 10:46). Thus the task of the social philosopher is to encourage the development of the method of social intelligence; it is not to work out the solutions. That is the work of the public as a whole. Nor do the answers worked out by the philosopher, or the public for that matter, have to be good for all time. They are responses to specific needs at specific times. If they meet those needs, then they have done their job.

Conclusion

For some Dewey is a moral as well as a philosophical hero. They, I should think, are embarrassed by some of Dewey's statements on and actions in regard to racial matters. It is not that he was terrible. Far from it. Rather, in matters of race he was sometimes out front (his analysis of race as a practical but not a biological reality, the founding of the NAACP, and the Odell Walker case), but he was often less than heroic (the NAACP address, his failure to write for *Crisis*, and his lack of intimacy with African Americans). Racial prejudice was a concern of Dewey's, and he attempted to find its causes. He was disturbed by the lynchings that were all too common in his time, but he participated in no crusade against them. For those of us who are concerned about racial justice today and who consider ourselves Deweyans or pragmatists, the Dewey to whom we should be turning is primarily the social theorist. It may have been that a more confrontational strategy was needed in the first two-thirds of the twentieth century than what Dewey would have preferred. But now, given the progress that has been made, the conditions are such that Dewey's collaborative, deliberative, experimental, and educational model is very much in order. One set of conditions that is in place that enables me to say this is the changed legal situation. Now acts of racial violence can be dealt with by the criminal justice system.

But my rather sanguine judgment will not be acceptable to those who think that racial prejudice is so pervasive, deep-seated, and enduring that it can be suppressed only for a time. It will sooner or later break out again with full force. Here I take my stand with Dewey in regarding racial prejudice as an acquired social characteristic rather than a fundamental feature of human nature. To his credit, as early as 1909, he was arguing that race is not a biological fact but a culturally conditioned "practical reality," as he termed it a decade later when speaking in China. If so, then it can be dealt with in practical ways. We do not have to live forever with the fiction that is race. We can come to think and behave in a different way. Thus there is something to be appreciated in Dewey's theorizing about race, but the way that this gets appropriated today is by using current social science research and employing the methods of social intelligence that Dewey encouraged.

NOTES

1. The best compact account of Dewey's recommended method of social reconstruction is James Campbell, "John Dewey's Method of Social Reconstruction," chap. 4 of *The Community Reconstructs: The Meaning of Pragmatic Social Thought* (Urbana: University of Illinois Press, 1992), pp. 38–58. My more positive assessment of the extent to which Dewey's method has been adopted is developed in an expanded version of "Social Reconstruction and Philosophy," which was presented at the Central European Pragmatist Forum: Second International Conference, which met at Jagiellonian University, Kraków, Poland, 6–12 June 2002.
2. Nashville: Vanderbilt University Press, 1998.
3. References to Larry A. Hickman, ed., *The Correspondence of John Dewey* (the material through 1939 has been published by InteLex in two volumes) are cited by year.month.day and accession number. Thus the letter from Wilkins to Dewey was written on 19 October 1949, and the Center for Dewey Studies' accession number is 11410. Searching by the latter number is an efficient way to locate items on the CD-ROM. This particular item, however, since it was written after 1939, is available at the Center for Dewey Studies, Southern Illinois University Carbondale. The Wilkens and White telegrams are quoted with the permission of the John Dewey Papers, Special Collection Research Center, Morris Library, Southern Illinois University Carbondale.
4. Much earlier, his first wife, Alice, held a meeting in her apartment "for the purpose of interesting the colored women in the suffrage" [1911.02.28 (03651)]. Dewey's involvement in this is not known. I am indebted to Hickman's introduction for this reference.
5. "John Dewey's Pragmatist Feminism," in Larry A. Hickman, ed., *Reading Dewey: Interpretations for a Postmodern Generation* (Bloomington: Indiana University Press, 1998), p. 197.
6. See also Nancy Fraser, "Another Pragmatism: Alain Locke, Critical 'Race' Theory, and the Politics of Culture," in Morris Dickstein, ed., *The Revival of Pragmatism: New Essays on Social Thought, Law and Culture* (Durham: Duke University Press, 1998), pp. 157–75. Fraser distinguishes Locke's views from "the mainstream tradition of classical pragmatist social thought," which is limited by "its neglect of power, its emphasis on culture at the expense of political economy, and its tendency to posit imaginary holistic 'solutions' to difficult, sometimes irreconcilable conflicts" (173).
7. For a brief account of the current debates in the broader field of critical theorizing about "race," see Fraser's essay on Locke in Dickstein, *Revival of Pragmatism*, p. 158.
8. Seigfried, "Dewey's Pragmatic Feminism," p. 197.
9. "John Dewey's Social Philosophy," in Steven M. Cahn, ed., *New Studies in*

the *Philosophy of John Dewey* (Hanover, N.H.: published for the University of Vermont by the University Press of New England, 1977), pp. 4–5.

10. Eldridge, *Transforming Experience,* pp. 73, 87–91, 80, 91–97.
11. Ibid., p. 75.
12. "Dewey's Interpretations of the History of Philosophy," in Paul Arthur Schilpp, ed., *The Philosophy of John Dewey* (Evanston, Ill.: Northwestern University, 1939), pp. 90–91.
13. Schilpp, p. 592, n. 57; LW 14:75.

2 Distance, Abstraction, and the Role of the Philosopher in the Pragmatic Approach to Racism

Gregory Fernando Pappas

What should be the role of philosophy (and a philosopher) in the social inquiry about racism? Taking as my starting point Dewey's suggestive comments about racial prejudice in a 1922 article, I will make some specific suggestions about the direction which the pragmatic philosopher needs to take in her inquiry about racism as a problem. In the process I will consider some issues that arise when one takes seriously the pragmatic-empirical method of dealing with the problem of racism.

Dewey was acquainted with many kinds of racial prejudice throughout his life, such as the prejudice against Orientals, blacks, and Jews. He lived in a nation of immigrants where each wave of newcomers (Irish, Italians, etc.) was first the object of prejudice and later the ones responsible for prejudice. He was one of the founding members of the NAACP and in public spoke against racism. In 1909 he participated in a National Negro Conference (with W. E. B. Du Bois and other social leaders) to demand equal opportunity for all blacks. However, there are very few places in his philosophical writings where he actually discusses racial matters at all. This silence may be perplexing to many. It is only in a 1922 lecture that he gave in China titled "Racial Prejudice and Friction" that Dewey explicitly addresses racial prejudice as a philosophical issue.[1] Yet a careful look at what we can find discloses a promising and interesting view of how an adequate investigation should be conducted, and about the role of the philosopher in this type of inquiry.

Most of his analysis consists in criticizing some common approaches and showing why racism is a very complicated problem. Dewey insists that instead of wasting our energies in "vigorous condemnations" (MW 13:242) about its evil character we should inquire into the conditions of the problem. The difficulty with racism is that it is usually experienced as a problem with a plurality and unique set of causes or factors, where none are reducible to the others but coexist in an "organic" relation to each other.

Dewey was aware of the tendency to reduce the problem to a matter of psychology and of changing people's minds (belief). Hence, he stressed the importance of the economic and political factors. He said,

> Without the economic and political changes which are fundamental, these factors would not produce the effect of completely eradicating racial discord. (MW 13:439) The cultivated person who thinks that what is termed racial friction will disappear if other persons only attain his own state of enlightenment and emancipation misjudges the whole situation. Such a state of mind is important for it is favorable to bringing about more fundamental changes in political and economic relationships. (MW 13:253)

However, for Dewey, it is equally mistaken to assume that the psychological-belief factor is only a consequence or a by-product of any of these other factors, as if to ameliorate the problem of racism we can just put our efforts in changing these basic factors. We may be unable to effectively ameliorate the economic and political factors without modifying racist prejudice as a psychological disposition.[2] Dewey's methodological prescription is that inquirers must avoid the tendency (temptation) to reduce the problem either to a problem of individual psychology or as a social, economical, or political problem. Instead, racism is a problem that must be engaged at *all* ends of the spectrum of factors that can be distinguished by reflection. While theoreticians would like to be able to argue that one factor is the foundation of all racial prejudice and racism while talk of any other factor is merely a verbal mask, equally simplistic is the approach of those who argue that even though each of the factors under consideration is different and present, if we try to ameliorate the most basic factor, all of the others will be affected and eventually disappear.

But Dewey's conception of the problem must also be contrasted with pluralistic but "linear" approaches, in which racism is simply a "many sided" problem requiring simply a "multiple" or "eclectic" approach.[3] In other words, each side is to be considered separately, as if the sides exist independently of each other. What is missing in the latter view is the interdependent relation among the many factors that are distinguished as a result of analysis. Dewey did not simply uncover multiple causes and factors in racial prejudice. He pointed out their mutually reinforcing "organic" relation. A complex "organic" problem requires an intelligent organic approach; that is, it requires not only that we ameliorate the problem from all sides but that we are alert to how one side affects, sustains, nourishes the other.

Dewey's analysis amounts to an advice against reductionism, oversimplification, and intellectualism regarding racism. It is consistent with the central tenet in his philosophy that the philosopher's foremost concern should be with the method of inquiry. Instead of searching for "the solution" or even addressing particular instances of racism he focused on method, that is, how to approach the problem. Mistakes in method are obstacles to effective amelioration of racism as a problem. However, one may find this wanting, empty, and in the end perhaps not very useful. Is this all that we can expect from philosophy? Is the role of the philosopher merely one of interdisciplinary guardian against certain methodological mistakes? Should not we expect more from Dewey? How could an American philosopher who cared so much about democracy in America not have had much to say in his philosophy about the particular problems of racism during his time?

Whether Dewey's silence about racism in his philosophy is or is not justified is not my main concern in this essay, although my conclusions may be relevant to this historical issue.[4] I am concerned with a broader issue, one that is of interest to contemporary Deweyans eager to apply their distinctive philosophical approach to racism as a problem. What can one really expect from a pragmatic approach to racism beyond criticism of method? How much more could Dewey have done? Given our pragmatic commitment, what are our limitations as philosophers? But, also, are there any untapped potentials and functions we can perform as philosophers? What particular tasks remain unexplored?

Let's begin by considering what particular limitations and practical issues are entailed by our commitment to pragmatism. The pragmatist opposition to fixed and universal rules or truths is a consequence of asserting the importance of context-sensitive reflection. One striking feature of Dewey's brief analysis is its universal or general scope. Is not this antithetical to the historical-contextualist thrust of his philosophy? Can a philosophy committed to sensitivity to context really engage in a general account of racism? Strictly speaking there is no general problem of racism but specific problems suffered by particular individuals or communities. The racism experienced by blacks in the North may be different in its conditions than the one experienced by blacks in the South. Even among a particular community there may be important changes in the problem across time. Inquiring about the racist or racism in general is a dangerous abstraction. We cannot forget that there are only particular racists embedded in unique historical and social circumstances, that racism varies from group to group, time, and expression. A contextualist holds that the relative importance of the psychological-individual factor and the collective causes (e.g., competition or oppression) in the amelioration of racism as a problem is to be determined by the particular racism that is under consideration, and not by a universal theory about racism.

If the intelligent thing to do is to study each particular racism in its contextual uniqueness, then this seems to be in conflict with the general and abstract character of any philosophical inquiry into racism. Have we discovered a possible inconsistency in Dewey? Is it even worthwhile to try to come up with an analysis of universal-general validity given that race prejudice varies from group to group, time, and expression?

I do not think there is an inconsistency in Dewey, and I find a general inquiry about racism to be appropriate and useful of a pragmatist philosopher. Pragmatism today is often portrayed as antitheory and opposed to any inquiry about a problem that is general or universal in scope. This is as if we were committed to the idea that the nonpractical character of a philosophy is proportional to its comprehensive, general, or speculative character. This is the same assumption that could lead one to believe that moral theory becomes of use for "practical" moral intelligence only if it becomes applied ethics, that is, if it addresses particular problems instead of the usual general ones. However, there is no reason to think that, for example, a moral theory about the problem of abortion will assist better the particular decisions about abortion than a theory that addresses the generic traits of moral problems.

Since the 1970s it has been assumed that making our students read essays in an anthology where different philosophers take a particular stand on the issue of abortion is more "practical" than discussing broader issues such as what are moral decisions or what we should usually consider when we have to make them. Is there any reason to assume that this is a better preparation to confront the unique and sometimes tragic decisions that are the concrete problems of abortion? Dewey would even be more suspicious of this applied ethics approach since it usually tries to replace individual-contextual reflection. Trying to fit some particular rule or argument that one has learned through considering philosophically the particular problem of abortion is often an obstacle to direct sensitivity to the problem.

The association of what is general and broad with what is speculative and useless is unwarranted. When one views theories as tools, as a pragmatist does, there is room for specialized tools as well as for tools that have a wide range of application and reference. Either tool can be an obstacle to moral practice. Philosophy cannot be disregarded as a speculative waste of time simply because it is concerned with formulating hypotheses that have the widest possible range of reference. On the contrary, Dewey finds this to be one of the reasons why philosophy is important:

> It is designated "philosophy" when its area of application is so comprehensive that it is not possible for it to pass directly into formulations of such form and content as to be serviceable in immediate conduct of specific inquiry. This fact does not signify its futility. . . . Historical facts prove that discussions that have not been carried, because of their very comprehensive and penetrating scope, to the point of detail characteristic of science, have done a work without which science would not be what it now is. (MW 12:263–64)

Of course, this is not to deny the futility of philosophical inquiries that are too abstract and detached from everyday experience. But usually the problem with these inquiries has nothing to do with being abstract or general per se. Dewey was aware of this common misunderstanding about pragmatism. He corrected C. I. Lewis once on this issue:

> Abstraction is the heart of thought; there is no way—other than accident—to control and enrich concrete experience except through an intermediate flight of thought with conceptions, relations, abstracta. What I regret is the tendency to erect the abstractions into complete and self-subsistent things, or into a kind of superior Being. (LW 7:216)

Problems stem from the tendency to reify theoretical abstractions over ordinary experience. Hence, one can argue that, so long as we understand the functional (instrumental) importance and limitations of a general inquiry about racism (with all of its abstractions and generalities), it can be a legitimate task.

But let me suggest a reason why it might even be worthwhile to have such an inquiry. It is the way of intelligence to study each problem of racism in its contextual uniqueness and that there be as many approaches to the problem as there are kinds of inquiry (in academic disciplines). However, attachment to one's own theoretical tools, and their success in application to a particular context, can tempt inquirers to forget their selectivity and the context-bound nature of what they are doing. This is why theoreticians are liable to a reductionism, one-sidedness, and oversimplification of concrete problems (such as racism). Hence, it might be a good idea to counteract this tendency by keeping the notion of an interdisciplinary inquiry about racism in general.

This would not result in a theory which in some sense has to be true to all instances of racism. But it would be a theory about what needs to be looked at if one is to approach and better understand particular instances of racism. It would be a theory mostly about method in the sense of how to proceed in an inquiry into this sort of problem. This general inquiry could serve as a reminder of the context-specific nature of our inquiries and our proposed solutions in confronting particular prejudices. It would not be able to prescribe anything about the individual and the particular instances of prejudices. Yet the general inquiry would be informed by insights gained in particular inquiries. It can preserve for future use the elements or conditions which have been present in past racism, so that when a new racist problem appears we are better prepared to approach its complexity. For instance, since economic conditions have been so central to so many cases of racial friction we have learned to look into that factor every time a new form of racism emerges.

To keep the abstraction of a general problem of racism is useful because it allows individuals affected by a particular racism to learn from racism in other contexts and times. Racism in Latin America is very different than racism in the United States, but a general inquiry makes possible learning from both the similarities and differences. One could, of course, refuse to engage in this sort of general inquiry. For instance, racism is sometimes conceived as merely a white-versus-black problem, but this is to cut short the possible lessons learned from similar problems. This refusal is also implicit in conferences about racism where participants are more concerned with arguments about whose racism is more "real" than with trying to learn from each other's experience.

What I am proposing is consistent with Dewey's conception of the relation and function between a general theory of inquiry (logic) and particular inquiries. The general theory is derived from ongoing observation of particular kinds of inquiries in all of their diversity and uniqueness, but it also serves as a tool to deal with the particular.[5] Dewey is against fixed and final rules, but principles and postulates can be generated in any general inquiry. They are generalizations in the form of formulation of conditions discovered in the course of inquiry itself. A general theory (with its generalizations) is "derived from what is involved in inquiries that have been successful in the past, it imposes a condition to be satisfied in future inquiries, until the results of such inquiries show reason for modifying it" (LW 12:25). Hence, a general inquiry about racism can be one that generates and applies principles but without undermining the ultimate importance of context-sensitive inquiry. Methods of inquiry to deal with racism can originate from the experience of past inquiries.

Let's assume that I have made a good case for having a philosophical approach to racism that is general. What does this entail in terms of what particular things we need to do as philosophers committed to such an inquiry? I have assigned two very different tasks to the philosopher that may be very difficult to adopt without one undermining the other. On the one hand, the philosopher must be sensitive to the unique, changing, and pluralistic nature of racism. On the other hand, its distinctive and useful role (qua philosopher) is to remain general, abstract, and interdisciplinary. This second task would seem easy (second nature) to a philosopher. It is the first task, of sensitivity to the particular, that raises some interesting challenges and issues.

The requirement that the general inquiry must be guided by the particular and concrete cases of racism follows from Dewey's empirical commitment that philosophy must begin and return to "primary experience." A genuine empiricism in philosophy entails that, no matter how abstract and remote our philosophical speculations might turn out, we need to start from and terminate in directly experienced subject matter. Hence, for Dewey experience is a "*starting point* and *terminal point,* as setting problems and as testing proposed solutions."[6] The concrete and unique problems of racism are the starting point and end point of an empirical philosophical inquiry about racism. This still leaves open and vague what it means to start with the experience of these unique problems. Does this mean that only those philosophers who have personally suffered a problem of racism (firsthand and in some direct and specific context) can be said to have the adequate "primary experience" to engage in a philosophical inquiry about racism? It may be relatively easy for someone like Dewey, who experienced privilege and not prejudice because of his color, to think abstractly about the logic of racial inquiry. But not being "caught up" in the question from a personal standpoint may well be the reason not to trust his more abstract and general conclusions. Indeed, it is questionable whether Dewey's speculations about racism originated from the sort of direct qualitative acquaintance with a problem that he stressed so much as a condition for genuine empirical inquiry.

There are in fact two different ways in which a philosopher's "distance" from the concrete problems of racism can be problematic. There is the personal or biographical "distance" of the philosopher, and the one that comes from merely thinking too abstractly or philosophically. The "distance" of philosophy as a mode of inquiry from particular problems and situations has always been the liability of philosophers. Dewey himself explains why:

> Thinking takes place in a scale of degrees of distance from the urgencies of an immediate situation in which something has to be done. The greater the degree of remoteness, the greater is the danger that a temporary and legitimate failure of

express reference to context will be converted into a virtual denial of its place and import. Thinking is always thinking, but philosophic thinking is, upon the whole, at the extreme end of the scale of distance from the active urgency of concrete situations. It is because of this fact that neglect of context is the besetting fallacy of philosophical thought. (LW 6:17)

This "distance" of philosophic thinking makes philosophical inquiry about any social problem difficult but not impossible. Pragmatism tries to remind us of the importance of a return to the concrete problems that originated the "flights" of thought. But in the case of racism there is also the problem of the philosopher's biographical "distance" from the concrete and lived problem. This is not just Dewey's problem (if it is a problem). In the history of philosophy racism has not been considered a serious subject matter of philosophical investigation simply because most philosophers have not suffered racism in a close and intimate way. To investigate the reasons for this "distance" requires a study of history as well as the social and economic conditions of philosophers as a group.

My concern here is more prospective and methodological. Let's assume that more philosophical inquiry about racism is needed and that it is a legitimate and worthwhile task. Who among us is better prepared to take on such a task? What would be required? The requirement that philosophical "distance" should begin with concrete and particular racism as "primary experience" suggests that, for example, an African American philosopher affected by racism is in a better position to philosophize about racism against blacks in America than a white person who only reads about it in the newspaper. American philosophy has been segregated in many ways, leaving black philosophers like Du Bois, Alain Locke, and Cornel West with the task of doing race theory. The segregation may be regrettable, but perhaps they are better prepared for the task. There is, however, something else to consider in a pragmatic inquiry about racism.

In such an inquiry how "close" does a philosopher need to be to some specific problem associated with race? Is there such a thing as being "too close" to some specific problem of racism? An African American philosopher may be so personally "caught up" that it does not allow him or her to have the required "distance" to engage in a general inquiry and learn from how racism is manifested in other contexts. This is possible, and it is similar to situations in our personal lives in which we are so consumed by a problem that we need others to help us think. To be sure, the needed "distance" is not the traditional dream of an "objective" standpoint (provided by "reason") outside of one's particular historical situation. For pragmatism, as Samuel Eames says, "reason is a balance of the impulses of detachment and attachment [involvement], a balance which experience shows is not very easy to accomplish."[7] The "distance" provided by reflection is merely a phase in the process of inquiry by an agent involved in a situation, not by a detached spectator. Inquiry is a process constituted by mutually dependent phases of "doing" and "undergoing." We "undergo" some concrete problem of racism, and the "distance" provided by reflection is a result of the operation ("doing") of habits of inquiry on the problem that is "had" (or suffered). This temporary and functional "distance" can be as abstract and as remote as our reflective and imaginative capacities allow, but its function is to return to illuminate and perhaps help resolve the problem that is being "undergone."

Ideally one must procure a certain balance between "doing" and "undergoing" in a philosophical inquiry about racism. One must be "caught up" enough in some particular problem of racism to obtain the qualitative material and the data that guide a general philosophical inquiry about racism. Otherwise, to think abstractly about the logic of racial inquiry can become a vice. But is it necessary that a philosopher personally suffer racism as a problem for her inquiry to be legitimate or of any use? Can we set some criteria about this? I do not think so. The required "closeness" and "distance" are matters of degree, and a pragmatist need not provide any definite or fixed "cutoff" point to make sense of the idea that there is better and worse, and that there must be some sort of balance between these two phases in a philosophical inquiry about racism. There is no one measure of "closeness" or "distance" to strive for even if it is clear that there are some undesirable extremes to be avoided. In fact, a general communal inquiry can benefit from having individuals coming from different racist experiences and from different degrees of "distance." It could be argued that since the problem of racism is a problem about human interaction (its quality), it is a problem that in a sense affects everyone in a community. But those who directly suffer the problem and those who suffered it in a more indirect fashion may have something different to contribute because of their particular "closeness" and "distance."

Now let us turn to the problem of whether the philosopher is too abstract. This last requirement of "balance" in the ideal inquiry about racism allows plenty of room for philosophers who are more or less "close to" (i.e., directly or indirectly affected by) the problem of racism. This does not change the fact that philosophers are usually more liable to one extreme rather than another. Since too much "distance" is usually our danger, it makes sense to prescribe more "closeness" to the concrete and unique problems of racism suffered by many. On the other hand, the source of our vice is also the source of our function and virtue in the context of communal inquiry. Our capacity to inquire and criticize in the most general and abstract direction can be of significant use within the communities that are most directly affected by racism. Blacks and Hispanics in many of our cities have not engaged sufficiently together in a more general inquiry about racism. Many somehow find it difficult to "distance" themselves enough from the particular problem they suffer to learn from the similar problem of others. This is most evident when in the discussion each tries to make hersef the genuine victim of "real" racism instead of making an effort to move inquiry in a more general and inclusive direction. But this is precisely the direction pursued by a philosophic mind. It may be argued that individuals from other disciplines are also capable of this task. Perhaps, but the general type of inquiry needed must not only be *inter*communitarian but *inter*disciplinary. The role of the philosopher is needed because academics in different fields find it difficult to distance themselves from the methods, goals, and tools of their particular type of inquiry. I am arguing that the capacity of a philosopher for a wider scope and even abstraction can be a virtue in a communal inquiry about racism, but I cannot deny that it usually functions as a vice and a reason to keep philosophers away from the conversation.

The communal role of the philosopher is an issue that concerns especially pragmatist philosophers. We are aware that according to Dewey philosophers should attend to the particular problems of the day, but the important issue is how? What would it mean to advance beyond Dewey's very incomplete inquiry about racism? What particular tasks or direction should we (Deweyans) pursue today? Being too close to the concrete problem of racism is hardly our problem. We could accuse Dewey of "distance" and even "silence," but how much better are we? If we are serious about engaging in an inquiry about racism, we need to find ways to get "closer" to these problems. It does not help that members of the communities suffering from racism are not well represented in our general community of academic philosophers. However, I strongly resist the implication (and I have argued here against it) that they are the only ones capable of genuine inquiry into this problem. Racism is a problem that affects us all, and "getting closer" to it is a matter of just opening our eyes and making ourselves be more "caught up" in the problem.

We could get closer to experiencing the problem through an open and sympathetic communication with those who are more directly affected, but when has a philosophical conference been a place to nurture this sort of conversation? The academic isolation of philosophy from the concrete problems of public life continues to provide the "distance" between pragmatic philosophers and racism. With a few exceptions (one of them is Cornel West), most of us (Deweyans) continue to limit ourselves to the problems of our profession (as "primary experience"), instead of also opening ourselves to experience the problems of the communities we are embedded in. I am at a loss as to how to fix this, except to suggest that the philosophical organizations in support of pragmatism (for example, the Society for the Advancement of American Philosophy) must at least resist "going with the flow" of the larger academic organizations (such as the American Philosophical Association).

As imperative as it is today for pragmatist philosophers to find ways to get "closer" to the problem of racism, it does not follow that philosophy must abandon the most general, abstract, speculative topics of inquiry. It is in fashion today among professional philosophers to believe that a pragmatist must proclaim the death of all theory (especially metaphysics and epistemology) as a necessary condition for getting in touch with concrete problems. Pragmatism does not become "practical" by becoming antitheory and by just making explicit reference to particular social problems in our philosophies. This does not guarantee that our philosophies are grounded in concrete "primary" experience. One does not get closer to *experiencing* the problems of abortion and racism by just talking about them. Dewey was aware of how philosophers have used the content of their philosophy as an excuse (rationalization) against a more genuine practical engagement in concrete problems.[8] Writing philosophical treatises about specific problems of racism is no guarantee that one is "caught up" enough in the particular problems that one writes about.

Deweyans today must go beyond Dewey by getting "closer" to the problem of racism, but I have argued that this does not imply that a pragmatist should abandon the same general character of Dewey's inquiry. We do need to be careful with our propensity toward abstractions, but by abandoning the relative "distance" or general character of philosophy we may be abandoning how philosophy can be most useful. To give philosophers the task of inquiry about specific problems at specific places and times may even be counterproductive to an effort to ameliorate problems intelligently. Perhaps Dewey just found no use for a philosophy of racism beyond one that gives general warnings about methods of dealing with the problem. This would hardly excuse him from the charge of not pursuing the inquiry enough (however general its character). On the other hand, he initiated many tasks left undone, hoping we would continue them. How then can we excuse our relative "distance" and "silence"?

What each one of us can and must do in order to ameliorate the problem of racism is a different issue than what we can and must do *qua* philosophers. This is, of course, an abstraction, but it is a very useful one. It helps us inquire about the potentials and limitations we share with other pragmatic philosophers, even if our personal circumstances and responsibilities are very different. We must be clear about our limitations on what we can do *as* philosophers against racism, but there are also tasks ahead of us. I have made here some positive suggestions that go beyond Dewey's "negative" advice to avoid certain mistakes. We must continue to defend the importance of context-sensitive inquiry while engaging in a very general inquiry about racism. The focus on method (i.e., how to approach the problem) still leaves many possible tasks. Beyond serving as an interdisciplinary guardian against certain common methodological mistakes in this area, a pragmatist philosopher can suggest how to proceed in learning from particular instances of racism, and how to refashion the conceptual tools needed to face the particular problems. But none of these suggestions have a chance as long as there is a gap (and not a continuity) between our philosophical inquiries and those people who suffer the problem of racism in the most direct and local way. We must rectify our problem of "distance" to this awful problem suffered by many in order to procure the required "balance" for a fruitful inquiry. We must get "closer" but use our "distance" *qua* philosophers as our greatest resource.

NOTES

1. This was a paper read before the Chinese Social and Political Science Association and first published in *Chinese Social and Political Science Review* 6

(1922): 1–17. In the critical edition it appears in MW 13:242–54. In this same volume there is an appendix titled "A Philosophical Interpretation of Racial Prejudice" (437–42). This small essay summarizes many of the same ideas as the one published in the Chinese journal.

2. For Dewey the psychological factor is in itself complex. For instance, he stresses how much of the racist prejudice is grounded on a natural psychological aversion to what is experienced as strange or foreign.

3. Allport, *The Nature of Prejudice* (Cambridge, Mass.: Addison-Wesley, 1954), p. 514.

4. There is an ambiguity in this issue. In judging Dewey's silence on the question of race are we judging his body of work or his personal character? If it is the latter, then one would have to look for evidence beyond what he wrote. We would have to examine what he did (or did not do) in light of his time and place and given his status as an American social philosopher. My concern here is only indirectly relevant to the first take on this issue. Let us assume that personally a pragmatist (like Dewey) is fully sensitive to racism as a serious problem. What should we expect from him or her in their capacity or role as philosophers? What is his or her best use of philosophy in the fight against racism and in light of his or her commitment to pragmatism?

5. Dewey's search, for example, with the pattern of inquiry is "checked and controlled by knowledge of the kinds of inquiry that have and that have not worked" (LW 12:108).

6. *Experience and Nature* (LW 1:14, emphasis added).

7. Samuel Morris Eames, *Pragmatic Naturalism* (Carbondale: Southern Illinois University Press, 1977), p. 52.

8. "But now the doctrine of 'higher' ends gives aid, comfort and support to every socially isolated and socially irresponsible scholar, specialist, esthete and religionist. It protects the vanity and irresponsibility of his calling from observation by others and by himself. The moral deficiency of the calling is transformed into a cause of admiration and gratulation" (MW 12:178).

3 "Discovering a Problem": A Pragmatic Instrumentalist Approach to Educational Segregation

Donald F. Koch

I am constantly surprised by how much I hear racism talked about and how little I actually see it.

—Dinesh D'Souza (2002)

New World African Modernity consists of degraded and exploited Africans in American circumstances using European languages and instruments to make sense of tragic predicaments—predicaments disproportionally shaped by white-supremacist bombardments on black beauty, intelligence, moral character and creativity.

—Cornel West (1993)

For a scientific man may reason and experiment for the express purpose of discovering a problem upon which to exercise inquiry.

—John Dewey, "An Analysis of Reflective Thought" (1922)[1]

Current discussions of race relations reflect a complex and contested state of affairs. This situation is illustrated by two widely divergent alternatives. One position is that, both morally and legally, there are no large-scale social difficulties involving race. To be sure, there are occasional incidents of racial violence and racial prejudice, but these are isolated actions which run contrary to a broad-based social consensus against racism. African Americans can and do get prestigious jobs and take on significant leadership roles. The alternative position is that racial oppression, prejudice, and even violence against minorities, especially African Americans, are persistent, pervasive, and seemingly permanent features of American social life. Accordingly, efforts of individuals, voluntary organizations, and government should be enlisted in a continuing campaign to deal with these problems. Probably most persons stand somewhere between these two positions and lean toward one or the other.

This essay will develop the thesis that we should abandon discussion of this disagreement and instead focus upon the task of securing adequate universal education for all people. Discussion will point out the central role of adequate universal education in doing away with difficulties experienced by many African Americans. I do not make specific suggestions as to the way in which this goal can be achieved. Our first practical task is make the case that the lack of adequate universal education constitutes a problem upon which to exercise further inquiry.

Both parties to the aforementioned disagreement admit that there are difficulties associated with the lives of many African Americans. In comparison with the population at large, significant numbers of African Americans have lower incomes and less capital accumulation, more menial and presumably less interesting employment, are more likely to be unemployed, share in a less stable family life, suffer from poorer health and inadequate health care, have less formal education, and engage in more crime.[2] For the sake of brevity, these will be referred to as "the difficulties" as short for "difficulties endured by a significant number of African Americans" in the discussion to follow.

Adherents to the first alternative tend to reject the claim that these difficulties are a consequence of racist individuals, laws, and policies. We can only guess how many of these adherents also believe that a significant number of African Americans have limited intelligence, little desire to succeed, and/or participate in a culture which encourages the "easy life" over the quest for hard work and success. Strictly speaking, beliefs like these cannot be designated as "racist" so long as they are represented as "fact."

Advocates of the second alternative are prone to cite racism as the explanation for the persistence of the difficulties. Perhaps the most prominent is that many (but not all) African Americans continue to endure the consequences of slavery, segregation, Jim Crow laws, and past white prejudice. So even if some blacks can—and indeed have—overcome these obstacles, many are unable to do so. There is something unfair, unjust, and just plain wrong about their situation, and something should be done about it.

One observation about both explanations for the admitted difficulties endured by African Americans is that all too often they are not subjected to and evaluated by any experimental test. Dewey has asserted that often what passes for a psychological explanation of human nature is really a branch of political doctrine which is "appropriate to the purposes and policies a given group wanted to carry through."[3] Similarly, what passes as explanation sorting out the cultural traits of different groups into, respectively, laudatory and deficient cultural traits is actually a branch of preestablished political doctrine a group wants to carry out. All too often the favored political doctrine *taken as such* is not regarded as the "kind of thing" that can be tested. It is instead expressed in generic terms as a fundamental vision, faith, self-evident moral principle, inherited set of political principles such as expressed in the Constitution or other written work, the word of God, or commonsense wisdom accumulated over time and so regarded as authoritative. This vision, faith, etc., often is associated with some set of assumptions about the capacity (or lack of capacity) of individual humans, communities, and nations (and, of course, African Americans) to reconstruct and enrich their experience.

These observations are relevant to discussion of our two widely divergent alternatives about race relations. Those who deny that the aforementioned difficulties within African American life are associated with racism must take for granted some so-called "factual" explanation of the situation. But the proffered factual explanation is often not subjected to a genuine test in which confirmation is sought through actual observation. Rather, those who deny that racism is a significant factor in leading to the difficulties can cite the difficulties themselves as evidence for whatever "facts" they cite as the cause of these difficulties, that is, limited intelligence, cultural limitations, desire for the easy life, etc. Those who take the other alternative and claim that the difficulties are associated with the contemporary effects of slavery, segregation, and racism face a similar problem. Is the occurrence of the difficulties themselves the sole evidence for the "facts" that allegedly cause those difficulties? In both cases the explanation of the phenomenon which calls for an explanation is a reiteration of the phenomenon itself.

This conclusion is not to be taken as substitute for historical inquiries which seek to explain the current conditions of African American life or the quest for conformation of hypotheses which explain why humans, including African Americans, act the way they act. But I believe it will be more fruitful to instigate a search for proposals which attempt to deal with the difficulties which are the subject matter of this essay. These proposals must begin with "things as they are," and in this sense I welcome the quest for the best explanation of current conditions.

From the Occurrence of Difficulties to the Search for the Discovery of the Problem about Which to Inquire

We need a new formulation of the difficulties associated with race relations which will lead us to new and hopefully effective hypotheses leading to their resolution. How do we go about doing this? First, it is helpful to indicate a plausible explanation of our inability to resolve disagreement about race relations set forth at the beginning of this essay. Dewey asserts in his well-known 1909 essay "The Influence of Darwinism on Philosophy" that we tend to be caught up in the "hallucination . . . that all the questions that the human mind has asked are questions that can be answered in terms of the alternatives that the questions themselves presuppose."[4] The questions at stake in the disagreement we have been discussing are whether or not racism remains as a significant factor in sustaining the difficulties endured by African Americans and other minorities. Call this the standard formulation of the race question. It can easily lead us to blame others rather than inquire further about what to do. Either African Americans suffer from character and/or cultural flaws and they are to be blamed for failing to struggle harder, to "make better choices," or whites are blamed for failure to do something about repressive racist practices and the adverse conditions of life which they allegedly sustain.

In *Logic: The Theory of Inquiry* (1938), Dewey asserts that "approach to human problems in terms of moral blame and moral approbation, of wickedness or righteousness, is probably the greatest single obstacle now existing to development of competent methods in the field of social subject-matter."[5] He holds instead that the search for "methods by which the material of existential situations may be converted into the prepared materials which facilitate and control inquiry is . . . the primary and urgent problem of social inquiry."[6] What is involved in this task?

When there is disagreement, it is helpful—as I will indicate in more detail later—to seek out a generic or shared difficulty (or difficulties) upon which all inquirers can focus. In this discussion all agree upon the aforementioned list of difficulties endured by a significant percentage of some African Americans. How do we advance the inquiry from the recognition of the occurrence of existing difficulties to the location of a problem about which we can inquire further? Adherence to the standard formulation constitutes a de facto admission that inquiry about what to do is unlikely to be forthcoming. Instead, parties to the disagreement continue to argue with each other about which of the incompatible positions is correct.

Moreover, suppose for the sake of discussion we admit the case of those who say there are no large-scale problems about racial relations in America. The outcome is that we are left with the status quo, and no effort is made to deal with the difficulties endured by African Americans. But what hypotheses are called for in order to deal with these difficulties? Now, admit the case for the side which argues that racism is permanent and pervasive. Admit further that somehow this racism can be, through the exercise of some kind of magic, done away with. We have yet to establish a connection between attaining this result and resolving the difficulties. What advocates of this view must really mean is that if racism disappears entirely, everyone would be more amenable to supporting their hypotheses for social change in the service of the relief of the difficulties. But what *are* these hypotheses? It seems that we still need to find a way to inquire which will help us find them.

Anyone familiar with editorial and "Op Ed" pages knows that the standard approach to inquiry taken therein is to call into question some law, policy, or action which is being considered by legislatures, executives, state agencies, businesses, etc. In addition, proposals for new laws, etc., are initiated and justified. This approach gives rise to the question, Why should those to whom criticism and new proposals are directed make any change at all? What is the link between defending a criticism or proposal, publishing it, and getting those who are called upon to do something about it? Why should those called upon do anything at all? Inquiry at this point relates to a logical question rather than an immediately practical question. How can we find a way to inquire which links the presumed moral recommendation with action? The common assumption seems to be that since our editorial has already shown that the preferred recommendation is a moral recommendation, no further answer to this question is called for. After all, moral recommendations are recommendations that, by definition, persons ought to act upon.

The expression "by definition" expresses an imagined tautological link between the establishment of a proposed behavior as moral and the attainment of a stimulus for persons to act upon that behavior. Unfortunately, resort to a tautology leaves out any reference to the empirical conditions for the appropriate behavior to actually place. No characterization of the sought-after stimulus (or series of stimuli) has as yet been made. What else is called for if the "others" who are asked to respond to the request for a changed behavior are to respond in the first place and then begin to "follow through" in pursuing the required task? How, over the long run, can the conflict between those making a moral claim and those who would initially ignore or resist it be restored?

Answering this question requires that we temporarily postpone our immediate interest in questions of racism. Instead, we will attempt to explore the logical conditions for an effective inquiry as they relate to the formulation of proposed hypotheses for the resolution of the difficulties suffered by African Americans. As a start, discussion will begin with perhaps the most significant generic element in creating a successful life experience for *any* person in a contemporary advanced society. Our hypothesis is that this element is universal education in the broadest sense of the term.[7]

The search for generic subject matter in moral inquiry is not an original standpoint. Mainstream moral and political theorists have, as stated earlier, sought for some *generic solution* to a particular moral question in the form of a fundamental vision, moral principle, etc., which unites all humans and so serves as the basis for a common moral and political will. Even relativists and pluralists who deny that there is such a common often seem to admit the need for basic principles of morality and justice which otherwise divergent persons, races, ethnic groups, communities, and nations are asked to accept. By contrast, the pragmatic instrumentalist approach to inquiry seeks out a *generic difficulty* or set of difficulties which all persons encounter. The generic difficulty which concerns us here is the need for universal education in the broadest sense of the term.

Indirect evidence for this approach is to be found in the suggestion that rational persons will covet their quest for the best education and try to exclude others from getting it. Call this the "Harvard syndrome" or view that everyone wants to get into Harvard but not everyone can go to Harvard. The basis of this syndrome is that there is fundamental segregation between classes, races, rich and poor, educated and uneducated, which divides persons. So long as this segregation is sustained there is no universal education. Moreover, like the old-fashioned racial segregation once practiced in this country, those who benefit from educational segregation can and do struggle to shut out those who suffer from it. They do so by trying to preserve access to the best forms of education for themselves.

Humans have always required education to survive and prosper. Youth in so-called primitive cultures must master the skills of hunting and gathering, and the complexity of these and other skills required for success in such cultures is not always acknowledged.[8] But what do we require of an educational system in a complex modern society? Taking an evolutionary perspective can be helpful. Given a series of cold winters and limited food supplies, why do some squirrels survive? Because they benefit from genetic mutations which provide them with functional characteristics called for in order to survive. These observations entail that individual squirrels who do not possess these characteristics will not survive. Humans are different. They have the ability to transform their environment. They can respond to difficulties by using creative intelligence to transform their environment. They need not rely upon the vicissitudes of an evolutionary process which, through no fault of their own, endows them with inadequate characteristics to deal with cold, disease, or famine.

These observations are relevant to the understanding of the overall educational process in a complex contemporary society. Many different vocations or specialized careers are called for if the society is to continue to function well. There must be some social process through which people discover specific vocations which best suit them and also contribute to the social good. To make "good choices" in this sense of the term is to participate in an educational process which makes choices available to them as plausible opportunities. A good deal of this educational process involves rejection of proffered alternatives. The person who becomes a mechanical engineer rejects a career as a teacher of literature, accountant, social worker, day laborer, etc. A good educational process, including family life, community life, and formal educational institutions, is a process which provides a way for people to grow and, moreover, to develop their unique capacities for growth along available pathways which are most productive in meeting the needs of society.

Competition among humans in America is not like the competition of squirrels who must compete against each other to gain access to a limited food supply and available shelter. Americans participate in a competition to evolve into a suitable vocation. It is a competition in which, at its very best, most or even all of the competitors can find opportunities to evolve in a more fruitful way.

Education in America does not live up to this standard. In places where there are difficulties in family life, community life, and bad to worse public schools, there is de facto educational segregation. Widespread political pressure for "local school districts" and "local education control" utilizes these euphemisms to disguise acceptance of widespread differences in educational opportunities. The poorest towns, cities, country school districts are in fact names for places where educational opportunity is not the best. Ask any real estate agent for confirmation of these points. To be sure, this educational segregation does not effect African Americans exclusively. It does affect them disproportionately.

The thesis here is that the difficulties in African American life can best be alleviated by creating a satisfactory educational process made available to *all* Americans. Whether this improvement can be attained is another matter. But reflection upon ordinary experiences demonstrates that repeated failure to get another person to do something leads us to invoke a distinction between *telling* that person to do something and *getting* the person to do it. The mainstream theorist can avoid further discussion of the matter by invoking something called morality or "justified morality" to "defend" what is told in spite of the fact that it is resisted or even ignored. But we are interested in getting things done, and this interest suggests a reconstruction of the mainstream approach to moral inquiry.

Getting something done was a major preoccupation of the founders of the philosophical movement that we refer to as pragmatism. Charles S. Peirce was a working scientist who participated in a working scientific community. His conception of beliefs as leading to habits which guide future action is central to his thought. William James was the great defender of the individual as a significant working factor in his or her self-reconstruction. His belief that a difficulty can be overcome by acting as if it could be overcome is central to his thought. Dewey's lifelong goal was to enlist thought in service of intelligent action. He does this by developing an account of inquiry which utilizes a "scientific treatment" of experience to reconstruct that experience, and by developing a melioristic psychology and account of social interactions which makes clear the opportunities for progress.

This is not the place to tell the full story of Dewey's attempt to develop an account of human experience which is instrumental in getting things done. My discussion is restricted to four aspects of his theory of inquiry which have a bearing upon the quest for educational equality by doing away with educational segregation.

Difficulties as the Generic Element in All Inquiry

The ancient warriors who initially designed catapults to toss boulders over the wall of a fort were presumably limited to trial and error experiments. As science progresses, general scientific laws and principles such as the theory of gravity, the conception of the effects of friction upon moving bodies, the effect of the rotation of the earth upon an object in motion, etc., were utilized to develop the accurate projectiles of the present day. These generic factors did not literally tell weapons manufacturers how to make better shells in the same sense that written instructions for assembling a bicycle tell you how to go about the task. But the factors were utilized, taken up, made use of by practical-minded persons to produce more accurate projectiles.

Can there be a similar use of generic elements in a moral inquiry? Earlier in this essay it was stated that it is common for the proposed generic element to be found in some form of basic moral knowledge as expressed in the will of God, a self-evident moral principle, etc. Since every intelligent person who is party to a moral inquiry is presumed to have access to this generic knowledge, they presumably can reach an agreement in its application to specific situations which call for moral judgment. On this view, the occurrence of continuing moral disagreement may be a question about our failure to apply the moral knowledge in difficult cases. It may also be a sign that those who disagree with us are either not intelligent or deliberately immoral.

How does Dewey respond to this unsatisfactory (from the practical standpoint) conclusion? The question is significant because it amounts to the de facto admission that a moral ideal cannot be attained. In his 1895 lectures on the logic of ethics he formulates the view that when inquiry breaks down, we need to "go back of the problem." This is an early development in his new approach to inquiry which leads him to the above-cited conclusion in "The Influence of Darwinism on Philosophy" that we should reject the standpoint that inquiry must always attempt to deal with a problem in terms of the alternatives proposed in the formulation initially presented to us. In our case the alternatives are whether America does or does not remain a racist society. We will not, in the words of Dewey's 1895 lectures, "take it [this formulation of the problem] and try to solve it."[9]

But what does it mean to "go back" of the problem? The problem or difficulty in this case is how to get from "telling" a person what to do to "getting" the person to do it. The same difficulty applies to the question of getting an organization to do something or creating a new organization for the purpose of getting something done. How is equality in education to be achieved? What kind of inquiry is called for if we are to get this job done?

Suppose, as was already hinted, that *the generic element lies in the conception of a difficulty* rather than a ready-made generic moral solution. In the case at hand the difficulty, or rather difficulties, are the above-cited adverse elements in the lives of many African Americans and others who experience similar problems. These difficulties—as will be explained—lead us to locate the problem to be dealt with as a problem about securing a better education for all. Fifty years ago we probably would have located the problem *at that time* as a problem about the elimination of state- and community-sponsored segregation. Today the situation is different, and similar difficulties require fresh proposals.

Difficulties as Indeterminate Situations Which Provide the Impetus to Get Something Done

But how do these abstract considerations about the character of inquiry lead us to "getting it done" where the "it" refers to any proposed task at all, including the task of dealing with the difficulties that are the subject matter of this essay?

The term "difficulty" is ambiguous. To be sure, all difficulties interrupt and affect adversely the ongoing course of experience, but sometimes the interruption can be easily dealt with, and other times it resists further inquiry. If a headache can be relieved by taking aspirin, the difficulty of enduring one is resolved by walking to the medicine cabinet and taking an aspirin. If it persists, we are moved to do something, but we don't know what to do next.

In *Logic: The Theory of Inquiry,* Dewey utilizes this second sense of a difficulty by referring to it as an "indeterminate situation." He distinguishes between "the antecedent conditions of inquiry" involving an "indeterminate situation" and "the institution of a problem."[10] An indeterminate situation is a situation which is "disturbed, troubled, ambiguous, confused, full of conflicting tendencies, obscure, etc." It is a situation in which "we do not know, as we say, where to turn, we grope and fumble."[11] In inquiry, "the indeterminate situation becomes problematic in the very process of being subjected to inquiry." The characterization of the situation as problematic "is but an initial step in the institution of a problem." So "to find out *what* the problem and problems are which a problematic situation presents to inquire into is already to be well along in an inquiry."[12] As illustration, an indeterminate situation which is a cause or source of suffering, injury, or destruction to a human or class of humans is a difficulty which may or may not be transformed into a problem.

From this standpoint, reference to the "problem of race" in the title of this book is ambiguous. Are so-called "problems of race" simply intractable difficulties, tragic evils to be endured permanently? Or can we find a way to transform these difficulties into problems upon which to exercise a scientific inquiry? What would such an inquiry be like? The question is a crucial one for Dewey and for us. Dewey asserts in *Logic: The Theory of Inquiry* that "the heart of the entire theory developed in this work is that the resolution of an indeterminate situation is the end, in the sense in which 'end' means *end-in-view* and in the sense in which it means *close* [of an inquiry]." Moreover, "inquiry effects *existential* transformation and reconstruction of the material with which it deals; the result of the transformation, when it is grounded, being conversion of an indeterminate problematic situation into a determinate resolved one."[13] The subject matter of this essay is the question as to what is involved in the transformation and reconstruction of difficulties associated with racial relations. The question is whether we can transform these difficulties into problems upon which to exercise inquiry.[14]

So in an indeterminate situation some kind of action is going on: "we turn, we grope, we fumble." The point is crucial to getting something done. If, from the standpoint of any inquiry whatsoever, that inquiry begins with activity, then the apparent dichotomy between thought and action, telling and doing, is rejected. If inquiry begins with activity, subsequent inquiry seeks control of current activity in the service of a proposed satisfactory activity. There is no gap between generating ideals and getting things done. Inquiry is inherently active and is concerned with the control of its own activity.

How do these remarks pertain to the proposal for the equality of adequate education? The goal is elimination of educational segregation. What is involved in this task?

The Generic Element in a Moral Inquiry

Discussion so far has made reference to scientific and moral illustrations, without setting forth the distinction between a factual difficulty and a moral difficulty. The generic element of a difficulty or indeterminate situation has been invoked as providing an impetus to do something. But if the difficulty is genuine, that impetus or tendency to act has as yet no specific subject matter at all. The questions that arise next are "When do we call the difficulty a *moral* difficulty?" and "How does our answer contribute to getting something *moral* done?"

Every situation, indeterminate or not, includes an individual who is the subject of an experience and a setting or immediate environment which constitutes the subject matter of an experience. An indeterminate situation supplies the impetus to all inquiry. It does not supply an answer to the question about what to do to initiate a successful inquiry.

When caught up in an indeterminate situation we can try to advance the inquiry by making a distinction between factual or scientific inquiry in which the future experience of the inquirer is a practical condition for conducting a moral inquiry (but not the subject matter of the inquiry) and a moral inquiry in which the working out of their character, their anticipated future experience, becomes the subject matter for the inquirer.[15] For example, recent news reports say that a giant asteroid is nearing the earth and may or may not collide with us in 2019. The scientific question is whether or not it will hit and how much damage it will do. When we try to answer these questions it is a practical matter to find scientific inquirers to investigate the matter. However, inquiry with regard to the asteroid becomes moral when someone (possibly the scientific inquirers themselves) ask what action they will take with regard to its anticipated arrival. Will they support more research to find out whether the asteroid will collide with the earth and what damage may be done? If the asteroid indeed threatens us, will they seek ways to divert it? At this point it is important to bring out Dewey's view that the determination of working ends is related to the development of available means. What a person or persons propose to do about the asteroid is a function of whether we can work out means to divert it and the costs of doing this.

These points seem abstract, theoretical, nonpractical unless and until we take up the suggestion that if you can control the way a person inquires you can go a long way toward controlling the person's behavior. From this standpoint, our characterization of an inquiry as moral could lead others to think and act in ways which would serve the cause of doing away with educational segregation and promoting equal education for all. Until we have some idea of the conditions which are called for if such control is to be achieved, any proposal for change is likely to meet with resistance from others. Further discussion of this problem leads us to a discussion of the instrumental function of conflict and resistance between persons in an ongoing moral inquiry.

The Generic Conditions for an Inquiry Involving Conflict

We turn now to William James's vivid discussion of demands in his 1891 essay "The Moral Philosopher and the Moral Life." Dewey heartily approved of the essay,[16] and his 1930 essay "Three Independent Factors in Morals" placed James's argument in the social setting of Roman life.

In the early part of the essay James asserts that in a universe with a "single sentient being . . . so far as he feels anything to be good, he *makes* it good." Suppose a second being—James refers to the being as a "thinker"—comes into this world, but each being "is indifferent to what the other may feel or do." He characterizes this situation as a world "without ethical unity," a "moral dualism."[17] James's account also applies to distinct memberships of any sort. Take, for example, the isolated hill tribes of New Guinea, which, because of the impossibility (even in the relatively recent past) of traversing the rugged terrain that divides them, never had contact with each other. They never made demands upon other social units. This is a situation in which one class of people or race is morally no better than any other.[18]

Friction between memberships previously separated or indifferent to each other occurs when one membership makes a demand upon the other. In James's colorful words, "Take any demand, however slight, which any creature, however weak, may make. Ought it not, for its own sole sake, to be satisfied? If not, prove why not. The only possible kind of proof you could adduce would be the exhibition of another creature who should make a demand that ran the other way."[19] A demand is a form of behavior which initiates an interaction with another party. James's use of the term seems to cover a wide range of actions from making an initial request to, after persistent refusals, threatening to utilize violence if the request is not met. If, on the other hand, the demand is immediately accepted and acted upon, then an obligation is created.

Any demand, whether it be that of a slave for freedom, the demand of the civil rights marchers for the end of Jim Crow laws, or a prospective student's demand for affirmative action, is apt to meet with rejection in the form of a counterdemand. The resulting conflict situation calls for the introduction and use of creative intelligence to resolve the conflict. From this standpoint, the employment of civil rights marchers and passive civil disobedience during the civil rights revolution of the 1960s was an intelligent hypothesis, a hypothesis which involved risk but eventually proved successful. In a sense it had to create friction in order to bring out a previously latent and unrecognized friction.

These remarks lead us to Dewey's use of James for his account of the origin of specific obligations and rights in the social and historical context of ancient Rome. We have seen that Dewey holds that moral inquiry in the generic sense involves situations in which the working out of the future conduct of the inquirer is at stake. Following James, determination of a new obligation is initiated when a party makes a demand upon another party and the demand meets with resistance. The ancient Romans, with their need to control a great empire, were among the first to call attention to difficulties associated with the formation of new laws needed to secure order in newly conquered countries:

> Men who live together inevitably make demands on one another. Each one
> attempts, however unconsciously by the very fact of living and acting, to bend

others to his own purposes, to make use of others as cooperative means in his own scheme of life. There is no normal person who does not insist practically on some sort of conduct on the part of others. . . . From the standpoint of the one making the demand, the demand is normal for it is merely part of the process of executing his purpose. From the standpoint of the one upon whom the demand is made, it will seem arbitrary except as it happens to fall in with some interest of his own. But he too has demands to make upon others and there finally develops a certain set or system of demands, more or less reciprocal according to social conditions, which are generally accepted—that is, responded to without overt revolt.[20]

How far along does this account lead us in the quest for universal and equal education? The demand that educational segregation be overcome will doubtless be met by resistance or even indifference. The question before us is whether others can be enlisted to work out a specific formulation of that demand which will, in Dewey's words, create a "a certain set or system of demands . . . which are generally accepted."

Concluding Remarks

The difficulties endured by many African Americans impede their introduction into the workplace and so harm many other aspects of their experience. Emphasis upon the workplace acknowledges the significant role of the working life in the American experience. Work is not simply a source of salary, fringe benefits, and prestige. In terms of time spent together with fellow workers and cooperative efforts to deal with tasks, work constitutes the most enduring of human relations—often surpassing time spent with the family. Most philosophers tend to ignore or even reject ordinary work as a suitable subject matter for inquiry. Dewey points out that Plato created a demarcation between the "economic pursuits, superimposed upon the dense mass of serfs, artisans and labors" and the "superficial [higher] layer of cultured citizens" as practitioners of moral theory. His advocacy of "back-and-forth give-and-take discussion [among workers] until final decisions represented a workable consensus of the ideas of all who took part" is at the heart of his account of democracy as "the method of achieving community by processes of free and open communication."[21]

Philosophers tend to ignore the significance of the process just described. As stated earlier, mainstream inquirers tend to take for granted a separation between moral inquiry which deals with exclusively moral subject matter and factual inquiry including "practical activity that enters into the construction of the object known."[22] The latter is to be taken up *after* the moral ideals are established. The philosopher stands apart from the scene of action as commentator on what goes on there. So philosophers who take the first alternative on the race question are *telling* everyone else to do little or nothing about race. Those who take the second position are *telling* everyone else to shape up and do something. For example, philosopher-advocates of equal opportunity in job placements and advancement, of greater public services provided for those who are less well-off, and of affirmative action to address lingering remnants of racial prejudice are content to explain and (when they can) justify the positions they take on these matters. Both positions neglect discussion about the practical use of available materials and obstacles encountered to actually achieve the changes they recommend.

The workplace, taken in the broadest sense to include all the activities by which humans earn their bread, constitutes a significant playing field for social change. Responses to difficulties are worked out and changes instituted on the job. The contemporary workplace is served by a formal, mandatory, and largely state-sponsored educational system which prepares individuals for the opportunities and challenges presented on the job. It is, as we have suggested, the major area of human experience where individuals function together in cooperative endeavors. In so doing, they develop their capacities and enlarge the capabilities of their fellow workers. Indeed, the workplace is perhaps our most significant test of the hypothesis that humans are capable of treating other humans with respect and dignity.

Slavery and other forms of semibondage such as sharecropping and backbreaking factory labor are associated with a stage in the development of technology such that massive amounts of hard (often unskilled) labor were requisites for achieving wealth and power. This is no longer the case. Educated and skilled workers are called for. The latter fact is significant for anyone who has a regard for the difficulties in the form of adverse experiences endured by many African Americans. Universal and uniform education is proposed here as an alternative to the uncertainty and ambiguity about whether there is a contemporary race problem in America. Both sides in the dispute cited at the beginning of this essay are invited to start with the difficulties of race and then to go on to locate in more detail the problem of universal education as a problem upon which to exercise inquiry.

The task is not an easy one. The quest for a better approach to universal education, in both the informal and formal senses of the term, is perhaps the hardest human difficulty. Successful education is typically achieved when these circumstances are *already* favorable to it. Given careful nurturing of the infant, parental time spent in interactions with the young child, positive and safe community life with good schools at all levels, education is very likely to be successful. The search for an adequate education becomes a search for these elements in community life, and the search for adequate education is a quest for better communities.

Why not just skip over the abstract and technical discussion in this essay and "get on with it" by making specific suggestions? Consider the physician who practiced before the advent of modern medicine. In many cases he or she responded to disease by taking action, and the effort failed because the disease continued to successfully resist the treatment. In this sense the physician was irrelevant. In similar fashion, those who prescribe moral medicines must encounter and deal with the resistance they will encounter. From this standpoint, moral inquiry requires that we utilize intelligence to turn existing obstacles into existing means by creating a common task in which all involved are enlisted. Whether we go about the inquiry in a way which acknowledges the necessity of creating this common task is central to the achievement of success in the future.

NOTES

1. Dinesh D'Souza, *What's So Great about America* (Washington, D.C.: Regnery, 2002), p. 118, cited with approval by Thomas Sowell, *Lansing State Journal,* 5 June 2002, p. 7a; Cornel West, *Keeping Faith: Philosophy and Race in America* (New York: Routledge, 1993), p. xii; John Dewey, MW 13:62.

2. These difficulties are more explicit in so-designated "black ghettos" or "predominantly black inner cities." Because the prospects for reconstruction of individual and shared experience in these areas are so difficult, nothing much gets done to change the situation. There is need for large-scale coordinated social efforts to repair the ongoing damage, but the intelligence, effort, and large-scale enlistment of human resources which are called for to deal with the situation are currently regarded as beyond our ken.

3. *Freedom and Culture* (1939, LW 14:83–84).

4. MW 4:14.

5. LW 12:489. In "Racial Prejudice and Friction" (1922) he makes a similar point by criticizing those who "fancy we can get rid of moral evils by vigorous condemnation and by preaching to people about how evil they are" (MW 13:242).

6. LW 12:487.

7. Good health, political freedom, opportunities to succeed in life are very important to a successful life. My discussion takes these factors for granted. A critic might say that African Americans have very limited opportunities for success in American culture. My response is that this statement is false as regards educated African Americans. In any event, this disagreement is clearly a factual question to be settled by actual surveys and other empirical investigations.

8. See Dewey's article on "The Savage Mind" (1903).

9. Citations from Dewey's 1895 lectures are from *Principles of Instrumental Logic: John Dewey's Lectures in Ethics and Political Ethics, 1895–1896,* ed. Donald F. Koch (Carbondale: Southern Illinois University Press, 1998), p. 44, §50, and the editor's Introduction, pp. 12–17.

10. Dewey's discussion seems to be a reworking of the 1922 quotation cited as an epigraph to this essay.

11. LW 12:109, 186.

12. Ibid., pp. 111–12.

13. Ibid., pp. 160, 161.

14. This approach differs substantially from the mainstream approach to inquiry. The latter ignores those indeterminate situations which constitute difficulties associated with race relations. For the mainstream inquirer, existential difficulties are mere instigators or stimuli for a moral inquiry which

does not seek to *existentially* transform a difficulty into a more satisfactory situation. As I have already said, inquiry begins with conflicting moral positions already held and attempts to determine which of the two positions is really moral. The desired outcome is that those who advocate or practice the wrong position are shown to be morally incorrect, and, if they don't change their ways, we can pass moral judgment against them, to blame them, and even condemn them. To be sure, the mainstream inquirer hopes that those who contribute to existential difficulty, insofar as the difficulty reflects moral error, will change their ways. But the mainstream inquirer provides no specific way to accomplish the desired moral goal. Dewey realizes that this tendency toward justification of one's own position and condemnation of others was a common feature of discussions of racial matters. Instead, he advocates a "scientific treatment of morality," which is devoted to the task of destroying, doing away with the difficulty. See the important 1903 essay "Logical Conditions of a Scientific Treatment of Morality" (MW 3:3–39). See also "Racial Prejudice and Friction" (1922), where the goal of inquiry is the destruction of prejudice itself (MW 13:242).

15. The argument stated here is worked out in slightly different language in "Logical Conditions of a Scientific Treatment of Morality" (MW 3:23); *Ethics* (1908), pp. 191–95; *Human Nature and Conduct* (1922), p. 31.

16. See Dewey's 3 June 1891 letter to William James in praise of this essay (Dewey Correspondence, I, CD-ROM version, 00460).

17. "The Moral Philosopher and the Moral Life," in *The Study of Ethics: A Syllabus* (1894), pp. 145–46.

18. Dewey makes this point in *The Study of Ethics: A Syllabus*, p. 261. Questions about better and worse can only arise when there is conflict, that is, between old and new, habit and proposed new way of acting. Accordingly, there is no way to say one class or race is better than another until they come into conflict with one another and the conflict about goods leads to an inquiry as to which way of life, medical treatment, food, etc., is better.

19. "The Moral Philosopher and the Moral Life, p. 149.

20. "Three Independent Factors in Morals" (1930, LW 5:284).

21. See "Intelligence and Morals" (1908, MW 4:33); "The One-World of Hitler's National Socialism" (1942, MW 8:443).

22. *The Quest for Certainty* (1929, LW 4:18).

4   Dewey's Vision of Equal Opportunity for Education in a Democracy

John R. Shook

America's system of public education has been a constant object of close scrutiny. Since its origins in the nineteenth century, the growth and evolution of public education could not go unnoticed or proceed without controversy.[1] Basic questions are now being asked about the purpose and methods of schooling, and fundamental principles that originated with public education over one hundred years ago have been challenged. A multitude of answers to these difficult and pressing questions have been emerging, from a wide variety of public sectors.[2] Among the many social and political issues in which public education has perennially been embroiled is the integration of blacks and voluntary immigrants into American society. Today's calls for reform in public education, and proposals to supplement (or even supplant) public education with private institutions of schooling will inevitably impact minority and underprivileged portions of society. These groups are increasingly aware that substantial alterations to public education could deeply impact their future in American society. Foremost among the many concerns is how proposed changes will affect the vision of just and equal opportunity that public education has promised, and whether democracy will be weakened as a result. John Dewey's philosophy, I argue, can help us to assess the principles grounding public education and judge reform proposals in light of current social contexts.

To visionaries born with each new generation, education appears to be a manifest panacea for solving perceived social problems of the era. Wiser heads may scorn such romantic idealism, but it is true that very few other social structures can establish as deep and lasting transformations of a country's way of life. Education in its broad sense, Dewey long ago explained, is achieved for better or worse by all forms of social interaction that perpetuate culture over generations. To would-be dictators and totalitarians, control of education is not incorrectly perceived as essential; after seizing political power, their zeal for taming and harnessing the media, churches, and schools (and even the family, if possible) is indicative of education's real power. A democracy is not misguided to discern in education the possibility for real and lasting social change.

A totalitarian government typically prefers ruling a rigid and static society and thus promotes lifeless and conformist modes of education. Democracies instead embrace the freedom of dynamic social relations and institutions that follow the novel opportunities that continually emerge. Democratic education, as Dewey persistently demanded, must be as dynamic as democratically possible. This general principle has direct application to answering key questions about the role of education for attaining primary democratic aims. Freedom, self-reliance, citizenship, opportunity, and many more such traditional democratic values must not be disconnected from any democracy's educational processes, since those values are preserved and transmitted through education.

This clashing juxtaposition of democracy's *dynamic* nature against democracy's *traditional* aims is not intended to be a criticism of Dewey's stance toward education's responsibilities. The precise meaning of democratic values, like any values, fortunately can be modified over time as a democracy evolves. A democracy surely stands for freedom and opportunity; yet what freedom or opportunity pragmatically signifies in actual social relations has dramatically changed across a century or even a generation in America. Furthermore, these changes are rarely uniform across all segments of society. Explaining political clashes often requires noticing how disputing groups understand the same value quite differently.

Controversy over education's role in advancing "equal opportunity" is a shining illustration of this variability. It is hardly enough to favor "equal opportunity" without specifying what an opportunity is *for*. Opportunity does not exist in the abstract (neither does freedom) since it exists only in relation to something toward which people can aim. What should people have an "opportunity" to do? The slogan "freedom of opportunity" can further compound confusion if freedom is conceived as an abstract capacity or property as well. A pragmatic approach to social philosophy recommends that a democratic society should examine actual existing living conditions to determine the range and extent of real freedoms of opportunity to achieve various concrete ends of living, so that these freedoms may be usefully compared against social ideals. Competing groups will not let the other side more loudly proclaim allegiance to the ideal of "freedom of opportunity." What is needed for intelligent public deliberation is at least clarification of what each side pragmatically means by this phrase and practically proposes to improve existing conditions.

John Dewey's social philosophy is highly relevant for understanding the possible use of the democratic principle of "equal opportunity" as an argument for reconstructing our nation's public education system. Dewey was America's foremost public philosopher during the first half of the twentieth century, a pioneering visionary who forcefully and persuasively argued for education's central role in democracy. He constructed a powerful and comprehensive theory of democracy's progress which required the establishment of one public education system for all children.[3] Although it is true that social conditions now are not the same, since social groups have newer priorities in addition to perennial goals, Dewey himself would have expected as much. That is why Dewey's social philosophy can still illuminate current issues and proposed changes confronting public education, and it can aid our evaluation of the long-term consequences of such potential changes.

The expanding concern over the proper destiny of public education has raised philosophical questions about the purposes and methods of schooling in America. Many long-held assumptions about public education, from its benefits, costs, and even its necessity, are now being challenged. Should it continue to attempt to be truly public by dominating the educational possibilities and funding in this country? Would reducing public education's scope and systematicity improve student performance and outcomes? Could private education play a larger role in the production of young citizens more capable of adult success? Should there be some uniform standards of educational achievement across the nation? These emerging issues are deeply connected with many other foundations of our democratic society, further elevating the importance of the debates over education. Naturally, the principle of "equal opportunity for all" is a major aspect of these debates.

Dewey was not merely a spectator and commentator on the explosive expansion of public schooling around the beginning of the twentieth century. He was an energetic and persuasive voice supporting the idea that schooling should be both public and systematic. As I will try to show, Dewey's philosophical arguments display a heightened sensitivity to the needs of underprivileged and minority groups. His views also illuminate why those needs must play a major role in our nation's pursuit of genuine living equality, and why systematic public schooling can be best designed to meet those needs.

Can Dewey's views on equality of opportunity for minorities be trusted? How well could Dewey understand this issue's complexities in his own day, much less in ours? This essay does not attempt to comprehensively survey public schooling's problems and roles in current society, but only to ask whether Dewey's own grounds for supporting public schooling are still relevant. These grounds, the principles of free association and public deliberation, do indeed require attention and careful consideration today. Perhaps Dewey was not a philosopher of race, if that label requires preeminent devotion to racial/ethnic issues. However, it is simply wrong to say that he never wrote about the issue of race in America,[4] and Dewey cannot be justly lumped together with so many other prominent American philosophers who turned a blind eye to racism and violence. Dewey was one of the founders of the National Association for the Advancement of Colored People in 1909,[5] and his efforts on its behalf won him the admiration of black leaders.[6] Furthermore, Dewey's educational theory has influenced several black social philosophers.[7]

The primary conclusion of this essay is that, from Dewey's perspective on the proper evolution of a progressive democracy, the erosion of public schooling would harm efforts to eliminate prejudice and second-class citizenship. Two additional pressing issues will also be considered as the argument proceeds: whether minority groups should pursue integration with the dominant way of life in America and whether a truly progressive democracy would demand tight ethnic integration instead of a looser, more pluralistic society of broad tolerance and group rights.[8]

The transmission of values and capacities for citizenship undertaken by all of society's educational processes should be carefully inspected and controlled by the public. Schooling must receive special scrutiny because of its special powers of shaping character and intelligence. The wider context of education will be treated first because most of Dewey's views on schooling are measured applications of his more general arguments about equal opportunity in democratic education.

Education and Equal Opportunity

Dewey distinguished between education in the broad sense and formal education.[9] Education results from the normal contingent interactions of people in their community. Formal education, or "schooling," constructs a controlled and simplified environment for learners in which social situations are deliberately structured to stimulate and guide problem-based learning. In Dewey's time most schools instead tried to instill the habits of self-control, attentive listening, rote memorization, and skill imitation. These skills were best fitted to the kind of learning expected: the mastery of a body of information and skills most relevant to the student's expected social role in adulthood. Dewey noted the contrast between the kind of schooling for the children destined for labor with schooling for the children destined for leadership. The purpose of this contrast was primarily to criticize the deficient education for the laboring class, which suppressed independent and constructive thinking in favor of the passive acceptance of factory conditions upon entering the workforce. However, Dewey was not recommending that all children instead receive the aristocratic schooling either.

Dewey's deeper critique of both aristocratic and proletariat schooling questioned how both systems shaped students into adults who could apply a uniform method of evaluating facts. The laborer's stock of fixed knowledge of facts serves as the test of truth. The aristocrat's stock of fixed logical principles in addition to fixed facts likewise provides the method of testing truth. Eternal verities were thus supplied for both sides: an unquestionable body of facts to be accepted, and an unquestionable list of principles to be obeyed. Dewey saw in this division the remnants of a medieval and monarchical form of society in which eternal truths were bestowed by powerful authorities upon an obedient population. Modern democracy should view education as far more than the memorization of facts and also beyond the acquisition of skills of learning. Neither a stock of facts nor a body of skills could by themselves be the goal of education. Instead, the source of all facts and skills, which is problem solving, must itself be the focus of education. But since problem solving and its improvement is a lifelong task, education must be lifelong even if formal schooling can have some relatively fixed duration.

Some education reformers in Dewey's time saw that students did not need the body of information typically bestowed by schools because most of the students were destined for work in industry. But this vocational learning simply substitutes the passive duplication of skills for the passive acceptance of facts. What is missing from all of these systems of education is the appreciation for the student's need to develop sound skills of problem solving. Genuine participation in a democracy requires these skills, because a modern democracy does not offer a fixed form of life with guaranteed social structures and relations throughout a person's lifetime. Thus a democracy cannot make the dangerous assumption that there is some fixed amount of information, or a fixed body of skills, that will permit an adult to function well for an entire lifetime. What then is to be learned in education? In a society of ever-changing social relations and institutions, the most important learning exists within the context of the individual's adjustment to such changes, and the resolution of the inevitable conflicts caused by these changes. Adjustment and conflict resolution are necessarily social endeavors. They are social not only in their effects but also social in the very process of deliberation. Because democracy is a form of life that provides extensive opportunities for intelligent problem solving, democracy itself is a vital process of education for adults as well as for children.

Education in this broad sense is even more essential to democratic life than these important considerations can reveal. Dewey's theory of progressive democracy is a vision of the intelligent methods of public deliberation that permit genuine "self-rule" by the body of citizens. Education in Dewey's sense as developing capacities for problem solving is essential to the proper functioning of a democracy. Any political structure must among other things aim at social problem solving or what may be accurately referred to as public conflict resolution. Democracy's capacity for conflict resolution is vitally grounded on the citizens' powers of intelligent conflict resolution. Dewey's basic political orientation aligns him with the political tradition of republicanism. Republicanism stresses that citizenship is not defined by the citizen's relationship to a government, but rather by the citizen's relationship to fellow citizens. That relationship must be one of equality among peers, so that the body of citizens may have the capacity for self-ruling power. The republican conception of "equal opportunity" accordingly finds that each citizen should have an equal opportunity for meaningful political participation. This political equality is Dewey's primary understanding of equal opportunity. Equality of political participation comes in many forms; there are numerous capacities for political involvement besides public conflict resolution that will not be discussed here. However, given that democracies will contain social groups pursuing diverse values, stable and peaceful democracies should pursue public conflict resolution. Education according to Dewey is the instrument making such public deliberation possible in a republican democracy. Other kinds of democracies, which do not take "self-rule" as the political standard, accordingly do not see in education the mainspring of democracy, and they would not construct a vision of ideal education as fundamentally political.

Against rights-based libertarianism, republicanism does not start from trans-social inherent rights that must define political relations, and thus does not frame political issues in terms of placing limitations on the powers of government. Limitations may be needed; but from republicanism's perspective, it is the capacity for citizens to stand equally together as a self-ruling and self-determining group which defines democratic government. Hobbesian liberalism depicts a fragmented aggregate of individual selfish citizens confronting a powerfully unified government capable of either tyranny or peace keeping. Lockean liberalism likewise ponders how the individualized rights of each citizen can be best protected so that every person may have an opportunity to prosper. But these liberalisms assume that the primary problem is how to guard against unjust interference and enslavement by the state and by other citizens. Negative liberty, the freedom from interference, is the sole type of freedom receiving consideration. However, Dewey and the republican tradition agree that democracies flourish where citizens can meaningfully participate in public deliberation, and hence negative liberty might not be a good measure of democratic life. Merely guarding against interference does nothing to ensure that all, or even many, citizens have the genuine capacity to influence democratic discussion and decision making. The parallel in free-market economics is obvious: protection against interference in a capitalist system does little to prevent poverty and economic helplessness. Although a free-market economy may be comfortable placing vast economic decision-making power in the hands of a few wealthy citizens, democracies should not be as comfortable doing likewise in the political sphere. Republicanism goes further than promoting noninterference by advocating the establishment of "nondomination" between citizens to guarantee effective political participation.[10]

Dewey's political philosophy attempted to delineate several specific components (especially education) of a republican model of self-rule that could distinguish mere majority rule by simple voting (rightly derided by antidemocratic thinkers since Plato) from the more sensible intelligent practices of group deliberation. It must be noted first that the concept of group deliberation is hardly a settled and stable notion in political theory. Rights-based liberalism, for example, does not lag behind other theories in esteem for group deliberation (or education). However, this type of liberalism naturally shapes this concept to fit its characteristic assumption that a citizen engages in group deliberation only to attempt to protect her own interests. The tempting slogan that "group deliberation must have group aims" would be therefore false, because rights-based liberalism would hardly assume that any group aims, other than the aims of factional segments, motivate public deliberation. Rights-based liberalism was, after all, formulated to provide functional governing for a pluralistic country lacking much social agreement on important ends. Strategic compromise among citizens along broadly utilitarian lines was the natural interpretation of group deliberation's optimum contribution to political progress.

Prominent descendants of classic liberalism, notably including John Rawls and Jürgen Habermas, have rejected utilitarian political foundations in favor of a Kantian requirement that deliberation must be "rational" in some stronger sense than mere strategic negotiation. These philosophers have accordingly demanded that a democracy must by definition engage in a form of group deliberation leading to consensus which excludes appeal to factional or individual values (commitments to a vision of "the good" and the "good life"). Such values are illegitimate on the grounds that appeal to them could never produce consensus in a deeply pluralistic country. Only values held by all citizens may be used to justify policy proposals. Thus it appears that Rawls and Habermas have rehabilitated the notion of group deliberation toward group ends, yet paradoxically they have actually emptied the concept of group deliberation of any meaning, since the exclusion of value commitments from deliberation leaves the questions "toward what does group deliberation aim?" and "upon what basis could consensus be reached?" quite unanswerable in any concrete way.[11] No one denies that social conflicts deserve a public consensus on a potential resolution —but praising consensus is not the same as displaying some actual conditions under which consensus would occur. These forms of rights-based political liberalism encourage us to think of a democracy as a procedural process that first and foremost protects the right of an individual against those public deliberations grounded in others' values that could never sound persuasive to him. But why should individuals have the right to veto reasons for policies (and thus to prevent consensus) using their private or group values, but at the same time be forbidden from advancing their own values as reasons for policies? Either one's view of "the good" is politically relevant or not. Rights-based procedural liberalism simply guarantees that a sufficiently recalcitrant faction need never worry about being confronted with a reasonably persuasive argument for any policy that goes against its basic interests.

Rawls and Habermas are only recent examples of a long-standing trend in modern social philosophy that surrenders any possible hope of rational deliberation about important values when confronted by pluralism. Not surprisingly, such surrender assumes that all reasoning is instrumental: we can reason only about means and never about ends. Given an instrumentalist notion of reason, and a country that is sufficiently pluralistic, then rights-based political liberalism appears to be the only option. Many advocates of republicanism seem impressed by this inference and ally themselves with forms of communitarianism that require in advance some basic values held in common by all in order to prevent deep pluralism. But Dewey was never forced into these limited options. His social philosophy's staunch opposition to rights-based political liberalism is predicated on the possibility of reasoning about both means *and* ends, plans *and* goals, and ways of life *and* concepts of "the good." Dewey's pragmatic moral theory is designed expressly to show how "final" goals and "highest" goods are amenable to revision in light of practical experience. While this theory cannot be explored here, the possibility that public deliberation can reasonably modify even the most staunchly held basic values permits Dewey to evade the dilemma of republican communitarianism versus procedural liberalism. Dewey indeed viewed his republican philosophy as following the spirit of liberalism, because his story of liberalism is an account of the pursuit of liberating capacities for meaningful citizenship. Dewey's political theory is a liberal republicanism, and his theory of education is thus founded on the imperative to create free (both free from domination and the will to dominate) citizens capable of self-rule:

> The original use of liberal in anything like a technical sense was in connection with schools and studies, when the word meant that which was adapted to the character and needs of free men in distinction from training that was imposed from without, that was routine and that fitted men for mechanical and subservient pursuits. The association of liberalism with liberty remains a permanent deposit. The historic signification of the word is associated also with liberality and generosity, especially of mind and character. It points to an open mind, to emancipation from bigotry and from domination by prejudice.[12]

Dewey's liberal philosophy of democracy might be termed "procedural republicanism," if that phrase does not sound too self-contradictory. A procedural democracy has a paramount respect for the process of free, open, and reasonable public deliberation. A republican democracy emphasizes that public deliberation requires the establishment of social equality and freedom from domination for all citizens. Provided that public deliberation can (under the right conditions) reasonably question and modify commitments to the good, then a procedural republicanism does not need to specify any inherent individual rights for protection, nor does it need to require that some vision of the good must be shared by all citizens. A procedural republicanism must account for the public desirability of public deliberation in the first place, which is something that too many political thinkers have simply taken for granted. If a democracy wants to foster valuable public deliberation, then it must strive for intelligent and purposeful deliberation about real problems. What is needed is an explicit connection drawn between democracy and practical social intelligence. Procedural republicanism establishes this connection through what Dewey termed "social intelligence."

Social intelligence requires two features of a society to be present: the society is sensitive to social problems, and the society permits public investigation into ways of resolving problems. Democracy, according to Dewey, is the way of life that prominently displays both features. Democracy is impossible if there is not enough sensitivity to the problematic experiences of portions of society, and democracy is also impossible if public investigations into possible conflict resolutions are obstructed. Authoritarian and totalitarian societies typically lack public sensitivity and public scrutiny. Only a democracy expects that those people who experience social problems should be the people who participate in the investigation of possible solutions and decide whether the experiments of proposed solutions are successful. Social intelligence is therefore possible only in a democracy. Dewey's vision of the proper functioning of democracy is grounded on the possibility that goods can be evaluated, reevaluated, and mutually adjusted in an intelligent and experimental social inquiry:

> Democracy is a way of personal life controlled not merely by faith in human nature in general but by faith in the capacity of human beings for intelligent judgment and action if proper conditions are furnished. . . . For what is the faith of democracy in the role of consultation, of conference, of persuasion, of discussion, in formation of public opinion, which in the long run is self-corrective, except faith in the capacity of the intelligence of the common man to respond with commonsense to the free play of facts and ideas which are secured by effective guarantees of free inquiry, free assembly and free communication?[13]

For democracy to be intelligent, it cannot be merely the process of polling of individuals who vote only in light of their subjective desires. Democracy is the experimental method applied to the question, How can a society preserve and expand the shared experience of cooperation in the face of inevitable difficulties and conflicts? The society must apply democratic social intelligence in every aspect of its life.[14]

Education is essential to democracy because it represents the progressive aspect of democratic problem solving. The explicitly political institutions of a democracy have an important role in value inquiry and conflict resolution, but education is the more fundamental engine of democracy. Education is essential to intelligent public deliberation because, through education, citizens are better prepared for appreciating and resolving social problems. As in Dewey's own time, many people since have assumed that education's responsibility is simply the instruction of basic facts and primary skills necessary for the young adult's entrance into the working world. Many people have also assumed that it is government's responsibility to notice social problems and provide solutions. Because of the combined prevalence of such assumptions, the idea that education is the most effective way to resolve social problems has not been obvious and immediate for most Americans. But Dewey's vision of an educational system permits it to teach facts and skills through the activities of problem solving in group deliberation.[15]

Perhaps a fragmented realm of education, divided by public and private, secular and religious, and pluralist and ethnic categories, might deliver problem-solving skills for all children. But, as Dewey explains, such a realm would be much more likely to produce a fragmented society of adults who are less willing and able to respectfully deliberate with any other adults from a different portion of society. Minority and underprivileged groups would suffer further from the widespread consequences of living in that sort of dysfunctionally segregated society. Of course, our nation today displays appreciable fragmentation. As a result, it suffers from failures of respectful communication, to varying degrees. Democracy can and should promote pluralism but cannot long withstand segregation in any form. For Dewey, the most pernicious corrosive to public deliberation is discourse segregation obstructing mutual comprehension and understanding. Constitutional rights can bring down visible barriers to free communication, but effective speech requires respectful listeners:

> Democracy is a way of life controlled by a working faith in the possibilities of human nature. . . . That belief is without basis and significance save as it means faith in the potentialities of human nature as that nature is exhibited in every human being irrespective of race, color, sex, birth and family, of material or cultural wealth. This faith may be enacted in statutes, but it is only on paper unless it is put in force in the attitudes which human beings display to one another in all the incidents and relations of daily life. . . . Merely legal guarantees of the civil liberties of free belief, free expression, free assembly are of little avail if in daily life freedom of communication, the give and take of ideas, facts, experiences, is choked by mutual suspicion, by abuse, by fear and hatred.[16]

What is the foundation for mutual comprehension and understanding? Dewey argued that cooperative and productive social interaction (in Dewey's terminology this is "shared experience") is the minimally necessary ground for the sort of mutual appreciation and respect which can in turn nurture the capacities for mutual comprehension and understanding. The higher levels of collaborative problem solving, unified consensus, and community solidarity may or may not be possible with further careful and constructive communication.[17] But these prized democratic accomplishments of public "self-rule" by citizens will surely wither if the ground is parched by a deficiency of shared experience. The following quotation exemplifies Dewey's definition of democracy in terms of a society's capacities for facilitating shared experience and peaceful problem resolution. Education is essential to developing these democratic capacities:

> Since education is a social process, and there are many kinds of societies, a criterion for educational criticism and construction implies a particular social ideal. The two points selected by which to measure the worth of a form of social life are the extent in which the interests of a group are shared by all its members, and the fullness and freedom with which it interacts with other groups. An undesirable society, in other words, is one which internally and externally sets up barriers to free intercourse and communication of experience. A society which makes provision for participation in its good of all its members on equal terms and which secures flexible readjustment of its institutions through interaction of the different forms of associated life is in so far democratic. Such a society must have a type of education which gives individuals a personal interest in social relationships and control, and the habits of mind which secure social changes without introducing disorder.[18]

Democratic education cannot be value-neutral—indeed, Dewey explicitly claims that the central democratic values of respect for free cooperative association, equal political participation, and peaceful social change must be exemplified in the processes of education. Any government or social group that restricts citizens' free association, diminishes political participation, or condones violent behavior violates the foundations of liberal democracy in general and undermines the principles of procedural republicanism in particular. Therefore, both imposed segregation and self-segregation cannot be tolerated and should be equally condemned.

The values inherent in democratic education should be animated by a combination of two axioms. First, moral character formation is an essential task of any educational process that contributes to the perpetuation of a society. Second, a crucial component of moral character in a democracy is an ability to intelligently reevaluate values and ends in group problem solving. Both axioms have been strongly rejected again and again in the long course of debate over education in this country. Social groups which do not find their own traditional moral principles to be the subject matter of civic education often complain that moral character cannot result. Many liberals who desire civic education free from any social group's particular moral principles also do not expect production of moral character. The long history of religious conflict behind the American doctrine of separation of church and state is partially responsible for the widespread assumption that moral principles have no place in secular education. Dewey himself did not regret the gradual elimination of religious indoctrination from public education. However, there are numerous nondenominational character norms deserving recognition as "moral" that should be universally held since they make democratic life possible. Among these character norms is the ability to reflect critically on the values of oneself and others. Value-neutral liberalism has no place for this ability. To advance mutual toleration for divergent values, it is claimed, criticism of moral values must not be tolerated. Minority social groups that cannot achieve segregated moral education may also understandably prefer value-neutral civic education and its underlying premise that basic moral values are by their nature immune from rational evaluation. Dewey believed that democracy and dogma can never be coherently combined, since the vitality of one automatically limits the range of the other.[19]

Value-neutral liberalism may be inspired by the liberal value of toleration, but toleration for its own sake leads to unacceptable results, such as the toleration of racial prejudice. Determining intolerable values can be accomplished by balancing toleration against other democratic principles mentioned above. This determination should be done democratically. No a priori method could fix the proper boundaries of toleration since the pragmatic meaning of democratic principles gradually shifts over time. Our present-day legal toleration for demeaning epithets in the name of free speech, for example, must be understood in its proper context of actual conditions of social equality. This particular application of freedom of speech may require alteration in the future if further progress toward full social equality is at stake.

Value-neutral liberalism is constitutionally incapable of formulating a comprehensive philosophy of education for a democracy. Setting all values off-limit for deliberation, by taking some for granted (democratic principles) and placing others in a criticism-free zone (any specific group values like ethnic or religious morals), only guarantees that students will never acquire robust powers of critical inquiry into values. Value-neutral education therefore cannot develop young adults who have the capacities necessary for genuine democratic deliberation. Of course, such capacities are not highly valued by some minority social groups, revealing their illiberal tendencies. Social groups grounded in dogma (religious or otherwise) are perfectly capable of formulating comprehensive philosophies of education, but these would never be philosophies of education for a democracy.

Can a comprehensive philosophy of education for a deeply pluralistic democracy be achieved? Dewey's efforts notwithstanding, some political thinkers have been persuaded that only a rights-based political philosophy that prevails over any conception of the good could ground democratic institutions. Dewey did not agree that "the right" should prevail over "the good." But Dewey did not believe that "the good" should prevail over "the right" either, since Dewey characteristically could not hold that a democracy must first have secured one "good" for all members of society. Communitarians have protested that no conception of the right can be divorced from people's actual commitments to life goods. Dewey would find this partly congenial to his project but also somewhat misleading. He did forcefully argue that there is no such thing as individuality in the abstract since real people cannot be justly treated as political units stripped of social relationships. What individuals find valuable and worthy of effort gains significance only through modes of social experience:

> The conditions of a vitally valuable experience for the individual are so bound up with complex, collective, social relationships that the individualism of the past has lost its meaning. Individuals will always be the centre and the consummation of experience, but what an individual actually *is* in his life-experience depends upon the nature and movement of associated life.[20]

This communitarian manifesto implies that education in a democracy must always look to the development of social capacities serving community needs instead of private wants:

> As the material of genuine development is that of human contacts and associations, so the end, the value that is the criterion and directing guide of educational work, is social. The acquisition however perfectly of skills is not an end in itself. They are things to be put to use as a contribution to a common and shared life. They are intended, indeed, to make an individual more capable of self-support and of self-respecting independence. But unless this end is placed in the context of services rendered to others, services which they need to the fulfillment also of their lives, skills gained will be put to an egoistic and selfish use as means of a trained shrewdness for personal advantage at the cost of others' claims and opportunities for the good life.[21]

After rights-based justice is set aside, the communitarian perspective cannot be used to force a choice between homogeneous countries grounding justice on one single vision of the good and heterogeneous countries abandoning justice. There is another alternative sketched in Dewey's writings: a country containing any number of flourishing social groups engaged in a mixture of cooperation and conflict can maintain a working system of justice that protects social equality and nondomination. This system of justice is the unfinished and imperfect product of a society's historical experience of resolving past social conflicts, and hopefully for democracies this system of justice continues to be improved and expanded. The concrete provisions of justice may usefully be termed "rights" in Dewey's theory, so long as such rights are not taken to be grounded in some notion of "human nature" or some a priori reasoning from dogmatic premises.

Dewey's theory of justice is therefore rooted in a democracy's never-ending construction of deeper and more permanent rights that guarantee nondomination, freedom of cooperative association, and opportunity for participation in peaceful problem solving. These are the "freedoms of opportunity" worth having. There are social groups in America that do not respect these freedoms—can they justifiably cry "Oppression!" against the establishment of democratic justice? Perhaps these illiberal social groups do not find any irony in desiring freedom for their group from external forces while denying that freedom to their internal members. Be that as it may, the charge of hypocrisy can be supplemented by the observation that very few domestic ethnic/religious groups deserve protections from American liberal democracy, such as special status and group rights. As Will Kymlicka explains, there is an important distinction demarcating three candidates for protection: (1) geographically established "nations" involuntarily enveloped by conquering country, (2) the descendants of involuntary immigrants, and (3) voluntary immigrants. Voluntary immigrants appear not to have sufficient justification for subsequently demanding special group status and protection, whereas conquered peoples, such as Indian tribes, may likely have such justification. African Americans that fall into the second category, in Kymlicka's view, may justifiably consider forming a separate "people" and negotiate for special status.[22] The practicalities of such "nation forming" are weighty, and relatively few African Americans at present are seriously interested in that option, preferring to continue the pursuit of fully equal citizenship. If such a nation were formed, it is highly unlikely that it would become an illiberal authoritarian society. If no nation emerges, then it remains the grave responsibility for America to proceed at full throttle toward equal rights and opportunities for all citizens.

The subject of Dewey and multiculturalism would require a long book; I will limit discussion here to the question of what sort of multiculturalism could find support in Dewey's educational philosophy. Many of Dewey's fellow pragmatists and progressives used the terms "pluralism," "multiculturalism," and "melting pot" with a bewildering variety of meanings. Dewey should not be lumped together with those who sought the elimination of distinctive ethic customs. In one his earliest statements (1902) on immigration and education, Dewey expressed concern for the loss of native customs and values:

> The power of the public schools to assimilate different races to our own institutions, through the education given to the younger generation, is doubtless one

of the most remarkable exhibitions of vitality that the world has ever seen. But, after all, it leaves the older generation still untouched; and the assimilation of the younger can hardly be complete or certain as long as the homes of the parents remain comparatively unaffected. Indeed, wise observers in both New York and Chicago have recently sounded a note of alarm. They have called attention to the fact that in some respects the children are too rapidly, I will not say Americanized, but too rapidly de-nationalized. They lose the positive and conservative value of their own native traditions, their own native music, art, and literature. They do not get complete initiation into the customs of their new country, and so are frequently left floating and unstable between the two. They even learn to despise the dress, bearing, habits, language, and beliefs of their parents—many of which have more substance and worth than the superficial putting on of the newly adopted habits.[23]

Like Horace Kallen, Dewey rejected the "melting pot" metaphor and "Americanization" as a legitimate goal. Shortly after Kallen published his key essays defending pluralism in 1915, Dewey applauded his efforts, saying that

I want to see this country American and that means the English tradition reduced to a strain along with others. . . . I quite agree with your orchestra idea, but upon condition we really get a symphony and not a lot of different instruments playing simultaneously. I never did care for the melting pot metaphor, but genuine assimilation *to one another*—not to Anglo-saxondom—seems to be essential to an America. That each cultural section should maintain its distinctive literary and artistic traditions seems to me most desirable, but in order that it might have the more to contribute to others.[24]

Dewey exposed the key issue confronting education by questioning whether the concept of the new "hyphenated American" really respects the individual's own experience of life in this country:

The American nation is itself complex and compound. Strictly speaking it is interracial and international in its make-up. It is composed of a multitude of peoples speaking different tongues, inheriting diverse traditions, cherishing varying ideals of life. This fact is basic to our nationalism as distinct from that of other peoples. . . . The way to deal with hyphenism, in other words, is to welcome it, but to welcome it in the sense of extracting from each people its special good, so that it shall surrender into a common fund of wisdom and experience what it especially has to contribute. All of these surrenders and contributions taken together create the national spirit of America. The dangerous thing is for each factor to isolate itself, to try to live off its past, and then to attempt to impose itself upon other elements, or, at least, to keep itself intact and thus refuse to accept what other cultures have to offer, so as thereby to be transmuted into authentic Americanism.

In what is rightly objected to as hyphenism the hyphen has become something which separates one people from other peoples—and thereby prevents American nationalism. Such terms as Irish-American or Hebrew-American or German-American are false terms because they seem to assume something which is already in existence called America to which the other factor may be externally hitched on. The fact is the genuine American, the typical American, is himself a hyphenated character. This does not mean that he is part American, and that some foreign ingredient is then added. It means that, as I have said, he is international and inter-racial in his make-up. He is not American plus Pole or German. But the American is himself Pole-German-English-French-Spanish-Italian-Greek-Irish-Scandinavian-Bohemian-Jew- and so on. The point is to see to it that the hyphen connects in-stead of separates. And this means at least that our public schools shall teach each factor to respect every other, and shall take pains to enlighten all as to the great past contributions of every strain in our composite make-up.[25]

In all of his writings on education, despite the setbacks suffered by progressivism in the face of increasing xenophobia after World War I, Dewey consistently dem-onstrated the compatibility between preserving genuine pluralism, expanding social cooperation, and guaranteeing equal rights. Some critics have tried to de-pict Dewey's view of education as inimical to individualism because they view the process of promoting social cooperation as the repression of uniqueness.[26] But Dewey's plan for fostering favorable conditions for voluntary cooperation where individuals find such cooperation valuable is a very different project from coercively congregating people into foreordained social structures. All too often such critics have come from the standpoint of an established illiberal social group seeking protection for its own field's flock instead of genuine personal freedom and uniqueness. Uniqueness cannot be sensibly equated with aloofness from social relationships; indeed, a larger diversity of possible social relations permits an exponentially greater number of possible life plans. It is democracy, and education for democracy, that permits the only kind of individuality worth seeking, no matter the pleas of illiberal authoritarians claiming to know which life plans possess final validity and which chosen people deserve equality.

Schooling and Equal Opportunity

Dewey's philosophy of democracy requires that all modes of education should (1) foster the opportunity for cooperative shared experience and (2) de-velop the capacity for intelligent problem solving, especially conflict resolution over values. We can outline the workings of a mode of education completely antithetical to democracy by reversing these functions: a completely antidemo-cratic mode of education would (1) tightly constrict a person's opportunity for social engagement with anyone except for those quite similar in background and social status and (2) carefully restrict a person's material for thought to the memorization of "established" facts and the application of "authoritative" prin-ciples to particular situations. It should be unnecessary to describe at length Dewey's diatribes against the education of his time for embodying these me-dieval antidemocratic mechanisms. Segregation and dogma, both rooted in elit-ism, are the degenerative diseases fatal to healthy democratic life. Dewey de-fended one system of public education, guaranteeing a universal proficiency in respectful public cooperation, discourse, and problem solving, as the best pro-tection for a democracy against the corrosive powers of elitism of every kind.

Public education in America has had to overcome two primary obstacles: resistance to the notion that public funds should support education for all portions of society, and resistance to the idea that public schools should not be segregated by gender or race or religion. Historically, most minority groups have had to fight these kinds of resistance to truly public education. But the attitude toward public education has hardly been uniform across all minority groups. Minority social groups that cannot achieve a degree of segregation sufficient to implement their own educational systems may appreciate a compromise with the dominant civic educational system if that system centers on basic skills and positive knowledge. The knowledge and skill base useful for functioning in a country's economy has long been regarded by many liberals and minority social groups as the obvious curriculum for all children. In the past two decades in America such liberals and social groups have been joined by some conservatives for a common cause of advocating that public education should exclusively focus on producing able workers. Paradoxically, this newfound anxiety and energy directed toward public education's basic curriculum of reading, writing, mathematics, and science has been matched in volume by proclamations announcing that the time has come for establishing vigorous competition to public education in the form of private schools.

Conservatives worried about government intrusion into the allegedly private realm of moral values have found allies in liberals worried about the survival and self-respect of minority social groups. Many of these conservatives are also supporters of religious minorities which have long desired their own segregated educational systems. The collision of liberal forces backing value-free public education with conservative forces advocating segregated religious education produced a remarkable synthesis of ideas—why should the government be forbidden from using tax money to support private religious educational institutions? So long as that public money is ostensibly paying for the same secular education that a student would have received in a public school, students can at the same time also receive the moral character training approved by parents. Society appears to be repaid thrice-over by this arrangement. A student is prepared for entering the workforce; a student has developed moral character; and a student is well formed for perpetuating a minority social group. Furthermore, the backlash against value-neutral liberalism was inevitable: couldn't the lack of virtue in our children be the result of public education's failure to teach morality? If what this nation needs is more moral virtue, and if public education shouldn't or couldn't teach moral virtue, then this country must offer an alternative to public education (or abolish public education altogether). If public schools cannot be as effective in teaching the basics, and cannot approach private schools' ability to develop virtue, then private schools deserve consideration.

The equality of opportunity principle is always useful for enhancing this argument's persuasiveness. Suspicious of conservative motives for advocating private schooling, many minority groups wonder how their members could meet the expenses of adequate private schooling. Will poorer segments of society continue to be burdened with impoverished schools, regardless of whether the school is public or private? If the government guaranteed that each student could pay a certain amount each year, such as a school "voucher," with this guarantee grounded in the principle of equal opportunity ("no child deserves to be trapped in a failing school"), then minority groups might be reassured. However, the wealthy could still purchase as much high-quality private schooling as they could afford, and with the government's assistance guaranteed for all students, far more families could suddenly find expensive private schooling within their reach. This arrangement does not really provide for equality of opportunity, but rather equality of minimum opportunity. Equality of education will not be achieved, since quality of education is (roughly) proportional to expenditures.[27] If competition by private schools will only produce equality of minimum opportunity, where is the advantage over the current public education system? If what is needed is simply equality of minimum opportunity, then that could probably be achieved far more effectively and cheaply by upgrading existing impoverished schools now. The suspicions of minorities are not diminished when it is noticed that proposals to upgrade "failing" schools rarely arouse as much conservative fervor as proposals for funding school vouchers. The chasm between the minimum schooling available for disadvantaged minorities and schooling for elites would only expand if the government supported private schooling.[28]

Another type of argument for privatization encourages family control over education in order to advance freedom of religion. Many parents are hearing a seductive plea for privatization in the claim that private schools rightfully return control over education to them. Instead of education dictated by the government, private schools would provide the education of choice made by each family. This "state of families" kind of argument, as termed by Amy Gutmann, gains its appeal by extolling both freedom of choice and liberation from government. However, this kind of choice and liberation, when practiced by many, would have unintended yet foreseeable consequences. What might be the long-term effects of revived self-segregation? Those who predict among other results a continuation of improving religious and racial harmonies may be making a vital mistake, rashly presuming that past gains may be easily preserved. Gutmann provides a useful thought experiment demonstrating how public education should receive due credit for lowering religious prejudice:

> Many public schools in the mid-nineteenth century were, to say the least, disrespectful of Catholicism. . . . Imagine that instead of becoming more respectful, public schools had been abolished, and states had subsidized parents to send their children to the private school of their choice. Protestant parents would have sent their children to Protestant schools, Catholic parents to Catholic schools. The Protestant majority would have continued to educate their children to be disrespectful if not intolerant of Catholics. The religious prejudices of Protestant parents would have been visited on their children, and the social, economic, and political effects of those prejudices would have persisted, probably with considerably less public protest, to this day. There may be little reason today for Catholic parents to worry that privatizing schools will reinstitutionalize bigotry against Catholics, at least in

the short run. But one reason that Catholics need not worry is that a state of families today would be built on the moral capital created over almost a century by a public school system. That moral capital is just now being created for blacks and Hispanics, and even more well-established minorities might reasonably fear that returning to a state of families would eventually squander the moral capital created by public schooling.[29]

The moral capital for blacks and other racial minorities is of recent origin indeed, especially in the South. The staunch resistance to desegregation in the South continued for decades after the 1954 decision *Brown vs. Board of Education* formally eliminated "separate but equal" educational systems. Several states, including Virginia, Georgia, Mississippi, and Alabama, funded tuition grant plans, scholarships, and other similar voucher programs that effectively permitted white parents to keep their children in segregated private schools. It required a long series of federal decisions stretching well into the 1970s to close off the more transparent routes funneling public money to segregated private schools in the name of "school choice."[30] To this day hundreds of private schools in the South, most operated by religious denominations, make freedom of choice a reality for white families that can afford them.[31] Proponents of education's privatization must struggle with this distressingly resilient feature of contemporary American society. Granted, some private schools are presently more integrated than inner-city schools which draw from ethnic enclaves and ghettos. But unless funding for all schools is roughly equalized, until private schools compete for inner-city students, and when family racism is neutralized, universal school choice could not magically produce widespread integration.

The recent dramatic elevation of "civic virtues" to political prominence has also become intertwined with the debates over school choice. No less a figure than William Bennett, Secretary of Education in the Reagan administration, has explicitly stated that private school choice is essential to restoring respect for the civic virtues of liberty and equality, along with a host of specific moral virtues. Bennett holds that (1) schools must instill these civic virtues and (2) parents should have the power of school choice aided by government vouchers. As Michael Engel points out, Bennett does not realize the contradictory nature of these two propositions, even as he strangely appeals to nineteenth-century common schools as exemplary models of virtue instruction. The tendency of those common schools only to perpetuate prejudice has apparently been forgotten—replaced by a curious confidence in every American parent always to choose private schools which instill toleration and respect.[32] Dewey persistently argued that public education, answerable to a democracy and responsive to democratic ideals, is the obvious and natural conduit for shaping virtuous citizens. If today's public schools do not sufficiently shape virtue, then public forums on curriculum reform are needed, and not a panic retreat to the hidden agendas of private schools.

Further arguments for privatization portray education's aim as equality of economic opportunity. When viewed through the lens of economic advantage, two key considerations become paramount. First, how can education be improved through economic forces? Second, how does education deliver economic value to its consumers? The first question may be answered by applying a theory of open markets, in which fair competition (such as private schools) can force improvement or elimination of any educational institution. The central article of faith for open market theorists is that choice automatically forces improvement. However, there is hardly any evidence that private schools, *when teaching the same kind of students,* provide enhanced educational value. Some proficiency increases can be easily measured when the selected students of private schools are compared to the students of public schools which must admit all. But the much-heralded elimination of bureaucracies, teachers unions, tenure, desegregation orders, affirmative action, or due process for student expulsions has had little impact on academic achievement when similar groups of students are compared.[33] The second question may be answered by applying a theory of individual free consumption of goods, in which the consumer prefers some degree of choice over no choice at all, in order to maximize value for each person. Both considerations of market ideology go well beyond the obvious fact that schooling provides valued preparation (more or less) for employment, by treating education as primarily a private good instead of a public good. If schooling produces an important public good that must be provided by the government where private suppliers fail, then market analysis is inappropriate. What public good does schooling produce? If done well, schooling achieves its democratic aims of (1) fostering the opportunity for cooperative shared experience and (2) developing the capacity for intelligent problem solving, especially conflict resolution over values. Private schools tend to jeopardize or abandon these aims, while public schools (again, where well designed) do not. Therefore, schooling should be regarded as a public good immune from market forces.

Gutmann agrees with Dewey's assessment of liberal republicanism that full political participation must be the primary goal of K–12 education. Tracking, racial segregation, gender discrimination, and narrowly vocational training all stand condemned, even if they might in some cases improve academic achievement:

> The most devastating criticism we can level at primary schools, therefore is not
> that they fail to give equally talented children an equal chance to earn the same in-
> come or to pursue professional occupations, but that they fail to give all (educable)
> children an education adequate to take advantage of their political status as citi-
> zens.[34]

Naturally, many parents and students may individually prioritize other goals, such as achieving employment or forging a unified ethnic or religious community. Advocates of market ideology do not fail to highlight the desirability of school choice by promising to satisfy individual needs and priorities. As Jeffrey Hening explains, the "choice" label carries associations with freedom of movement, freedom of thought, religious freedom, and cultural pluralism. These associated ideas naturally have a strong appeal for Americans, but in actual practice the abstract ideals of choice and freedom do not automatically translate into a demand that government withdraw from education.[35] Furthermore, any concrete plan for erecting private schools next to public schools only redistributes choice without increasing the overall amount of choice. In the absence of unlimited funding for education, one family's enhanced educational choice eliminates a possible choice for another. A well-funded magnet school in my neighborhood does not guarantee a place for my child, and my child may instead be transported to a distant poorer school. The ideology of market choice is always blind to preexisting financial and social disparities, and disadvantaged minority groups should carefully examine the reality behind the rhetoric of "choice."

Could private schools in principle satisfy the basic democratic aims and avoid exacerbating the harmful effects of segregation? Undoubtedly so, provided that careful public scrutiny ensures that a private school's admittance policy, educational curriculum, and social atmosphere are all consistent with the promotion of free association, mutual respect, and democratic deliberation. To prevent the evaporation of the precious "moral capital" for minorities, private schools could not be as free from government oversight as market advocates desire. Indeed, under these criteria for operation, private schools would not look very different from public schools, apart from the possibly variable quality of faculty and facilities.

Dewey was also concerned with the vexing question of class and wealth gaps in relation to education. Minority groups which seek genuinely equal citizenship for their members should not ignore the widening chasm between the wealthy and middle-lower classes. They rightly view education as a means to achieving and solidifying middle class status, but this goal requires possessing full citizenship in addition to employment opportunity. Dewey never failed to stress both aspects of social progress. Occasionally his claim that economic disparity is a source of racial prejudice is taken to be his only analysis.[36] Granted, one must look elsewhere for a psychological analysis of emotional disturbances such as prejudice and hatred, since Dewey never tried to be a philosopher of irrationality. However, the notion that breaking down economic barriers would go a long way toward ameliorating prejudice as well as moving blacks toward full citizenship was hardly mistaken or shortsighted.[37] Since economic class unfortunately has largely determined educational opportunity in America, heightened economic status and its concomitant social integration have been essential to educational progress.[38]

The dismal record of prejudice and violence against blacks perpetrated by whites unwilling to bestow full citizenship has understandably forced numerous black communities to construct separate educational institutions since emancipation. But at this crucial juncture in America, after the slow but sure progress of civil rights and racial integration of the twentieth century,[39] it may be unwise for any minority group to seek refuge in the kind of educational privatization that would harm democracy if available to all segments of society. Instead, a Deweyan philosophy would recommend that minority groups seek ways to achieve their common interests for improved schooling, which should include increased funding linked to accountability, greater community involvement, higher teacher quality, curriculum reform, and a recentering on civic morality.[40]

Nothing in this analysis and critique of school privatization should be construed as a repudiation of greater parental involvement in schooling. The spirit of Dewey's vision of democratic participation supports parents' participation in schooling as essential to community life. When this valuable activism is supported by the democratic principles of free association and equal citizenship, then citizens can master the process of deliberative democracy, instead of feeling dependent on government action. It is this capacity for exercising responsible participation in the democratic life of a society which characterizes equal freedom and opportunity. Education multiplies this investment of effort many times over, where it is well designed to develop the skills of democratic life:

> In ultimate analysis, freedom is important because it is a condition both of realization of the potentialities of an individual and of social progress. Without light, a people perishes. Without freedom, light grows dim and darkness comes to reign. Without freedom, old truths become so stale and worn that they cease to be truths and become mere dictates of external authority. Without freedom, search for new truth and the disclosure of new paths in which humanity may walk more securely and justly come to an end. Freedom which is liberation for the individual, is the ultimate assurance of the movement of society toward more humane and noble ends. He who would put the freedom of others in bond, especially freedom of inquiry and communication, creates conditions which finally imperil his own freedom and that of his offspring. Eternal vigilance is the price of the conservation and extension of freedom, and the schools should be the ceaseless guardians and creators of this vigilance.[41]

NOTES

1.   For surveys of the public school movement, see Richard Pratte, *The Public School Movement: A Critical Study* (New York: David McKay, 1973); David Nasaw, *Schooled to Order: A Social History of Public Schooling in the United States* (Oxford: Oxford University Press, 1979); and Charles L. Glenn, Jr., *The Myth of the Common School* (Amherst: University of Massachusetts Press, 1988).

2.   Informative accounts of proposed reforms and their implications are provided by Jeffrey R. Henig, *Rethinking School Choice* (Princeton: Princeton University Press, 1994); Peter W. Cookson, Jr., *School Choice: The Struggle for the Soul of American Education* (New Haven: Yale University Press, 1994); John B. Williams, *Race Discrimination in Public Higher Education: Interpreting Federal Civil Rights Enforcement, 1964–1996* (Westport, Conn.: Greenwood, 1997); and William Lowe Boyd, "The 'R's of School Reform' and the Politics of Reforming or Replacing Public Schools," *Journal of Educational Change* 1 (2000): 225–52.

3.   The larger story of public education and the progressive education movement is told by Maurice R. Berube, *American School Reform: Progressive,*

Equity, and Excellence Movements, 1883–1993 (Westport, Conn.: Praeger, 1994). Dewey had mixed reactions to the explosion of "progressive" private schools in the 1910s and 1920s. Too many schools, in Dewey's view, applied suspect formulas of "child-centered" romanticism without designing curricula, involving parents, or considering surrounding social contexts. See Dewey, "How Much Freedom in New Schools?" (LW 5:319–25).

Dewey's own Laboratory School, founded at the University of Chicago in 1894, was never meant to be a private school but was a teaching environment designed for studying possible reforms for public schools. See Laurel N. Tanner, *Dewey's Laboratory School: Lessons for Today* (New York: Teachers College Press, 1997). It should also be noted that Dewey's praise for the achievements of black educators and schools, like those of W. E. B. Du Bois, was not intended as an oblique endorsement of the "separate but equal" doctrine.

4. As curiously pronounced by John P. Diggins, "Proceduralism, Pragmatism, and Postmodernity," *Hedgehog Review* 2, no. 1 (spring 2000): 102–103. I refer the reader to Dewey's "Racial Prejudice and Friction" (MW 13:242–54) and "Understanding and Prejudice" (LW 5:396–97). More than a dozen additional articles primarily concern race/ethnic relations and eliminating prejudice. A search through Dewey's *Collected Works* on CD-ROM produced over four hundred "hits" for paragraphs about racial issues both in America and in foreign countries from psychological, cultural, economic, and political perspectives. This is hardly an embarrassing publication record. The wider context of progressive education and race relations in the pre–World War II era is beyond the scope of this essay. Ronald K. Goodenow examines major figures and debates in "The Progressive Educator, Race and Ethnicity in the Depression Years: An Overview," *History of Education Quarterly* 15 (1975): 365–94.

5. Perusal of the signers of the NAACP's original declaration finds that Dewey was the lone academic philosopher, and together with W. E. B. Du Bois and W. I. Thomas one of the three university professors publicly endorsing the new movement.

6. One touching expression of gratitude for Dewey's work came from Walter White, who was an early leader of the antilynching campaign and later secretary of the NAACP. His telegram to Mrs. Dewey upon Dewey's death in 1952 deserves quotation in full: "We are profoundly grieved at the passing of your distinguished husband. We are proud that he was one of the founders of the National Association for the Advancement of Colored People and as you know unremittingly and uncompromisingly a supporter of the fight for full citizenship rights for the American Negro. We shall miss his wise and kindly counsel but we are grateful that he was spared enough years of life to advance so measurably the thinking of mankind." Walter White to Roberta Dewey, 2 June 1952, in *The Correspondence of John Dewey,* vol. 3: *1940–1952,* ed. Larry A. Hickman (Charlottesville, Va.: Intelex Corporation, forthcoming), #15984.

7. Early examples include Ambrose Caliver, "The Negro Teacher and a Philosophy of Negro Education," *Journal of Negro Education* 2 (1933): 432–47; and Charles S. Johnson, "On the Need of Realism in Negro Education," *Journal of Negro Education* 5 (1936): 375–82. The most prominent recent example is

Cornel West; see *The American Evasion of Philosophy: A Genealogy of Pragmatism* (Madison: University of Wisconsin Press, 1989).

8. Dewey's work on education in relation to countries other than America will not be discussed here. See Ronald K. Goodenow, "The Progressive Educator and the Third World: A First Look at John Dewey," *History of Education* 19 (1990): 23–40; and *Dewey and European Education: General Problems and Case Studies,* ed. Jürgen Oelkers and Heinz Rhyn (Dordrecht: Kluwer, 2000).

9. See Dewey, *Democracy and Education* (MW 9:9–10).

10. See Philip Pettit, *Republicanism: A Theory of Freedom and Government* (Oxford: Oxford University Press, 1997). Pettit does not elaborate on Dewey's contributions to this tradition, but see Blanche H. Brick's discussion of American thinkers on education's impact on the republic's fate in "Changing Concepts of Equal Educational Opportunity: A Comparison of the Views of Thomas Jefferson, Horace Mann and John Dewey," *Thresholds in Education* 19 (1993): 2–8.

11. See James Bohman's critique of Rawls and Habermas on this point in *Public Deliberation* (Cambridge, Mass.: MIT Press, 1996), pp. 80–89.

12. Dewey, "The Meaning of the Term: Liberalism" (LW 14:253).

13. Dewey, "Creative Democracy—The Task before Us" (LW 14:227).

14. Two recent books on Dewey should be consulted for further reading on Dewey's vision of social intelligence: Michael Eldridge, *Transforming Experience: John Dewey's Cultural Instrumentalism* (Nashville: Vanderbilt University Press, 1998), and William Caspary, *Dewey on Democracy* (Ithaca: Cornell University Press, 2000).

15. Sound expositions of Dewey's educational theory and curriculum design are given by Stephen M. Fishman and Lucille P. McCarty, *John Dewey and the Challenge of Classroom Practice* (New York: Teachers College Press, 1998); Jim Garrison, *Dewey and Eros: Wisdom and Desire in the Art of Thinking* (New York: Teachers College Press, 1997); Douglas J. Simpson and Michael J. B. Jackson, *Educational Reform: A Deweyan Perspective* (New York: Garland, 1997); and Harriet K. Cuffaro, *Experimenting with the World: John Dewey and Early Education* (New York: Teachers College Press, 1994).

16. Dewey, "Creative Democracy—The Task before Us" (LW 14:226, 228).

17. The complex relationships between shared experience, fruitful deliberation, and exposure of barriers to respectful communication, especially in light of the power of ideologically or prejudicially encoded rhetoric, are coming under the scrutiny of careful sociological research. See, for example, Tali Mendelberg and John Oleske, "Race and Public Deliberation," *Political Communication* 17 (2000): 169–91.

18. Dewey, *Democracy and Education* (MW 9:105).

19. A penetrating study of moral conflict and deliberation is offered by Amy Gutmann and Dennis Thompson, *Democracy and Disagreement* (Cambridge, Mass.: Harvard University Press, 1996).

20. Dewey, "What I Believe" (LW 5:275).

21. Dewey, "The Need for a Philosophy of Education" (LW 9:201).

22. See Will Kymlicka, *Politics in the Vernacular: Nationalism, Multiculturalism, and Citizenship* (Oxford: Oxford University Press, 2000).

23. Dewey, "The School as Social Centre" (MW 2:85).

24. John Dewey to Horace Kallen, 31 March 1915, in *The Correspondence of*

John Dewey, vol. 1: *1871–1918,* 2nd ed., ed. Larry A. Hickman (Charlottesville, Va.: Intelex Corporation, 2001), #03222.

25. Dewey, "Nationalizing Education" (MW 10:204–205). On Dewey's multiculturalism see Hilary and Ruth Anna Putnam, "Education for Democracy," *Educational Theory* 43 (1993): 361–76; J. Christopher Eisele, "John Dewey and the Immigrants," *History of Education Quarterly* 15 (1975): 67–85; and Ronald K. Goodenow, "Racial and Ethnic Tolerance in John Dewey's Educational and Social Thought: The Depression Years," *Educational Theory* 27 (1977): 48–64. A recent work exemplifying Dewey's vision is Duane E. Campbell, *Choosing Democracy: A Practical Guide to Multicultural Education,* 2nd ed. (Upper Saddle River, N.J.: Prentice-Hall, 2000).

26. See, for example, Eamonn Callan, "Education for Democracy: Dewey's Illiberal Democracy," *Educational Theory* 31 (1981): 167–75.

27. This axiom is accepted on all sides; those who prefer private schools despite the higher cost should think twice before challenging public education on the grounds that throwing more money at education does nothing. What is at stake is whether the *structure* of public education prevents greater expenditures from improving education. See note 33.

28. Of course, funding inequalities have long been an endemic problem in America because of school funding's origin in local property values. See, for example, Alonzo F. Myers's analysis in "The Democratic Ideal of Equality of Education and Equality of Opportunity," *Journal of Educational Sociology* 16 (1942): 3–14. For an argument that funded school choice would naturally result in meritocracy and stratification, leading to schools for elites and schools for mediocre students, see Alexander W. Astin, "Educational 'Choice': Its Appeal May Be Illusory," *Sociology of Education* 65 (1992): 255–60.

29. Amy Gutmann, *Democratic Education,* rev. ed. (Princeton: Princeton University Press, 1999), pp. 31–32.

30. Major judicial cases are summarized by Charles J. Russo, J. John Harris III, and Rosetta F. Sandidge, "*Brown v. Board of Education* at 40: A Legal History of Equal Educational Opportunities in American Public Education," *Journal of Negro Education* 63 (1994): 297–309.

31. David Nevin and Robert E. Bills examine post-1950s reactions to desegregation in *The Schools That Fear Built: Segregationist Academies in the South* (Washington, D.C.: Acropolis Books, 1976). The similarities to post–Civil War developments are striking; see Ward M. McAfee, *Religion, Race, and Reconstruction: The Public School in the Politics of the 1870s* (Albany: State University of New York Press, 1998), and William H. Watkins, *The White Architects of Black Education: Ideology and Power in America, 1865–1954* (New York: Teachers College Press, 2001).

32. This point is emphasized by Michael Engel, *The Struggle for Control of Public Education: Market Ideology vs. Democratic Values* (Philadelphia: Temple University Press, 2000), pp. 70–74.

33. See Albert Shanker and Bella Rosenberg, "Private School Choice: An Ineffective Path to Educational Reform," in *Privatizing Education and Educational Choice: Concepts, Plans, and Experiences,* ed. Simon Hakim, Paul Seidenstat, and Gary Bowman (Westport, Conn.: Praeger, 1994), pp. 59–73.

34. Gutmann, *Democratic Education,* pp. 287–88.

35. Jeffrey R. Henig, *Rethinking School Choice* (Princeton: Princeton University Press, 1994), pp. 189–93.

36. The key text is Dewey, "Racial Prejudice and Friction" (MW 13:242–54).

37. This theory was advanced before Dewey; see, for example, W. E. B. Du Bois, "The Economics of Negro Emancipation in the United States," *Sociological Review* 4 (1911): 303–13.

38. This is the conclusion, for example, of Charles H. Thompson, "Race and Equality of Educational Opportunity: Defining the Problem," *Journal of Negro Education* 37 (1968): 191–203.

39. A careful and detailed portrayal of progress and problems is "The Schooling of Black Americans," in *A Common Destiny: Blacks in American Society,* ed. Gerald D. Jaynes and Robin M. Williams (Washington, D.C.: National Academy Press, 1989), pp. 329–89. An early study was done by Earle H. West, "Progress toward Equality of Opportunity in Elementary and Secondary Education," *Journal of Negro Education* 37 (1968): 212–19.

40. Among the numerous discussions about the ethnic implications of education reform, a few can be mentioned here for further reading: Walter C. Farrell, Jr., and Jackolyn E. Mathews, "School Choice and the Educational Opportunities of African American Children," *Journal of Negro Education* 59 (1990): 526–37; Diana T. Slaughter-Defoe, "Parental Educational Choice: Some African American Dilemmas," *Journal of Negro Education* 60 (1991): 354–60; Faustine C. Jones-Wilson and Charles A. Asbury, "Why Not Public Schools," *Journal of Negro Education* 61 (1992): 125–37; Stanley C. Trent, "School Choice for African-American Children Who Live in Poverty: A Commitment to Equity or More of the Same?" *Urban Education* 27 (1992): 291–307; Pedro A. Noguera, "More Democracy Not Less: Confronting the Challenge of Privatization in Public Education," *Journal of Negro Education* 63 (1994): 237–50; Robert S. Peterkin and Janice E. Jackson, "Public School Choice: Implications for African American Students," *Journal of Negro Education* 63 (1994): 126–38; Dan A. Lewis and Kathryn Nakagawa, *Race and Educational Reform in the American Metropolis: A Study of School Decentralization* (Albany: State University of New York Press, 1994); Robin D. Barnes, "Black America and School Choice: Charting a New Course," *Yale Law Journal* 106 (1997): 2375–2410; Robert D. Winkle, Joseph Stewart, Jr., and J. L. Polinard, "Public School Quality, Private Schools, and Race," *American Journal of Political Science* 43 (1999): 1248–53; Salvatore Saporito and Annette Lareau, "School Selection as a Process: The Multiple Dimensions of Race in Framing Educational Choice," *Social Problems* 46 (1999): 418–39; "Is Voucher Education a Good Idea for African Americans?" *Journal of Blacks in Higher Education* 27 (2000): 116–17; Gilberto Q. Conchas and Kimberly A. Goyette, "The Race Is Not Even: Minority Education in a Post–Affirmative Action Era," *Harvard Journal of Hispanic Policy* 13 (2000–2001): 87–102; Jeffrey R. Henig, Richard Hula, Marion Orr, and Desiree Pedescleaux, *The Color of School Reform: Race, Politics, and the Challenge of Urban Education* (Princeton: Princeton University Press, 2001); and Peter C. Murrell, Jr., *African-Centered Pedagogy: Developing Schools of Achievement for African American Children* (Albany: State University of New York Press, 2002).

41. Dewey, "Freedom" (LW 11:255).

5 Situating the Self: Concerning an Ethics of Culture and Race

D. Micah Hester

It is not news to anyone who has studied issues surrounding "race" and "culture" that such concepts were not common to Western thought even two hundred years ago. It was primarily during the nineteenth century that biological scientists and sociologists began to show an interest in what became known as "race" studies (see Augstein 1997). The field determined to categorize human beings into "racial" groups, developing, at least at first, a rigid ontology of race—the now infamous distinction of three races in specific, "Caucasoid," "Negroid," and "Mongoloid." Although much has changed in the intervening years, many of the basic assumptions and logic of those nineteenth-century discussions carry forth to the current day.

K. Anthony Appiah has characterized this nineteenth-century scheme, and the thinking that has followed from it, as "racialism." He defines the concept as follows:

> There are heritable characteristics, possessed by members of our species, that allow us to divide them into a small set of races, in such a way that all the members of these races share certain traits and tendencies with each other that they do not share with members of any other race. These traits and tendencies characteristic of race constitute . . . a sort of racial essence. (Appiah 1990, p. 4)

Now, "heritability" can be either biological, cultural, or both. If biological, then scientific evidence must be marshaled to support the claim, and in the past decade some have argued that just such evidence is available and that fundamental racial characteristics "show" themselves in differences in behavior, intelligence, and biology. For example, studies like *The Bell Curve* (Hernstein and Murray 1994) purport to demonstrate through scientific research that intelligence is a function of race and go on to speculate about racially unique genetic causes for these differences, thus supporting a fundamental ontology of race itself.

Reactions to this "research" were swift and decisive, with some of the leading figures in science and sociology condemning the methods and findings of the authors (see, e.g., Fraser 1995). Furthermore, geneticists, biologists, anthropologists, and others have specifically addressed the question of racial biology in recent years. Particularly with the work of the human genome project, scientists have looked through the human genetic code in order to determine whether or not "race" can be determined within our DNA, but when they hold one genetic marker as constant, say, for skin color, no other genetic markers, say, for disease, appear with enough frequency to correlate to anything we might call race (see Cavalli-Sforza 2000; Kitchner 1999).

This blow to biological inheritance of race pushes racial characteristics, if inheritable at all, to the cultural, and if cultural, then (by definition) this heritability is constructed, historical, contingent. However, Appiah's own definition of "racialism" makes it an essentialism. As such, on Appiah's terms, racialism cannot be exclusively cultural. Thus, for Appiah, "racialism" cannot be true, and the elimination of an ontology of race is the logical consequence.

Based primarily on the (lack of) scientific evidence and a subsequent logic of essentialism, Naomi Zack (1995) has argued, similarly to Appiah, that there is a "fiction of race." Looking at the reality of "mixed race" individuals, Zack shows that we cannot continue to hold to an essentialist tradition of racial categories, and she goes on to take up what has been called an eliminativist position concerning race and racial identity. The eliminativist position argues that without a foundation for racial essentialism, racial categories (scientific or otherwise) should be eliminated, and through such elimination, individuals will be liberated from the tyranny of racial categorization and much of the racism that follows from it.

It is important to note the truths taken up by the eliminativist position: "First, the phenotypic characters used to demarcate races . . . neither have any intrinsic significance nor have been shown to correlate with characteristics of intrinsic significance. Second, . . . intraracial diversity is far more pronounced than interracial diversity" (Kitchner 1999, p. 87). And third, there can be no doubt that "race concepts have been used as a tool [*sic*] of oppression and domination, and we should want to get rid of those things that lead to domination" (Shuford 2001, p. 309). For eliminativists, then, these insights lead to the conclusion that the very concept of "race" is unnecessary and oppressive.

"Yet many have argued that race concepts can also be employed as resources toward racially liberatory practices" (Shuford 2001, p. 309). In fact, "race concepts" employed properly have the potential to overcome racial oppression itself. Thus, it may be the case that the immediate response to the destruction of racial essentialism is not, as Zack implies, the elimination of "race" as a category for social and ethical inquiry. Instead, as Lewis Gordon argues, "The constructivity of race does not in and of itself constitute the ontological conclusion of a fictitious reality" (quoted in Shuford, p. 307). Lucious Outlaw takes a similar stance when he states, "Too many . . . have become entrapped by an extreme reaction to racism that views the correction to racism as involving no reference whatsoever to national character [or race]. They are . . . assimilationists: a society free of racism involves no racial or ethnic distinctions." However, "Theory must reflect the reality of the (relative) independence of race and ethnicity as positive determinants of historical human existence, along with other factors" (Outlaw 1983, p. 126).[1]

Thus, it would seem that even *if* we have settled the scientific question of racial ontology in favor of its dissolution, such a scientific settlement does not in fact settle the sociophilosophical concern for what role, if any, race should play in political and ethical considerations. While scientific work will continue and new discoveries will be made—if only discoveries that continue to debunk the usefulness of a scientific category for race—and while such work cannot be neatly divided from cultural concerns since scientific endeavors are themselves cultural practices, philosophical questions about the nature of human beings, the ways of understanding the interests of individuals and groups, and the relationship of any such "nature" and interests to an understanding of ethics and the good life continue. In this vein questions concerning "racial interests" persist as well: How can we undermine racial prejudice? What is the value of "multiculturalism"? How best do we address tensions among people who identify themselves and/or others according to race (particularly where such identity itself creates tension)? These (and others) are the questions any ethic of race and culture must address. However, the very concept of race and its status in ethical deliberations open the door to more general concerns about human nature and conduct, and attempts to ground ethical deliberations have traditionally been supported by particular accounts of human beings and their relationships to their surrounding environments.

The Western philosophical tradition of attempting to ground ethical practice in general and a more recent ethic of race and culture in particular pits well-acquainted foes in battle. On the one hand, there are classical liberal theorists who argue that each individual self is a *rational* being, atomic and insular, clearly distinguishable and different from every other—that is, each of us is "autonomous," able to make *self*-legislating choices. To protect the autonomy of each individual self, no one person should be allowed to make pronouncements about the good of others. This means, for the liberal, that determining the good in social situations either leads to anarchy and chaos—wholly unacceptable for the philosophical mind—or must rely on some universal, objective feature of the human condition. The implications of liberal theory for an ethic of race and culture, then, are that considerations taken from a racially motivated perspective—whatever that would mean—must either be shown to be a part of the universal human condition or be excluded from ethical deliberations. In fact, most liberal theorists accept that "race" is not a fundamental condition but an "accident" of birth, social position, cultural upbringing, and so forth, the consideration of which acts as barrier to *objective* ethical deliberation—that is, most liberal theorists are eliminativists and assimilationists.

Many attacks on the liberal perspective have been set forth. A particularly vocal foe has been so-called "communitarians." Generally, the communitarian position takes seriously the function of social relationships as essential to selfhood: that is, each of us is, from the communitarian perspective, no more (nor no less) than the aggregate of social relations, cultural conditions, and environmental pressures we embody uniquely but dependently. Since individual goods primarily, if not exclusively, arise from our social natures and/or from our roles within the communities of which we are a part, determining the good demands a view toward the good of the community first and foremost. In grounding an ethic of race and culture, communitarianism places emphasis on the social aspects of what it means to be "African American" or "Hispanic" or "Asian" and takes the exploration of such meanings and their implications as central to any ethical deliberation, sometimes to the exclusion of personal interest and meaning. Such a position relies on either an assumed or expected homogeneity of values and interests among the members of a community.

Both the liberal and communitarian positions argue for particular understandings of the self and, thereby, the status of the interests expressed by any particular self, and at least in my brief account of these positions, the understandings they put forth are diametrically opposed. In the face of these conflicting views on ethical deliberation and the place of race concepts in them, I would like to explore what Dewey has termed, in another context, the "new individualism" and Mead has called "the self as social product" in light of the cultural aspects affecting the experience of race. Their pragmatic take on the self as not insular but situated requires an ethic different from the classical liberal's, for example, autonomy-based models. Contemporary liberals like John Rawls miss the point, for his account of a nonsituated "veil of ignorance" cannot ground a practical ethic, and racial interests, tensions, differences, issues, and bonds lost behind such a veil do an injustice to individuals qua social beings (see Rawls 1971). To ignore cultural identity is to lose individuality and deep diversity.

The communitarian corrective, on the other hand, threatens the same loss as well, where communal concerns ignore the novel individuality of expressed interests. Human "sociality," in Mead's terms, however, does not subsume the individuality of each person. Individuals are novel nexuses of communities, cultures, and perspectives; each one of us is unique in how he or she comes together and expresses interest in the world. Granting that the individuality of each person need not fracture us into atomic beings—our situatedness is part and parcel of who we are—and that being socially situated need not lose sight of individuality—each of us is unique—then an ethic of race or culture must take seriously two inextricable human conditions: differences *and* communality. I hope to show that such an ethic must take culturally based racial issues seriously without treating them as either fundamental or necessary.

Self as Situated Social Product

As just mentioned, the traditional liberal concept of autonomy holds sway as the basis for a liberal ethic of any sort and results in eliminativist tendencies when applied to an ethic of race.[2] Such an account is said to be positively liberating for rational individuals. Unfortunately, though autonomy does attempt to clear a space for individual choice, it is surprisingly empty of moral content and only minimally helpful in most moral encounters. It is incapable of any significant positive work, relying primarily on the negative dictum that others should "stand clear"—that is, autonomy's central demand is that rational beings be allowed to make decisions free of outside, coercive, influences—when someone is exercising personal choice because the account of the self upon which it relies is devoid of existential context in which deliberation and choice occur.

In response to these problems with autonomy and the nature of the self it assumes, I wish to reconstruct—à la Dewey and Mead—our notion of the self, not as an isolated entity, but as product and process of social interaction and community. Not unlike the communitarian position, this reconstruction will leave behind the too-thin idea of the insular individual, but unlike most communitarian theorists, the pragmatic, functionalist account will not lose individuality. Although intimately integrated with the social structures in and through which he or she develops, the individual is not subsumed under or consumed by them. Obviously, individual persons are distinguishable from each other, but further "there is not merely difference or distinction [between individuals], but something unique or irreplaceable in value, an unique difference of value" (MW 15:170). This value is not intrinsic (as in, for example, Kantian theory), but is developed, contingent, and ever-changing through the social interactions in which individuals participate. My alternative to traditional theories of the self offers a positive hope for future work in ethics and situates an ethic of race and culture avoiding many of the negative consequences that follow from a traditional ontology of race and, for that matter, some of the problems that have arisen in critiques of that ontology. It replaces the classical notion of the atomic self with a conception of self that is mediated through community and culture as contingent yet responsive to realities that both shape and are shaped by individuals.

I take the concept of the self not to be denoting some entity or substance, but a socially developed function that emphasizes and arises from specific occurrences, aspects, and processes in experience. It is impossible to set the individual self as fundamentally over and against society; each of us is inextricably developed by and continually develops community itself. Such an account allows for new understandings about the moral life to prevail.

Mead and the Self as Social Product

During the last decade of the nineteenth century and the first three decades of the twentieth, George Herbert Mead crafted his insightful philosophical psychology of social behaviorism. Influenced by William James's landmark work *The Principles of Psychology,* John Dewey's writings in functional psychology, and Alfred North Whitehead's process philosophy, Mead determined, like James before him, that the self is not an entity prior to social relations but instead develops in and because of social processes.

Mead's psychology explains that what we call the "self," rather than being an entity upon which attributes and relations are "hung," is actually an organized complex of attitudes that reflexively implicates both the individual and society. Certainly, biological, organic individuals are uniquely situated in and created out of complex biological processes: that is, at birth (or conception, if you wish—there is no need to argue this point here), the infant starts as a mass of cells and biochemical activities. However, this organic individual should not be mistaken for a "self"; he or she is no *self* at all. The newborn makes no immediate distinctions between his or her body or needs and the movements of the environment of which he or she is a part. The thumb is not *his or her* thumb; it is an object that appears, then satisfies, in a matter wholly foreign to the child. In this way the child *undergoes* experience but does not comprehend or control it.

The *self*, on the other hand, is a conscious, interacting being, in the world. He or she is a responsible and reflective character. The self makes distinctions and is conscious of its place in the world relative to its environment. However, these qualities do not and cannot arise until interactions with others occur: "Selves are essentially social products, products of phenomena of the social side of human experience" (Mead 1962, p. 1). Through social interactions, the individual organism (usually in the form of a baby or young child) begins to recognize and respond to others. At first, the child simply plays games that mirror the actions of others; he or she takes on roles and characters, merely imitating what he or she sees. Children smile at our smiles, laugh because we laugh, touch what we touch. Even later, this continues as they dress in our clothes, play with our tools, speak in affected voices because that is what they see and hear.

However, slowly individuals creatively separate the actions of others from their own. Rather than parroting others' actions, individuals look for responses from others to their own actions. Dogs growl and bare their teeth; children blurt out a noise. Mead calls these actions "gestures," and gestures gain their own meaning by the responses others have to them. The dog's growl *signifies nothing unless* we act scared because of it. The baby's cry means that it is time to change the diaper, not because of the infant's *intent*,[3] but because of the parent's (or caregiver's) *response*. The broken glass has no meaning to the child until an adult scolds him or her for breaking it; at that point, the broken glass *signifies* "trouble."

Soon the young individual becomes aware of the attitudes of others to the extent that he or she begins anticipating those attitudes in selecting gestures appropriate to the situation. This activity develops quickly into the use of what Mead calls "significant symbols," where the individual in making the gesture anticipates the response in others. Mead states, "Gestures become significant symbols when they implicitly arouse in the individual making them the same responses which they explicitly arouse, or are supposed to arouse, in other individuals, the individuals to whom they are addressed" (Mead 1962, p. 47). These "significant symbols" most often come in the form of "vocal gestures"— that is, language. Language, and all other significant symbols for that matter, objectifies within the conversation the individual who is speaking; it treats him or her as an object to him- or her*self*. Thus, the self first comes to be *reflexively*. The child says "bottle" in anticipation of the response by the parent to give the nippled object to him or her. But in saying "bottle" the child reacts to the object (if only internally) as he or she expects the parent to react. He or she leans toward it, reaches for it. The infant becomes as much a member of the audience for his or her response as the parents do.

The self arises, then, in "self-conscious" behavior that objectifies the self to itself. This objectifying move incorporates an awareness of the attitudes of the other. More specifically, it takes on the attitude of the community itself or, in Mead's language, the "generalized other": "The organized community or social group which gives to the individual his unity of self may be called the 'generalized other.' The attitude of the generalized other is the attitude of the whole community" (Mead 1962, p. 154). The self, then, arises by way of an awareness and an internalizing of the "attitudes" of the communities of which we are a part. Thus Mead states, "In this way every gesture comes within a given social group or community to stand for a particular act or response, namely, the act or response which it calls forth explicitly in the individual who makes it" (47).

The implications for the concept of "self," here, are obvious. Mead does not accept the prevailing modernist view of a prior self whose originary being comes fully formed. Instead, he takes the self to be a product of social interaction. Yet even this is misleading, for there is no "one" self, but

> We divide ourselves up in all sorts of different selves with reference to our acquaintances. We discuss politics with one and religion with another. There are all sorts of selves answering to all sorts of different social reactions. It is the social process itself that is responsible for the appearance of the self; it is not there as a self apart from this type of experience. . . . There is usually an organization of the whole self with reference to the community to which we belong, and the situation in which we find ourselves. (Mead 1962, pp. 142–43)

Community then is constitutive of and prior to the self. "It cannot be said that the individuals come first and the community later, for the individuals arise in the very process [of living] itself" (189). It is the taking on of community attitudes that makes us "who we are" in any important sense:

> This getting of the broad activities of any given social whole or organized society as such within the experiential field of any one of the individuals involved or included in that whole is, in other words, the essential basis and prerequisite of the fullest development of that individual's self. (155)

Community in Selves, Community of Selves

Mead's self arises in the very processes of organic community, but this community is defined in terms of Mead's "generalized other," which is both a dispositional (or "perspectival") and an ideal (or "normative") sense of community where there is an awareness among individuals that their interests are best satisfied in and through the satisfaction of others' desires.[4] It is a view of community that relates individuals to communities while recognizing that the individuals who are products of these communities have their own unique interests. As Beth Singer puts it, "The condition of community is one of sameness-in-difference, of partial commonality of perspective among persons whose perspectives as individuals also include other perspectives, some unique to themselves and some shared with members of multiple communities to which they belong" (Singer 1999, p. 83). The recognition of "sameness-in-difference" with emphasis on "difference" is important, for it requires of us that we take difference seriously when fashioning communities. Gender, sexuality, ethnicity, race, and other cultural aspects of individuals must be understood and taken into account in our moral deliberations. Such interests cannot be sorted out a priori as either good or bad, right or wrong. It is necessary to evaluate them in the context in which they are expressed.

It must be clearly noted that regulating individual activity according to community demands need not wholly subsume individual interests under community interests:

> Every individual is in his own way unique. Each one experiences life from a different angle than anybody else, and consequently has something distinctive to give others. . . . Each individual . . . is a new beginning; the universe itself is, as it were, taking a fresh start in him and trying to do something, even if on a small scale, that it has never done before. (LW 5:127)

Each of us, then, contributes uniquely to the community in a way that would be altogether lost to the community if that particular individual were not present. Pragmatists are pluralist, and though each of us is socially constructed, that very social construction creates a unique perspective for each one of us. The relationship between selves and communities is organic and transactional.

The key, then, in positive, progressive human interaction, it would seem, is to recognize the socio-individual character interests, finding ways to retain individuality of desires and values (in their vast multiplicity and diversity) while making them work within the social good.[5] The ideal here is a community of individually expressed interests that work together so that individual and social ends are contemporaneous (or coincident) and inclusive of each other.

Of course, the ideal is difficult to obtain. Interests are numerous, often competing. Many communal associations take complex negotiations and require well-stated arguments. These are not always pleasant and are rarely neat or clean. There are a vast array of factors that must be accounted for, factors that arise in the experiences of individuals and groups as well as the broader environments that support their existence, practices, and interests.

Clearly, this take on a communally situated self has important moral consequences, for interactions of any significance must recognize and respond to others as we take on their attitudes as our own. And the meaning of our actions comes, not by way of our intentions (though they may arise from our own impulses), but in how they are taken by others—that is, how they bear out in their consequences:

> If we look now towards the end of the action rather than toward the impulse itself, we find that those ends are good which lead to the realization of the self as a social being. *Our morality gathers about our social conduct. It is as social beings that we are moral beings.* On the one side stands the society which makes the self possible, and on the other side stands the self that makes a highly organized society possible. The two answer to each other in moral conduct. (Mead 1962, p. 386; my emphasis)

Moral activity occurs among social beings aware of this social self. Moral conduct and judgments must themselves be social such that "one can never [judge] simply from his own point of view. *We have to look at it from the point of view of a social situation. . . .* The only rule that any ethics can present is that an individual should rationally [and imaginatively] deal with all the values that are found in a specific problem" (387–88; my emphasis). In other words, since my activities are never exclusively my own—that is, they arise, in part, from the social conditions in which I find myself and will consequently affect others of my social group—if I wish to perform my actions to "the good," I must account for the many (and often competing) interests at play in the situation. Those interests arise from other selves who are part of the environment in which I wish to exercise my own (communally constituted) desires. As Dewey has said, it is not that morality *ought* to be social; "morality is social" (MW 14:219).

Experience, Culture, and Race

As just discussed, communities and selves have a transactional relationship where each exchanges with the other in the process of continual development of both. It will prove helpful to note that John Dewey described "experience" itself as transactional, as exchange between organism and environment (see *Knowing and the Known,* LW 16). Experience, then, is an active process that privileges neither organism nor environment but expresses the constitutive quality of each to the other. Furthermore, it is well known, by people who care about such things, that Dewey was, in the end, uneasy about his use of the term "experience" throughout his philosophy. Upon reflection, he suggested that the term "experience" be replaced by the term "culture," which better captured nonsubjective and transactional qualities (LW 1:361). This is an intriguing suggestion that, although dubiously effective in all cases, has implications from a pragmatic perspective for discussions of an ethic of race as cultural. Using Dewey's active and constitutive notion of "culture," I suggest that the process of selfhood is simply what Dewey means by culture—that is, Deweyan "culture" as the transactions between organisms and environments is what Mead means by the very processes of developing socially situated selves. The implication of this insight for an ethic of race where race is understood culturally is to make race concepts contingent, but not arbitrary, functional, not fundamental, and thus changeable, even eliminatable when, but only when, the environment in which they function changes to make their elimination possible and useful. Furthermore, the pragmatic view of socially situated selves demands, as I hope to clarify in the remainder of this essay, that ethical deliberation take all interests into account, which, in turn, implies that, although such interests are certainly individual and communal (and thus in Deweyan terms, "cultural"), those interests identified as "racial interests," no matter how contingent they are, be included as well.

For the pragmatist, to accept the self as social product demands that we analyze selves, their interests, activities, and the consequences of those interests and activities as they are expressed in and affect experience. William James knew this well when he demanded that any ethic worth its salt could only be built from actually expressed claims and desires, and must account for the consequences of fulfilling those claims in the complex of interests expressed in any given situation. In fact, it is the cornerstone of the Jamesian *Weltanschauung*, adopted by other pragmatists as well, that we take all experience seriously. Particular goods are prior to *the* good. All this shows experience to be communal in content and individual in expression. It is, as Dewey said, "cultural."

Thus, any ethic of race that recognizes socially situated selves must confront racial experiences, analyzing their sources, projecting the consequences of the interests expressed through racially motivated claims. This is a deeply cultural process—I shall argue, a *habit* of culture.

An example of racially charged experience may help. Every year I have the task of interviewing potential medical students for admission to Mercer University's School of Medicine. Mercer's is a unique medical school that has a very specific mission to provide primary care to underserved Georgia. The vast majority of our applicant pool is comprised of white, middle-class, twenty-somethings (all of whom must be legal Georgia residents), and in the course of the admissions conversation I often inquire whether they have applied to other medical schools in Georgia. In most cases, they have. Now, Georgia has four medical schools from which to choose: Mercer (private, problem-based learning format with our unique state-based mission), the Medical College of Georgia (our state medical school, traditional educational format), Emory (private, research-based), and Morehouse (private, one of three historically and predominantly black medical schools in the United States). However, even with those applicants who claim no desire to study outside the state, almost exclusively African American applicants have ever told me that they have applied to Morehouse as well as Mercer. Inevitably, to those who have not applied to Morehouse, I ask them why they have not. The typical answer is that they did not consider it since they were not sure they would "fit in." They are often concerned about being in the minority and thus feeling out of the loop *because* "*their* students are black, and I am not."[6]

Of course, any analysis of this example should lead directly to a discussion of power and control, two concepts at the heart of a critical analysis of race. And some would further argue that "race" is simply reducible to power and control. But it is more than that, for the concerns expressed by these students are not just about power but about being and confronting the "other," and all this is clearly stated in terms of "black" and "white." For these students, the complex of power, otherness, and culture is exhaustible by racial concepts of black and white. In fact, many people have no other conceptual scheme through which to experience social interaction than through race, and for them, at least (and as Cornel West has said) "race matters." Race *is* part of *our culture.* Such experiential reality does not make "race" a necessary part of the human condition, but it does, as James would insist, make it a necessary part of ethical analysis and deliberation so long as it continues to function within our culture.

Substantive (Fundamental) versus Functional (Instrumental) Ontologies

"Race," so the debate goes, is either a social construct of culture or a fundamental classification of human beings. I have already discussed in the first section the lack of support for accepting any fundamentalist or essentialist view of "race." In response to this essentialist void, then, classical liberal theorists, in particular, argue that "race" and "culture," since fundamental neither to humans nor to social institutions, should be ignored. Following contemporary scholars like Rawls, only behind a "veil of ignorance" should we determine the best course of action.

However, as William James has rightly pointed out, taking social context and experience seriously demands that we accept as real all experience. Such a demand implicates the need to include racial experience as well. The eliminativist position is misguided when it does not take the culturally habitual character of the experience of race seriously, while racial fundamentalism, against which the eliminativist rages, is mistaken because it does not recognize the historicity and contingency of race. These extremes both capture kernels of truth (though they may not see the truth they capture) and miss the central point. Racial experience and experiences of race are as real as the noncognitive cry of a newborn, while the meaning of such experience is tied falsely to sources taken as fundamental or absolute, when in fact they are historical and contingent. Like the baby's cry, society supplies the meaning of race and does so in purposeful ways that can be analyzed and critiqued.

The pragmatist position takes race as cultural (in the broadest sense), culture as transactional, and transactions as contingent. Thus, the pragmatist demands that contingent qualities of life be taken into account. To retain deep individuality is to take account of the interests of communities and the social structures in which we participate and which influence each of us, wittingly or unwittingly. In return, the transactional character of culture, in turn, not only puts our own values in play, it also calls into question the environment in which these values operate or attempt to operate.

Pragmatically, an ontology of selves neither accepts a substative account of selves nor denies that selves exist. Instead, a pragmatic ontology is always contingent, explaining that selves are what they are because of the historical and contextually, purposefully directed processes in which they find themselves and through which they operate. Social selves then are contingent but not arbitrary. They *could have been* something other than what they are, but given their histories, they *are what they are* now.

Coming from a different (existentialist) tradition, Lewis Gordon explains this well:

> In short, all ontologies asserted as ONTOLOGY may carry residues of the spirit of seriousness. . . . We have seen many instances of the perils of committing ourselves to what *must be the case* as far as existence is concerned. We lose sight of the contingency of being when we fail to appreciate that what is the case doesn't always have to be the case. No black has to be black. No white has to be white. But we must also stand back and add—provided we remember that the wide situation upon which these interpretations are based is itself contingent, although not necessarily "accidental." (Gordon 1999, p. 351)

The contingent character of being (in Gordon's terms), and specifically the being of race, makes no normative claim about whether it *ought* to be the case, nor does it condemn us to a future in which it *must* continue. However, that racial concepts and interests do exist and are expressed—that is, that they do arise from our history and function culturally—cannot and should not be denied, for their realities (contingent as they may be) cannot be changed in the future if they are not dealt with as they function now. The pragmatist does not see race (or class or gender, for that matter) as a fundamental social category. Such classifications perform instrumentally in particular social inquiries, but not necessarily in all social inquiries. Like any type of categorization, they are *purposeful*, and as purposeful, serve only when justifiable in the given situation.

As pragmatists have argued, however, instruments are not value-neutral. So it is important to note that simply arguing that "race" is functional/instrumental does not yet determine what values are inherent in such an "instrument." In fact, many argue that the moral values inherent in such an instrument are precisely the reason to jettison its use entirely. Shelby Steele and others have argued that it is precisely the conceptual instruments of race and racial difference that oppress blacks, for they manifest themselves in social institutions and public policy like, for example, affirmative action policies that ignore "the hard business of developing a formerly oppressed people to the point where they can achieve proportionate representation on their own (given equal opportunity)" (Steele 1990 [1996], p. 383). However, whereas Steele parenthetically throws away the phrase "given equal opportunity," sociologists still find a great deal of actual unequal opportunity abounding in hiring and admissions practices. Thus, the conditions that must obtain to make Steele's "color-blind" hiring practices come to fruition simply do not hold, which, it would seem by his own admission (parenthetical as it may be), undermines his position. Even an elimina-tivist like Zack admits that if affirmative action policies are to be useful as tools for improving professional and educational opportunities for historically un-derrepresented populations, then "mixed race" individuals, to the extent that they experience racial prejudice in hiring practices, would be well served to identify themselves along racial lines enhanced through affirmative action poli-cies (Zack 1995, p. 131). This kind of view captures the experience of present realities and understands racial issues as serving a positive social function. It demonstrates that it is not enough to recognize, in a vacuum, the vacuousness of a concept like "race," but that we must take the concept in context of the environing conditions that obtain here and now. Racial interests have a space in the discussion of professional and academic opportunities, and it is those very interests that not only often create the problems which set ethical inquiry in motion but are what must be satisfied in any successful ethical deliberation into issues like affirmative action policies. Elimination of any concept is possible only in an environment capable of supporting its elimination and beneficially filling its void. Thus, as the affirmative action example indicates, retention of race concepts in the current professional and academic environment may still perform a useful function in helping overcome injustices in hiring and admis-sions practices. Until significant environmental and cultural changes occur in Western societies, elimination of race from consideration in a deliberation over affirmative action is unwarranted.

It may be helpful to express the more general point about the instrumentality of race concepts in a different way. Namely, race concepts can be well described as what Dewey calls "collective habits" (MW 14:54). Such concepts form the basis for certain ways of thinking and acting because of the ways in which we have been enculturated. Their very existence betrays not only *what* we think but *how*. And how we think implicates not just the processes of ourselves but the conditions which make such processes function: that is, race concepts as hab-its say something about us, our communities, our political and economic sys-tems, and our world in general. What is important to note on this view, however, is that since selves are not isolated and atomic but socially constructed, every aspect of our lives and interests (race being just one among many) necessarily implicates all this as well.

Communities make selves, and to the extent that groups of people, based on either traditional or nontraditional racial characteristics and interests, arise out of and come together to form habitual race concepts and communities, "race" has a role to play in ethical inquiry where we must look at both each individual's expressed interests and the social situations that make individuals who they are. This role is cultural, having the contingency of human history, preference, and prejudice as its primary developmental support, and contingency is not arbitrariness. We cannot simply wipe the slate clean because we recognize the contingent and functional character of "race." Certainly, the contingent quality of race means that the very idea of race can be called into question, but it does not mean that racially motivated interests do not operate in some way upon the inquiry, for those interests are not arbitrary but situated within a community, arising from particular "racially" motivated environments. We rarely change habits willy-nilly or through a simple force of personal will. We must also reconstruct the environments that make such habits functional in the first place and dysfunctional in the second place. This is not always easy, for though we can and do change our environments (as they in turn change us), we do so *within* the environments we are attempting to change.

Epilogue

Clearly, the implications of the pragmatist account of the individual in relation to community are far-reaching for moral theory and practice. I, however, have not so much argued for the validity of the pragmatist position concerning situated selves and my concern for an ethic of race as I have attempted to elucidate it. For our purposes, this account situates an ethic of race and culture in such a way as to take seriously both the social interests of the communities that enculturate us and the novel way that those interests become embodied in each of us. Admittedly, then, this gives no answers to how to solve problems identified as concerning racial or cultural character, conflict, or communities. What this does do is provide an understanding of human natures that leads to the construction of methods for tackling such problems.

The pragmatic position gives value to the importance of a critical analysis of race (or class), but only if such an analysis is situated within a larger socioethical inquiry and punctuates the processive-transactional-functional character of such categories. In fact, as Outlaw has rightly pointed out, ignoring race/ethnic analysis runs important social, political, and ethical dangers. A thoroughgoing ethic of race demands that *neither* (1) we ignore race *nor* (2) we jettison the concept; instead, a deeper ethic of race demands a sociology of what function race plays in our ethical deliberations and in what ways it hinders or helps a particular moral inquiry and its outcome(s). In turn, such inquiry changes the character of the function of race through the outcomes we develop, and its consequences may further render the entire category functionless at some point in the future: that is, since race is cultural, and thus operatively transactional, it is affected by our endeavors. The concept changes with each new use and reconstructs with each inquiry. Of course, there is a danger that these changes solidify the negative (racist) consequences that have followed from the employment of race concepts throughout our history, but when properly situated in an ethical inquiry that takes the socially situated interests of all parties seriously, the possibility for deeper understanding of persons and the ability to move toward elimination of (the negative aspects of) race can be achieved. Thus the pragmatist take on race as cultural and the understanding of culture—read: "socially situated selves"—in ethical inquiry can satisfy the liberal who wishes to take individuality seriously, the communitarian who champions the concern for the common characteristics of selves, the historicist who recognizes the non-arbitrary and functional character of "race" in Western civilization, and the eliminativist (though maybe not today) who yearns to eradicate race concepts altogether.

NOTES

1. For reasons opposite those of Gordon's "race and ethnicity as positive determinants of historical human existence," anthropologists and bioethicists S. Lee, J. Mountain, and B. Koenig emphasize the "reality of race" since "Race is socially, not biologically, meaningful; it is 'real' because we have acted as if certain people, at certain points in time, were inferior based on innate or 'essentialized' characteristics" (Lee et al. 2001, p. 40).

2. This section has been edited and revised from Hester (2001), pp. 47–54.

3. We could say that children cry when they are "uncomfortable," but the *cognitive* character even this minimal description implies is simply not there for most infants most of the time. Children cry, and they *know* not why, but they do in fact *have* experiences that result in "discomfort" and crying.

4. Heather Keith in an unpublished paper (Keith 1997) on Mead's concept of "self" correctly points out that community involves not just individuals but the environment in which they live. Keith explains, "The experience of being human, philosophical and biological, depends on a variety of 'ecological' relationships," and she calls this "life in a social ecology" (1). This "ecological" aspect of community, though not explicitly discussed in its relationship to the "natural" environment within this essay, resides in the background of any discussion of "community" contained herein.

5. It is important to note at this point, a social "good" itself must have a certain character to it. In particular, I take the Roycean/Deweyan position that social goods must be developed out of the interests (as diverse and conflicting as they may be) of the members of the social group and must be, what we might call, "inclusive." That is, goals of a community must be of such a character that they do not intrinsically oppose or deny the worth of alternative communities' ends unless those ends are themselves exclusive, violent, or stifling of the possibilities for deeply enriching experience for both their members and, particularly, nonmembers—for instance, a band of robber barons or the Nazi Party. Josiah Royce sees this as constitutive of true "loyalty," and Dewey takes this to be the nature of a true democracy (see Royce 1995, particularly lecture 3, "Loyalty to Loyalty," pp. 48–69; and Dewey, LW 2:235–372, particularly chapter 5, "The Search for the Great Community," pp. 325–50).

6. This leads me to press them on why they believe they can serve the underserved when they are unwilling to put themselves in a position of vulnerability themselves. Whether white or black, are not the underserved precisely those who are left out of the loop? What part of the experience of powerlessness and otherness can they relate to in their future patients if they continually put themselves in positions that guarantee them the upper hand? There is no disputing that becoming a physician already places one in a posi-

tion of power and authority, and yet these white, middle-class students take on faith that they can relate appropriately to medically underserved Georgians, the vast majority of whom are African American and of lower socioeconomic standing. Is this not just their version of the "white man's burden" complex?

WORKS CITED

Appiah, Kwame Anthony. 1990. "Racisms." In D. T. Goldberg, ed., *Anatomy of Racism,* pp. 3–17. Minneapolis: University of Minnesota Press.

Augstein, Hanna F., ed. 1997. *Race: The Origins of an Idea, 1760–1850.* South Bend, Ind.: St. Augustine Press.

Cavalli-Sforza, Luigi Luca. 2000. *Genes, People, and Languages.* New York: Farrar, Straus and Giroux.

Fraser, Steven, ed. 1995. *The Bell Curve Wars.* New York: Basic Books.

Gordon, Lewis. 1999. "Antiblack Racism and Ontology." In L. Harris, ed., *Racism,* pp. 347–55. Amherst, N.Y.: Humanity Books.

Hernstein, R., and C. Murray. 1994. *The Bell Curve.* New York: Free Press.

Hester, D. Micah. 2001. *Community as Healing: Pragmatist Ethics in Medical Encounters.* Lanham, Md.: Rowman & Littlefield.

Keith, Heather E. 1997. "Pragmatism and Social Ecology: George Herbert Mead's Empathetic Self." Unpublished.

Kitchner, Philip. 1999. "Race, Ethnicity, Biology, Culture." In L. Harris, ed., *Racism,* pp. 87–117. Amherst, N.Y.: Humanity Books.

Lee, Sandra Soo-Jin, et al. 2001. "The Meanings of 'Race' in the New Genomic: Implications for Health Disparities Research." *Yale Journal of Health Policy, Law, and Ethics* 1, no. 1: 33–75.

Mead, George Herbert. [1934] 1962. *Mind, Self, & Society.* Edited by Charles W. Morris. Chicago: University of Chicago Press.

Outlaw, Lucious. 1983. "Race and Class in the Theory and Practice of Emancipatory Social Transformation." In L. Harris, ed., *Philosophy Born of Struggle,* pp. 117–29. Dubuque: Kendall/Hunt.

Rawls, John. 1971. *A Theory of Justice.* Cambridge, Mass.: Harvard University Press.

Royce, Josiah. 1995. *The Philosophy of Loyalty.* Nashville: Vanderbilt University Press.

Shuford, John. 2001. "Four Du Boisian Contributions to Critical Race Theory." *Transactions of the C. S. Peirce Society* 37, no. 3: 301–37.

Singer, Beth. 1999. *Pragmatism, Rights, and Democracy.* New York: Fordham University Press.

Stelle, Shelby. 1990. "Affirmative Action: The Price of Preference." In W. Shaw, ed., *Social and Personal Ethics,* pp. 381–87. Belmont, Calif.: Wadsworth, 1996.

Zack, Naomi. 1995. "Mixed Black and White Race and Public Policy." *Hypatia* 10: 119–32.

6 Tragedy and Moral Experience: John Dewey and Toni Morrison's *Beloved*

Eddie S. Glaude, Jr.

> When the future arrives with its inevitable disappointments as well as ful-
> fillments, and with new sources of trouble, failure loses something of its
> fatality, and suffering yields fruit of instruction not of bitterness. Humility
> is more demanded at our moments of triumph than at those of failure. For
> humility is not caddish self-depreciation. It is the sense of our slight inability
> even with our best intelligence and effort to command events; a sense of our
> dependence upon forces that go their way without our wish and plan.
>
> —John Dewey

Introduction

No one really questions John Dewey's commitment to democracy. His philosophical works and his political life stand as grand examples of his struggle for the formation of a genuinely cooperative society. But what do we make of his relative silence with regards to the problems of race in the United States? To be sure, Dewey's political choices reflected a desire to end racism. His participation in the formation of the NAACP and his 1922 essay "Racial Prejudice and Friction" showed an interest in the challenge race and racism posed to his conception of democracy. But Dewey was never truly attentive *in his philosophical work* to the problem of racism in America; in none of his major books on democracy did he grapple with the challenge that race presents to his ideas. How are we to think about Dewey's philosophical insights about democracy in light of this? Does he offer us any tools for thinking about contemporary problems of race in the United States?

I am more than convinced that Dewey's pragmatic philosophy can help us address some of the more intractable problems of race. From affirmative action debates, the difficulties of identity politics, to the conundrum of urban education, Deweyan pragmatism offers unique and innovative insights for creative, intelligent inquiry into these problems. But, I believe, an initial step has to be made: Dewey's philosophy of democracy must be reconstructed in light of the realities of race that have defined this nation. Indeed, if American pragmatism is to be understood, in part, as a specific historical and cultural product of American civilization, and as a particular set of social practices, as Cornel West argues, that articulate certain American desires, values, and responses, then it must address explicitly the tragedy of race in America. Dewey's philosophy of democracy—that everyday folk can interact for their mutual enrichment—is a hypothesis to be tested in action. The history of democracy in the United States is one of the continued exclusion of African Americans from full participation in that process, and that history seriously challenges Dewey's democratic faith. In short, Deweyan pragmatism must encounter what Cornel West describes as the "night side" of American democracy if it is to be a useful tool in our efforts to deal with the problems of race today.

But many scholars hold the view that Dewey's version of pragmatism was either an optimistic philosophy with a naïve faith in science or a philosophical position inattentive to the operations of power. His views, they maintain, are inattentive to the "night side" of life generally. Such descriptions trade on a misconception: that Dewey's undying faith in our capacity to work on our world means that he believed there are no limits to what we can do. It is certainly true that in reflecting on the meaning and value of American democracy Dewey emphasized, like Ralph Waldo Emerson, the heroic capacities of ordinary people in a world of radical contingency. But how we understand the place of contingency in Dewey's overall philosophical outlook frames how we ought to understand the scope of human agency in Dewey's thinking.[1]

This essay is divided into two parts. In the rather lengthy Part One, I argue that behind Dewey's notion of contingency lies what can be called a tragic sensibility: that is to say, Dewey held the view that uncertainty pervades our lives and involves us in the peril of evils, that there are dimensions of life that are far beyond our control, which deepen "a sense of our dependence upon forces that go their way without our wish and plan,"[2] and that this uncertainty defines our moral life in the sense that we don't have recourse to fixed, universal rules that resolve our moral dilemmas. Instead, our moral lives require us constantly to choose between competing goods and having to live with the consequences of those choices without yielding to despair. I suggest then that the underlying orientation of Dewey's work is predisposed to my efforts to reconstruct it in light of the tragedy of race in the United States.

Although I do not argue the case in this essay, I maintain that the view of tragedy I attribute to Dewey can be understood as a naturalized reading of Hegel's interpretation of the *Antigone*. Hegel recognized that the conflict between Antigone and Creon was one between competing goods (i.e., between the family and the state) and concluded that the harmony of these spheres "constituted the perfected reality of the moral life." For him, "the true course of dramatic development consist[ed] in the annulment of contradictions viewed as such, in the reconciliation of the faces of human action, which alternatively [strove] to negate each other in their conflict."[3] This Hegelian annulment and reconciliation effected a conflict-free harmony, as Martha Nussbaum notes, that negated the "terrible power of unconstrained contingency."[4]

Dewey's naturalism, however, discards the Hegelian impulse for harmony in this instance and emphasizes instead that there are no guaranteed satisfactory outcomes when we choose between competing values. Dewey holds on, then, to the Sophoclean insight about practical reason and refuses to streamline the complexity of our moral lives. He also recognizes that contingency forms the backdrop of our world of action, discarding the notion of guaranteed outcomes for intelligently guided experimentation. An idea of tragedy remains. However, it is reconstructed in light of Dewey's pragmatic commitments.

I defend this view against the arguments of Hilary Putnam and Cornel West. In *Renewing Philosophy*, Putnam claims, among other things, that Dewey's view of intelligence fails to capture what is really at stake in tragic moral situations: what kind of persons we take ourselves to be. Instead, Dewey's invocation of intelligence is simply about the maximization of goods and betrays, on Putnam's view, a naïve faith in science (broadly understood). West, in "Pragmatism and the Sense of Tragic," argues that Dewey simply fails to grapple seriously with tragedy and the problem of evil. For him, Dewey's pragmatism does not address the realities of dread, disease, and death which threaten our democratic ways of thought and life. And for West, Deweyan faith in critical intelligence simply fails to meet the challenge posed by the debilitating pessimism that can overtake us in the face of these realities. I maintain that both Putnam and West fail to grasp the importance of contingency and conflict in Dewey's philosophy of action and how his view of such matters limits the scope of critical intelligence.

In Part Two I deepen my reading of this view of tragedy with a brief examination of Toni Morrison's novel *Beloved*. First, I suggest that Sethe's choice to enable her children to escape slavery in death as opposed to living as slaves is best characterized by the sense of the tragic I am attributing to Dewey. Sethe's moral dilemma is between competing and conflicting values, and she has no recourse to any universal rules to decide the matter for her. Hers is indeed a tragic situation. Second, I examine Baby Suggs's exhortation to Denver to "Know it, but go on out of the yard." I maintain that Baby Suggs tells Denver that she must understand tragedy and evil as part of the moral exigencies of life. Both are ineliminable features of the world of action: know it, but act anyway. I read this as a particularly powerful reconstruction of what Dewey called intelligently guided experimentation. More specifically, my reading of Morrison's *Beloved* offers an outline of a pragmatic view of the tragic, which takes seriously the realities of race that have shaped this country. The lesson Morrison's novel holds for Deweyan pragmatism is that the problems of race in the United States are best dealt with by confronting our own past and the tragedy therein in order to intelligently invade the future: creative intelligence and an experimental approach enriched by the knowledge of our *racial* experiences allow us to locate and interpret the more serious conflicts that continue to plague

America, and offer up ways for dealing with them. Tragedy remains. We must simply "know" it and act anyway.

My use of Morrison's novel reflects a conviction that the complexities of race in the United States are often inadequately described in philosophical prose. The terror, the broken souls and promises that make up the history of race in this country are seemingly lost in the often stale language of the profession. I am not suggesting, like Stanley Cavell, that philosophy must become literature in order to respond to recognizable human problems. Instead, I hold the view that literary works provide us with particular "angles of insight" into human problems and predicaments. My turn to Morrison reflects this view.

The problems of race, at bottom, have everything to do with our refusal to recognize that we are a multiracial democracy. This refusal has resulted in beliefs, practices, and choices that butcher the ideals of this fragile democratic experiment. On one level, I am alluding to the formal exclusion of African Americans from deliberative processes—that black folks have been denied full participation in that flood of talk so central to Dewey's view of democracy. But, on another level, I am thinking about how this problem has tragically shaped our national imaginary: how we as a nation understand ourselves and how race, for good or ill, shapes that understanding. At the heart of this problematic is the legacy of slavery and our refusal to come to terms with it. No book, in my view, deals with this issue like Morrison's novel. So the novel and the pragmatic view of tragedy I am attributing to it are crucial to what I am trying to offer to contemporary discussions of race—a starting point of sorts.

Part One: Dewey, Tragedy, and Moral Experience

Sidney Hook argued in *Pragmatism and the Tragic Sense of Life* (1974) that William James and John Dewey held a view of tragedy which framed the central themes of their pragmatism—an open-ended universe, an accent on human agency, and the importance of critical intelligence—with the vital options, inescapable limitations, and piecemeal losses we all confront as we act in the world. Hook, drawing on the work of William James, suggested that "no matter how intelligent and humane our choices, there are real losses and losers."[5] The reality of our lives, the fact that we live in a dangerous world, and the seriousness that we attribute to life mean, as James noted in *Pragmatism*, "that ineluctable noes and losses form a part of it, that there are genuine sacrifices, and that something permanently drastic and bitter remains at the bottom of the cup."[6] Tragedy then is a part of the moral exigencies of life. It involves principally the moral choices we make daily between competing and irreconcilable goods, and it entails the consequences we must endure, if we live, and the responsibility we must embrace without yielding to what Toni Morrison calls "marrow weariness." Tragedy, in this view, is a moral phenomenon. As Hook argued, it is "rooted in the very nature of the moral experience and the phenomenon of moral choice. Every genuine experience of moral doubt and perplexity in which we ask 'What should I do?' takes place in a situation where good conflicts with good."[7]

Hook doesn't go very far to demonstrate how this notion of tragedy informs the work of James and Dewey. He simply assumes it and moves on. But one could easily see this particular view of tragedy in the work of William James. James's talk about the sick soul and his tortured attempt to hold off the view that the world is a sea of disappointment testify to his intense grappling with tragedy. In "The Moral Philosopher and Moral Life" James argues that the conflict of goods is an essential feature of our moral lives. He writes that

> the actually possible in this world is vastly narrower than all that is demanded; and there is always the *pinch* between the ideal and the actual which can only be got through by leaving part of the ideal behind. There is hardly a good which we can imagine except as competing for the possession of the same bit of space and time with some other imagined good.

And when we make our choices between them, some ideal is always butchered. "It is a tragic situation," he notes, "and no mere speculative conundrum with which [we have] to deal."[8] For James, the *pinch* is a constitutive feature of the world of action. Victories abound. But so do defeats. Everywhere we look we see what he describes as "the struggle and the squeeze," and our task is somehow to make them less. In this effort we do not have recourse to fixed principles or rules. In James's words, "every real dilemma is in literal strictness a unique situation; and the exact combination of ideals realized and ideals disappointed which each decision creates is always a universe without a precedent, and for which no adequate previous rule exists."[9] At that moment, we can only act on what we hold dear.

Making the case that John Dewey holds a tragic vision is a bit more difficult. Dewey's talk about scientific method and critical intelligence suggests, for some, that he was excessively optimistic about our capacities to resolve conflicts (particularly of the sort that concerned James). Interestingly enough, Dewey begins in the same place as James. He writes of genuine moral dilemmas in *The Quest for Certainty*:

> All the serious perplexities of life come back to the genuine difficulty of forming a judgment as to the values of the situation; they come back to a conflict of goods. Only dogmatism can suppose that serious moral conflict is between something clearly bad and something known to be good, and that uncertainty lies wholly in the will of the one choosing. Most conflicts of importance are conflicts between things which are or have been satisfying, not between good and evil.[10]

This view presupposes formulations laid out in the *Ethics* (1932), and I will turn to this book a bit later in the essay. But for my purposes here it signals that Dewey recognizes, like James, that our moral lives are characterized by conflicts of values. In "Three Independent Factors in Morals," for example, Dewey writes that uncertainty and conflict are inherent in morals—that conflict is internal and intrinsic to every moral situation. Dewey's talk about critical intelligence and method ought to be understood then in light of this recognition of the centrality of conflict in our moral lives. As he writes in *Human Nature and Conduct*:

> It is not pretended that a moral theory based upon realities of human nature and a study of the specific connections of these realities with those of physical science would do away with moral struggle and defeat. It would not make the moral life as simple a matter as wending one's way along a well-lighted boulevard. All action is an invasion of the future, of the unknown. Conflict and uncertainty are ultimate traits.[11]

To be sure, the conflict runs so deep for Dewey that it becomes all the more urgent to develop habits and virtues, which we can intelligently seek[12] to ameliorate problematic situations. Unlike James, Dewey's *faith* resides in our capacity to engage in intelligent action: he is reluctant to fix belief even in the face of conflict of goods. Also, for Dewey, *preoccupation* with the pinch—the struggle and squeeze of the world of action—can become debilitating. So we should take the world for what it is: uncertain, in process, and always acting on us, for weal or woe. This understanding of the precariousness of the world of action, I maintain, is absolutely crucial for understanding the tragic vision in Dewey's pragmatic philosophy of action.

On Dewey's view, we have responded to the hazards of this world of uncertainty in, at least, two ways. First, we have constructed rituals of supplication, sacrifice, and ceremonial rites with the hope that the uncontrollable forces that impinge upon us might be appeased. The aim here is to ally ourselves with powers that dispense fortune in order to escape defeat and, perhaps, to experience triumph in the face of destruction.[13] Second, we have invented arts in response to the hazards of our world. Housing, clothing, forms of irrigation are all examples of attempts to "construct a fortress out of the very conditions and forces" which threaten us. The first response is what Dewey calls the method of changing the self in emotion and idea, a method that informs traditional philosophical reflection. The second is the method of changing the world through action.[14] Both reflect our efforts to respond to a world of hazards. Yet we have often viewed the arts as an inadequate response to the perils of life.

Why? The world of action, of doing and making, involves us in various sorts of activities that in no way remove uncertainty. As Dewey writes, "The distinctive characteristic of practical activity, one which is so inherent that it cannot be eliminated, is the uncertainty that attends it. Of it we are compelled to say: Act, but act at your peril."[15] Practical activity involves change, and it has been our desire to escape the frightening consequences of change that has led to misguided quests for certainty. In Dewey's view, modern philosophy has conceived of knowledge, for example, as a private affair in which the disclosure of the invariant—the Real in itself—is the object of philosophical inquiry. Here philosophers strip away the imaginative formulations of a religious outlook, in which a sharp division between the ordinary and the extraordinary animates how we see ourselves in relation to our world and the universe, only to replace them with their own doctrine of the antecedently real, which, when grasped by thought, discloses fixed and immutable Truth. For Dewey, this search translated efforts to escape the exigencies of life into rational form. Deliverance from the vicissitudes of existence by means of rites and sacrifice gave way to a form of deliverance through reason, a theoretical affair which stood apart from our actual conditions of living.[16]

The world of action, then, is fraught with uncertainty. In it, events happen to us, without our wish or plan, that transform our lives. Circumstances may force us to choose wrongly or to betray those whom we love. People we cherish die. We die. Indeed, the contingency of our lives and the apparent indifference of nature to our efforts jeopardize human aspirations to live good lives.[17] Deliverance from the exigencies of life is, in some ways, deliverance from what some take to be the tragedy of brute chance. For, in the end, "the quest for certainty is a quest for peace which is assured, an object which is unqualified by risk and the shadow of fear which action casts. For it is not uncertainty per se which men dislike, but the fact that uncertainty involves us in peril of evils."[18]

This understanding of contingency forms the background for Dewey's philosophical formulations; it extends the Darwinian outlook, which presupposes that the world is processive. Dewey believes that Darwinian evolution dislodged an Aristotelian conception of the world in which all changes reflected an overarching order and were cumulative in the sense that they tended in a predetermined direction.[19] Darwin's influence on philosophy resided in his rejection of this particular view and its replacement by the principle of transition: that the environment exerts pressures on its inhabitants and that there are random variations among these living creatures that affect how they will get on in an environment that acts on them. Our activity in the world then is one of constant adaptation and adjustment in light of the limit conditions of existence.

Three crucial points for Dewey's philosophy follow from this principle: (1) philosophy must give up inquiry after absolute origins and fixed Truth and turn its attention to the actual conditions of experience that generate specific values. (2) Philosophy must abandon efforts to prove that life *must* have certain qualities and values, over and beyond experience, because of some predetermined end. Instead, we must look the facts of experience in the face and acknowledge seriously the evils they present and the goods they *may* promise. (3) Such an outlook introduces responsibility into intellectual life. Queries, for example, that idealize the universe at large suggest that we have thrown up our hands with regards to matters that directly concern us. As Dewey writes:

As long as mankind suffered from this impotency, it naturally shifted a burden of responsibility that it could not carry over to the more competent shoulders of the transcendent cause. But if insight into specific conditions of value and into specific consequences of idea is possible, philosophy must in time become a method of locating and interpreting the more serious conflicts that occur in life, and a method of projecting ways for dealing with them: a method of moral and political diagnosis and prognosis.[20]

The quest for certainty is seen for what it is: an effort on the part of fragile, finite creatures to secure themselves and their world in the face of unrelenting change.

Such efforts have led us to turn our backs on the world of action and, to some extent, absolve ourselves of the strenuous work of "making and remaking" our world. To be sure, fixed reality, complete in itself, provides us with a sense of assurance that order stands behind what we experience as contingent. It is similar to the relief from grief we feel when we know that our loved ones are resting peacefully in heaven. But Darwin's insights, Dewey maintains, force us to reject this view. Disclosure of the antecedently real does nothing to arrest the changes in our world (just as knowing that our loved ones are in heaven does not change the fact that they are dead and no longer with us). Change still happens—for better or worse. If we turn to experience, though, we give up efforts to secure our world by means of transcending it. The search for security remains. Our efforts, however, are located in practical activity, not in quests for absolute certainty.

On this view, knowledge is the fruit of our attempts to resolve problematic situations. It is understood in the context of communal inquiry, not in terms of a private mental activity. The turn to the actual conditions of our living then tilts our understanding of knowledge in a different direction. It is not about absolute certainty and fixed Truth. Instead, knowledge can be properly understood only as a functional activity in the context of our experience, that is to say, in the context of interactions with our environment. The qualities and values of these experiences are not predetermined and set. Nor are they reducible to an inner event or to a backward-looking affair in which the past counts exclusively. Experience, for Dewey, "is a matter of *simultaneous* doings and sufferings,"[21] a process of undergoing in which the agent-patient seeks experimentally to find the best tools to cope with the obstacles an environment presents and to anticipate future problems that may occur.

This connection to the future forms the primary basis for responsibility. For in the efforts to secure our world for our children and us, we employ methods that generate foresight to anticipate future consequences in our present doings and sufferings. We make moral and political diagnoses and prognoses with an eye toward securing and expanding for future generations the values we so dearly cherish. As Dewey writes in "The Development of American Pragmatism":

> Pragmatism . . . does not insist upon antecedent phenomena but upon consequent phenomena; not upon precedents but upon the possibilities of action. . . . The doctrine of the value of consequences leads us to take the future into consideration. And this taking into consideration of the future takes us to the conception of a universe whose evolution is not finished, of a universe which is still, in James's

terms "in the making, in the process of becoming," of a universe up to a certain point still plastic.[22]

Dewey's accent on human agency presupposes a world that is always evolving. No guarantees. No fixed truths. Just the fragile attempts of finite creatures to flourish in an environment that impinges upon them daily. Here the mystery and awe we have felt in the face of a universe that is extraordinary (which requires being approached with ceremonial scruples) is transferred to the human future.[23] And our primary responsibility is to act intelligently in order to ensure, as humanly possible, that this future is better than our present living.

Moral Experience and Hilary Putnam's Critique

Contingency then forms the backdrop for Dewey's philosophical reflection. Once we grasp its place in his overall outlook we get a sense of his view of human agency and the task of philosophy. That is to say, once we realize that there is never a metaphysical guarantee to be had for our beliefs, we give up efforts to discover the antecedently real and realize that what human beings do in the face of problems and how they go about doing it *is* the primary topic of philosophical reflection. Questions like Is the universe friendly to democratic possibility? are abandoned. And we ask instead how the consequences of our choices serve or defeat our efforts for genuine democratic living. The shift is "from an intelligence that shaped things once for all to the particular intelligences which things are even now shaping."[24]

It is important, however, to realize that uncertainty still remains even with all of Dewey's talk about intelligent action. Action involves risks and by no means guarantees satisfactory outcomes. He powerfully makes this point near the end of his Gifford lectures:

> At best, all our endeavors look to the future and never attain certainty. The lesson of probability holds for all forms of activity as truly as for the experimental operations of science and even more poignantly and tragically. The control and regulation of which so much has been said never signifies certainty of outcome, although the greater need of security it may afford will not be known until we try the experimental policy in all walks of life. The unknown surrounds us in other forms of practical activity even more than in knowing, for they reach further in the future, in more significant and less controllable ways. *A sense of dependence is quickened by that Copernican revolution which looks to security amid change instead of to certainty in attachment to the fixed.* (emphasis added)[25]

Dewey suggests here that our immodest pains to uncover the fixed and immutable principles of the universe provide a level of comfort (assurance) that is not available once we turn to the world of action. *This* world forces us to humble our efforts to the work of hypotheses for the amelioration of individual and social problems. We stand unprotected by the armor of traditional metaphysics only to encounter the full brunt of change and its potential misery and joy. Our best recourse in the face of these moments is not to escape to a haven in which we find rest from the storms of life—an asylum in which we take refuge from the troubles of existence[26]—but, rather, to act as intelligently as possible to secure for ourselves what we deem, at that moment, desirable. The problems of evil then are understood, for Dewey, within the stream of experiences, and we need only turn to his conception of *moral* experience to see how thoroughly tragic his philosophy of action is.

Conflicting moral demands characterize our moral experiences.[27] We confront situations that demand of us a choice between competing values, and the conflict produces a genuine moral dilemma. Moral experiences and deliberation then are always situated. They are located in the context of some particular problem—some perceived moral perplexity. For Dewey, there are at least two kinds of moral struggle. One, which is the most emphasized in traditional moral writings, is the case when the individual is tempted to do something she knows is wrong. Dewey uses the example of the bank employee who is tempted to embezzle money. She knows that what she is thinking about doing is wrong. The bank employee may even try to convince herself otherwise in an attempt to permit her desires to govern her beliefs. No real thinking, however, takes place in this circumstance, for, as Dewey suggests, there is no sincere doubt as to what should be done when she seeks to find some justification for what she has made up her mind to do.[28]

The other is the case when two values conflict. Dewey's example is worth quoting at length:

> Take . . . the case of the citizen of a nation which has just declared war on another country. He is deeply attached to his own State. He has formed habits of loyalty and of abiding by its law, and now one of its decrees is that he shall support war. He feels in addition gratitude and affection for the country which has sheltered and nurtured him. But he believes that this war is unjust, or perhaps he has a conviction that all war is a form of murder and hence wrong. One side of his nature, one set of convictions of habits, leads him to acquiesce to war; another deep part of his being protests. He is torn between two duties: he experiences a conflict between incompatible values. . . . The struggle is not between a good which is clear to him and something else which attracts him but which he knows to be wrong. It is between values each of which is undoubted good in its place but which now get in each other's way.[29]

For Dewey, moral theory represents an extension of the kind of reflection that goes on in such moments: it does not emerge in the conflict between right and wrong. We already know, by way of custom and habit, why one course of action is right and the other wrong. Moral theory takes place when we are confronted with situations in which opposing goods and incompatible courses of action seem to be morally justified.[30]

This particular approach evades some of the pitfalls of traditional moral theory. Dewey argues that traditional moral philosophy tends to isolate and reify specific features of our moral life in an effort to uncover one single principle of morality. These efforts, in whatever form, fail to acknowledge the centrality of uncertainty and conflict to our moral experiences. Instead, a litany of dualities—good and evil, justice and injustice, duty and caprice, virtue and vice—render moral conflict as only specious and apparent not as an inherent part of the good, the obligatory, and the virtuous.[31] On such a view, with its ready-made distinctions and dualities, "the only force which can oppose the moral is the immoral."[32]

Dewey argues that uncertainty and conflict in moral experience ought not to be understood in this way. Instead, he suggests that moral experience and the notions of moral progress and character development that attend it involve the activity of making "delicate distinctions, to perceive aspects of good and evil not previously noted, to take into account the fact that doubt and the need for choice impinge at every turn," and the mark of moral decline is the loss of an ability to make such distinctions. He goes on to suggest that there are at least three independent variables—good, right, and virtue—in moral action. Each has its own source of origin and mode of operation, and because of this, each can get in the other's way.[33] From this point of view, Dewey argues:

> Uncertainty and conflict are inherent in morals; it is characteristic of any situation properly called moral that one is ignorant of the end and of the good consequences, of the right and just approach, of the direction of the virtuous conduct, and that one must search for them. The essence of the moral situation is an internal and intrinsic conflict; the necessity for judgment and choice comes from the fact that one has to manage forces with no common denominator.[34]

For Dewey, in such situations the correct choice is rarely apparent. We stand somewhat ignorant of the end and the consequences that may follow from whatever choice we may make. Nevertheless, and this is a Sophoclean insight, we must choose. Not with the mind that our choice is based in some fixed, universal principle but that our choice is the best intelligent choice for the problematic situation in which we happen to find ourselves.

Hilary Putnam finds this dimension of Dewey's philosophy less than satisfactory. He argues that Dewey's emphasis on intelligence does not take us very far in resolving the moral dilemmas we often face, particularly when what's at stake is what kind of individual we take ourselves to be. Putnam writes:

> Consider the famous case of an existential choice that Sartre employed in his *Existentialism and Humanism*. It is World War II, and Pierre has to make an agonizing choice between joining the Resistance, which means leaving his aging mother alone on the farm, or staying and taking care of his mother, but not helping to fight the enemy. One of the reasons that Dewey's recommendation to use intelligently guided experimentation in solving ethical problems does not really help in such a case is Dewey's consequentialism. Pierre is not out to "maximize" the good, however conceived, in some global sense, he is out to do what is right. Like all consequentialist views, Dewey has trouble doing justice to considerations of the right. I am not saying that Dewey's philosophy never applies to individual existential choices. Some choices are just dumb. But Pierre is not dumb. Neither of the alternatives he is considering is any way stupid. Yet he cannot just flip a coin.[35]

For Putnam, when individuality is at stake—like the need for Pierre to decide who Pierre is—intelligently guided experimentation doesn't really help matters. Instead he turns to William James.

For Putnam, we need not restrict ourselves to "consummatory experiences which are brought about and appraised." Often times we have to act on our firm belief that this course of action is right (even though relatively little in our experience would suggest to do so or that we haven't the time to adequately assess the consequences of acting in this particular way). We sometimes have to "run ahead of the evidence." Putnam writes of James:

> James thought that every single human being has to make decisions ahead of the evidence of the kind that Pierre had to make; even if they are not as dramatic.... James argued again and again that our best energies cannot be set free unless we are willing to make the sort of existential commitment that this example illustrates. Someone who acts only when the "estimated utilities" are favorable does not live a meaningful life. Even if I choose to do something of whose ethical and social value there is absolutely no doubt, say to devote my life to comforting the dying, or helping the mentally ill, or curing the sick, or relieving poverty, I still have to decide not whether it is good that someone should do that thing, but whether it is good that I, Hilary Putnam, do that thing. The answer to that question cannot be a matter of well-established scientific fact, in however generous a sense of "scientific."[36]

Many people are duped by Dewey's language. He writes in such a way that the reader comes away from the text thinking that Dewey believes in inevitable progress and human capacities to transform any circumstance—that optimism about human potential blinds him to the real existential dilemmas that we fragile and finite creatures confront. But to read Dewey in this way obscures the tragic dimensions of his thinking. Putnam's reading, in particular, fails to grasp this dimension of Dewey's moral philosophy. He has been duped.

I have already gone to great lengths to demonstrate in Dewey's view the centrality of uncertainty and conflict in any situation that can be properly called moral. As I have mentioned, uncertainty and conflict are not the result, in most cases, of a conflict between good and evil. As Dewey puts it, "the moral agent knows good as good and evil as evil and chooses one or the other according to the knowledge he has of it." Instead both conflict and uncertainty arise because of the complexity of the problem of discovering what is good, what is right, and what is virtuous. For Dewey, the more thoughtful the moral agent is about the quality of her moral acts, the more the agent is aware of the complexity of the problem of discovering what is good. He goes on to say, sounding a lot like Putnam here, that the moral agent "hesitates among ends, all of which are good in some measure, among duties which obligate him for some reason. *Only after the event and then by chance, does one of the alternatives seem simply good morally or bad morally.*"[37] Dewey maintains that dilemmas of this sort are not recognized by moral theory because, whatever the differences that may separate different moral accounts, they all offer a single principle as an explanation of our moral lives. To put the point baldly, Pierre's sort of dilemma—the conflict between good and right in this case—is Dewey's point of entry into reconstructing moral philosophy.

But Putnam's worry goes beyond this. He would have to concede that, like James, Dewey recognizes the experience of a conflict between incompatible values as the starting point of his ethics. The problem, however, lies with Dewey's talk of intelligence in the context of such dilemmas. On Putnam's view, Dewey simply fails to capture what is really at stake when we are confronted with conflicting goods—that is to say, what is at stake is who we take ourselves to be.

This worry points to a problem in Putnam's description of Dewey's moral philosophy. He makes no mention of the importance of habit and custom to the formation and continued development of our *individual* characters. What's at stake for Dewey in situations like Pierre's, among other things, is precisely what kind of person Pierre takes himself to be and will become. Dewey makes this point quite explicit in *Human Nature and Conduct*:

> The poignancy of situations that involve reflection lies in the fact that we really do not know the meaning of the tendencies that are pressing for action. We have to search, to experiment. Deliberation is a work of discovery. Conflict is acute; one impulse carries us one way into one situation, and another impulse takes us another way to a radically different objective result. Deliberation is not an attempt to do away with this opposition of quality by reducing it to one amount. It is an attempt to uncover the conflict in its full scope and bearing. What we want to find out is what difference each impulse and habit imports, to reveal qualitative incompatibilities by detecting the different courses to which they commit us, the different dispositions they form and foster, the different situations into which they plunge us. *In short, the thing actually at stake in any serious deliberation is not a difference of quantity, but what kind of person one is to become, what sort of self is in the making, what kind of world is in the making.* (emphasis added)[38]

In light of this, I am a bit puzzled by Putnam's worry. Dewey, like James, begins with the conflict between values. He also, like James, understands that our deliberations in the face of moral dilemmas are, in some ways, deliberations about what kind of person one is to become. On both views, individuality is at stake. Putnam, however, makes no mention of Dewey's talk about character and its relation to conduct. He fails to see that, for Dewey, what we do—even if that entails running ahead of the evidence—depends on the history of the organism engaged in the action. Dewey's invocation of intelligence, then, goes beyond the maximization of goods. To use his language, intelligence is, in some ways, about discovery: our attempt to figure out, as best we can, given the circumstances, why one impulse carries us this way and the other that way.

Unlike James, Dewey is not willing in these critical moments—moments that are as much about who we will become as they are about who we are—to allow us to rest solely on already established habits. There may be cases where this is necessary. But we must not render the notion of "running ahead of the evidence" in such a way that it amounts only to a blind jab in the darkness. To run ahead of the evidence can very well be, and in some cases is, an intelligent act. Beyond this Dewey would agree with James:

We stand on a mountain pass in the midst of whirling snow and blinding mist, through which we get glimpses now and then of paths which may be deceptive. If we stand still, we shall be frozen to death. If we take the wrong road, we shall be dashed to pieces. We do not certainly know if there is any right one. What must we do? "Be strong and of good courage." Act for the best, hope for the best, and take what comes. . . . If death ends all, we cannot meet death better.[39]

The Problem of Evil and Cornel West's Critique

We could easily throw up our hands and become pessimists about any possibility of flourishing in such a world. To be sure, experiencing the dark side of nature is all too much a part of what it means to be an agent. Evil, absurdity, the hideously petty dimensions of our failures and losses, as Josiah Royce describes it, could easily lead us to conclude, with Schopenhauer, that "everything in life proclaims that earthly happiness is destined to be frustrated, or recognized as an illusion." And that "the grounds for this lie deep in the very nature of things."[40] For Schopenhauer, suffering is an ineliminable feature of this worst of all possible worlds. Here the nastiness of experience makes it such that—for each of us—it would have been better not to have been born. We need only take a serious look at our world: "Nine tenths of mankind live in constant conflict of want, always balancing themselves with difficulty and effort on the brink of destruction."[41] People die of hunger and of senseless wars. Pharmaceutical companies charge exorbitant fees for life-saving drugs. Corporate elites continue to pay starvation wages to their workers. Our world, as Schopenhauer put it, can be described quite accurately as hell, and we "are on the one hand the tormented souls and on the other the devils in it."[42]

Classical pragmatists[43] like Dewey reject the pessimistic conclusions drawn from the recognition of our precarious position in the world. Dewey, for example, would readily agree with Schopenhauer that suffering is a constitutive feature of the world of action, but would insist that it points to only one side of the "double connection" of experience. Of course, experience involves suffering. It is "primarily a process of undergoing: a process of standing something; of suffering and passion, of affection, in the literal sense of these terms."[44] But the process of undergoing is never merely passive: experience is not simply a matter of receptivity. We are also agents—reacting, experimenting, concerned with influencing the direction of our encounters in such a way that they will benefit and not harm. These actions involve us in peril: conflicts of ends will occur, and, more than likely, new sorts of problems will arise as old ones are resolved. But this is not necessarily a bad thing. It is part of what it means to be an organism interacting with its environment. Dewey would agree with Schopenhauer: our world is one in which suffering is inescapable. But, where Schopenhauer would conclude from this fact that it would have been better not to have been born, Dewey, like Emerson and James, responds with meliorism.

Meliorism is the belief that our circumstances at a given moment, be they comparatively good or bad, can be improved. For Dewey, such a view commends intelligent action in the sense that it encourages us to inquire into the amelioration of problems, individual and social, and the obstructions to their resolution. Such a view doesn't commit Dewey to a form of optimism. In his words, meliorism "arouses confidence and a reasonable hopefulness as optimism does not. For the latter in declaring that good is already realized in ultimate reality tends to make us gloss over the evils that concretely exist."[45] For Dewey, optimism with its view that our world is the best possible world "cooperates with pessimism . . . in benumbing sympathetic insight and intelligent effort in reform." Moreover, "it beckons men away from the world of relativity and change into the calm of the absolute and eternal."[46]

Dewey echoes William James here. James wrote in 1907 that "meliorism treats salvation as neither necessary nor impossible. It treats it as a possibility, which becomes more and more of a probability the more numerous the actual conditions of salvation become."[47] To put the point in Deweyan language, we can indeed reconstruct our experiences for the better—secure and stabilize some of the goods within them—once we grasp, through critical intelligence, the conditions that make for those experiences. But our efforts are not guaranteed. The world of action is a world of change, "a precarious and perilous place" in which, in spite of our intelligent efforts, when it is all said and done, its hazardous character remains modestly modified, but hardly eliminated.[48] As Dewey writes in *Experience and Nature*:

> Philosophy has its source not in any special impulse or staked-off section of experience, but in the entire human predicament, this human situation falls wholly within nature. It reflects the traits of nature; it gives indisputable evidence that in nature itself qualities and relations, individualities and uniformities, finalities and efficacies, contingencies and necessities are inextricably bound. The harsh conflicts and happy coincidences of this interpenetration make experience what it consciously is; their manifest apparition creates doubt, forces inquiry, exacts choices, and imposes liability for the choices made.[49]

We can never claim that intelligence will secure our lives once and for all or "save us from ruin or destruction." The strangeness and unexpected aspects of nature will continuously interrupt, irritate, and exact choices from us. To think otherwise would turn our attention away from the facts of experience and suggest an unreasonable hopefulness that would lead away from the task of reconstruction.[50] To be sure, our conditions of living, Dewey maintains, require "a certain intellectual pessimism, in the sense of a steadfast willingness to uncover sore points, to acknowledge and search for abuses, to note how presumed good often serves as a cloak for actual bad."[51] Ours is indeed a life of suffering. But suffering is only a part of our experiences. We must always be mindful of our capacity to act on our world.

If those efforts are frustrated—as perhaps they will be—or if they lead to other more complicated, nuanced problems—as they most assuredly will—such is the nature of our efforts to secure our world amid change. They are provisional and sometimes fail. But this fact should not lead us to turn our backs on this world or lead us to believe that nonexistence is better than existence. Responses like these reflect a desire for certainty and ultimate guarantees. For Dewey, despite our best efforts, neither is possible nor, if we truly care about *this* world, is desirable. Oliver Wendell Holmes states the position best, and Dewey quotes him at length in *Experience and Nature*:

> If we believe we came out of the universe, not it out of us, we must admit that we do not know what we are talking about when we speak of brute matter. We do know that a certain complex of energies can wag its tail and another can make syllogisms. These are among the powers of the unknown, and if, as may be, it has still greater powers that we cannot understand . . . why should we not be content? Why should we employ the energy that is furnished to us by the cosmos to defy it and to shake our fist at the sky? It seems silly. . . . That the universe has in it more than we understand, that the private soldiers have not been told the plan of campaign, or even that there is one . . . has no bearing on our conduct. We still shall fight—all of us because we want to live, some, at least, because we want to realize our spontaneity and prove our powers, for the joy of it, and we may leave to the unknown the supposed final valuation of that which in any event has value to us. It is enough for us that the universe has produced us and has within it, as less than it, all that we believe and love.[52]

This is where Dewey's philosophy of action begins and why I believe it is tragic at its very root. Because once we stop pondering God's intent or seeking to disclose that which supposedly lies behind the world of appearance, we are then confronted with the tragic choices of fragile human beings seeking a bit of security in the here and now and hoping, reasonably, for a better future for our children. His is a philosophy that begins with human agency and historical/natural limitations, accenting all the while that all we hold dear lies in this world, and that's all we need, with intelligence and a bit of luck, to flourish.

But for Cornel West, even with all of his talk about contingency, Dewey fails to grapple seriously with tragedy and the problem of evil. He argues that although Dewey recognized, with Jefferson, "the irreducibility of individuality within participatory communities," and acknowledged, like Emerson, "the heroic action of ordinary folk in a world of radical contingency," he failed to "meet the challenge posed by Lincoln—namely, defining the relation of democratic ways of thought and life to a profound sense of evil."[53] For him, the only American philosopher to take seriously Lincoln's challenge was Josiah Royce. He even suggests that Royce's post-Kantian idealism can be read as a sustained meditation on the relation of evil to human agency.

Royce and Dewey are linked, however, insofar as both thinkers begin with fundamental pragmatic notions. Voluntarism, fallibilism, and experimentalism are central to Dewey's instrumental pragmatism and Royce's "absolute pragmatism." Both thinkers stress the importance of human will and practice. And as West notes, this emphasis leads to two basic claims in their philosophies: (1) truth is a species of the good, and (2) the conception of the good is defined in relation to temporal consequences.[54] For both thinkers, what we believe matters, and what we do can make a difference in relation to our aims and purposes. Truth then has ethical consequences, and the future has ethical significance. West demonstrates the way both of these claims animate the absolute idealism of Royce and the instrumentalism of Dewey, and how each claim, particularly the prospective emphasis in their philosophies, results in the view that all facts are fallible and that efforts to better our world are experimental. This, for West, is the common ground between the two thinkers. Both hold the view that "unique selves acting in and through participatory communities give ethical significance to an open, risk-ridden future. . . . The 'majesty of community' [Royce] and 'the true spirituality of genuine doubting' [Dewey] combine to ensure that nothing blocks the Peircean road to inquiry."[55]

But when it comes to the fact of evil, Royce and Dewey simply go their separate ways. For West, the presence of evil affected Royce more than Dewey. This tortured struggle with evil and Lincoln's challenge attracted Royce to the work of Schopenhauer, and West sees the absence of references to Schopenhauer in Dewey's corpus as some sort of failure. For Royce and West, Dewey's faith in critical intelligence is woefully inadequate when confronted with a deep sense of evil, for the problem of evil demands of us a lifelong struggle with pessimism.

Royce attempted to hold on in a world of suffering and sorrow by way of his absolute idealism. He recognized that the irrevocable nature of our actions and the indeterminate character of the future made fulfillment at any present instant impossible. Yet Royce was "ready to accept the dear sorrow of possessing ideals and of taking [his] share of the divine task." For him, absolute reality ("the sort of reality that belongs to irrevocable deeds") and absolute truth ("the sort of truth that belongs to those opinions which, for a given purpose, counsel individual deeds, when the deeds in fact meet the purpose for which they were intended") grounded our actions in *this* world and made them sturdy. For West, though, Royce's idealism went beyond worries about skepticism and epistemic relativism. Instead, reality and truth had to be absolute because they are "the last and only hope for giving meaning to the strenuous mood, for justifying the worthwhileness of our struggle to endure."[56] Without absolute truth and reality pessimism is our only option.

At this point, West turns to a powerful moment in Royce's work in which he doubts his own response to the problem of evil:

For I do not feel that I have yet quite expressed the full force of the deepest argument for pessimism, or the full seriousness of the eternal problem of evil. . . . Pessimism, in the true sense, isn't the doctrine of the merely peevish man, but of the man who to borrow a word of Hegel's, "has feared not for this moment or that in his life, but who has feared with all his nature; so that he has trembled through and through, and all that was most fixed in him has become shaken." There are experiences in life that do just this for us. . . . The worst tragedy of the world is the tragedy of brute chance to which everything spiritual seems to be subject amongst us—the tragedy of the diabolical irrationality of so many among the foes of whatever is significant. An open enemy you can face. The temptation to do evil is indeed a necessity for spirituality. But one's own foolishness, one's ignorance, the cruel accidents of disease, the fatal misunderstandings that part friends and lovers, the chance mistakes that wreck nations:—these things we lament most bitterly, not because they are painful, but because they are farcical, distracting,—not foe-men worthy of the sword of the spirit, nor yet mere pangs of our finitude that we can easily learn to face courageously, as one can be indifferent to physical pain. No, these things do not make life merely painful to us; they make it hideously petty.[57]

For West, this constitutes recognition of a "deep," "profound" sense of evil, an intense grappling with its presence, which he remarks is entirely absent in Dewey's work.[58]

West believes "that a deep sense of evil must infuse any meaning and value of democracy," and that Dewey simply failed to see that "the culture of democratic societies requires not only the civic virtues of participation, tolerance, openness, mutual respect, and mobility, but also dramatic struggles with the two major culprits—disease and death—that defeat and cut off the joys of democratic citizenship."[59] Royce's insight is found then not in his absolute idealism—his quest for ultimate assurance—but, rather, in the recognition of evil that often leads us to seek that assurance. And, for West, such a recognition—stamped as it is with a Christian imprimatur—is required if we are to meet Lincoln's challenge.

Dewey would disagree. Evils are scaled down in his naturalistic philosophy. They are desires errant and frustrated: simply part of the vicissitudes of existence. To be sure, evils remain a powerful force in our lives—thwarting our efforts and oftentimes making our lives miserable and painful—but they are not thought of as a defect and aberration, as deviations from the perfect. For Dewey, the recognition of uncertainty displaces the assumption of an antecedent identity between the actual and ideal and all of the problems, particularly the problem of evil that follows from it. Dewey's starting point then is quite different from Royce's. It is not one in which the ideal is already and eternally a property of the real. Instead, ideals signal the possibility of modifying the current state of affairs; they take us back to Dewey's understanding of ideas as designations of operations and their consequences.[60] As he put it, "The sense of incompetency and the sloth born of the desire for irresponsibility have combined to create an overwhelming longing for the ideal and rational as an antecedent possession for actuality, and consequently something upon which we can fall back for emotional support in times of trouble"[61] and, if that support fails us at that moment, something to shake our fist at because we have now succumbed to pessimism.

The problem of evil, for Dewey, is not a theological or a metaphysical problem. It "is perceived to be the practical problem of reducing, alleviating, as far as may be removing, the evils of life," and the task of philosophy is to contribute "in however humble a way to methods that will assist us in discovering the causes of humanity's ills."[62] For Dewey, then, the world is neither wholly evil nor good. It simply is what is, and *our* actions infuse it with meaning. Unlike Royce, Dewey does not begin with "bitter lament" over the "tragedy of brute chance." He simply acknowledges uncertainty and all that attends it as *the* constitutive feature of the world of action, and our task is to act in such a world as intelligently as possible in order to secure some consequences and avoid others.

This exposes us to the peril of evils. We may have experiences that make us "tremble through and through"—even lead us to despair. But they would be *experiences*,[63] not abstract lamentations over the failure of the universe. Not ideals pitched too high, but moments of genuine defeat. Such moments concerned Dewey. He worried about despair. For Dewey understood that any turn to the world of action threatened debilitating defeat. I read his passionate insistence on the need for critical intelligence as, at times, a desperate attempt to equip us with the tools to withstand such moments. Does this constitute an answer to Lincoln's challenge? To my mind, yes. If we understand that the world of action involves us in the peril of evils and that democracy is a product of our making, then we must define democracy in relation to that world and the uncertainty that attends it. Our democratic way of life is by no means guaranteed nor is it perfect. As such, democracy must be understood apart from procedures and laws and seen as a regulative ideal toward which we strive (with all of the risks that striving entails).[64]

West would remain unsatisfied for at least two reasons. First, his preoccupation with the problem of evil is not about conclusions drawn from weighing evidence for and against the existence of God. His view stems not from a disconnection between the actual and ideal. Instead, West is more concerned about undeserved harm and suffering, and the inadequate grasp of this suffering (along with the complex operations of power that produce it) by classical and contemporary pragmatists. Second, I have yet to address what he takes to be the fundamental challenge of evil to our democratic way of thought and life: disease and death. Both of these ineliminable facts of life defeat and cut short the joys of democratic citizenship.

In the first instance, with this view of evil, I am puzzled by West's attraction to Royce and his criticism of Dewey. When West claims that to be mindful of the operations of power is to confront the tragic, that is, "to confront the individual and collective experiences of evil with little expectation of ridding the world of all evil,"[65] he sounds a lot like Dewey—particularly when he claims elsewhere that "suffering is understood only as a reality to resist, an actuality to oppose. It can neither be submitted to in order to gain contemplative knowledge nor reified into an object of ironic attention. Rather it is a concrete state of affairs which produces discernible hurt and pain, hence requiring some sort of action."[66] What differentiates this view from Dewey's? What makes Royce's idealist formulation of the problem of evil more compelling? Perhaps it is Royce's struggle with Schopenhauerian pessimism? But this form of pessimism discloses a view of the ideal and actual that West, by his pragmatist lights, should reject. The point to be made here is that West leaves unattended the ambiguities and ambivalences in his understanding of evil and tragedy. And these problems are only complicated by his invocation of depth metaphors as standards of judgments between thinkers who take on such matters (when he claims, for example, that classical pragmatists simply don't go "deep" enough when they address the problem of evil).

Moreover, West makes an interesting claim in his reading of Royce (interesting in the sense that, if we read the claim carefully, it may say more about West than about Royce). He suggests that Royce's idealism went beyond a concern about skepticism and epistemic relativism: he was more concerned with justifying the worthwhileness of our struggle to endure. But surely these two concerns are intimately related. Critics of relativism hold the view that unless something absolute stands behind the mess of our living, we have no reason to go on resisting evil. In fact, as Richard Rorty notes, "If evil is merely a lesser good, if all moral choice is a compromise between conflicting goods, then, they [critics of relativism] say, there is no point in moral struggle. The lives of those who have died resisting injustice become pointless."[67] But for Dewey this sort of wringing of the hands is unnecessary. Rorty states what I take to be Dewey's position quite well:

> To us pragmatists moral struggle is continuous with the struggle for existence, and no sharp break divides the unjust from the imprudent, the evil from the inexpedient. What matters for pragmatists is devising ways of diminishing human suffering and increasing human equality, increasing the ability of all human children to start life with an equal chance of happiness. This goal is not written in the stars, and is no more an expression of what Kant called pure practical reason than it is the Will of God. It is a goal worth dying for, but it does not require backup from supernatural forces.[68]

On this view, there is no need to justify the worthwhileness of our struggle to endure. The strenuous mood is maintained by our efforts "to modify what exists so that it will take on a form possessed of specifiable traits."[69] In other words, the recognition of the possibilities of existence and our passionate devotion to the cause of these possibilities sustain the strenuous mood. We must see that Royce's desire to justify our efforts to endure emanates from his worry about skepticism and epistemic relativism and the consequences of such views for our moral life. Why Cornel West, the prophetic pragmatist, finds Royce's efforts powerful and poignant is a bit curious. Perhaps it suggests a bit of hand-wringing on his part.

As for the challenge of death and disease to our democratic life, Dewey's response would be pretty straightforward. At a certain level of abstraction, the inevitability of death constitutes a natural limitation. Organisms live and they die. It's a fact of nature: no mystery there. At another level, however, the issue becomes What do we make of our time here? Death and disease are then understood in concrete terms—for example, the fact that AIDS is destroying a generation of Africans or that violent death threatens African American males at rates disproportionate to other segments of the U.S. population. These facts bring the issues of disease and death down to earth as problems that impede our attempts at genuine democratic living.

But I am sure West would claim that such a move does not speak to the individual struggle with disease and death—that the shudder that was evidenced in Royce's solitary moment is missing here. I will bracket my worries about the existentialist overtones of West's invocation of these terms and the problematic conception of the self they presuppose[70] only to make this point: that moving to such a level of abstraction does little to secure democratic forms of life and, more importantly, threatens those who ask such questions with a debilitating form of despair or helplessness precisely because the alternatives they make available force us, in some way, to turn our backs on this world.[71] We either give up on the possibility of our actions affecting any significant change or else look to some other force that will, in the end, save us from ourselves. In the case of the latter, those of us concerned with bringing about radical democratic change must remember Dewey's admonition: "[We] will have to ask, as far as [we] nominally believe in the need for radical social change, whether what [we] accomplish when [we] point with one hand to the seriousness of present evils is undone when the other hand points away from man and nature for their remedy."[72]

Dewey's naturalism rejects what I take to be the Christian impulse informing West's conception of the tragic. Like Royce, West holds on to something like the drama of salvation to stave off a debilitating form of despair and dread. Dewey requires no such drama. Yet I have maintained that he has a tragic sensibility, one that recognizes the ineliminable conflict of values that makes up our moral lives. By my reading, Dewey's view of moral experience begins with opposing goods and possibly justified, but incompatible, courses of action. He refuses, unlike Hegel, to reconcile such conflicts and see harmony in tragic situations. He also refuses to be paralyzed in the face of tragedy. Unlike Schopenhauer, "the inseparable pain, the wretchedness and misery of mankind, the triumph of wickedness, the scornful mastery of chance, and the irretrievable fall of the good and the innocent"[73] do not produce in Dewey resignation, but rather, a will to engage the world with a reasonable hope that our actions may make our world better than it would otherwise be. What is at stake in all of this, for Dewey, is not only what kind of person one is to become, but what kind of world is in the making.

Part Two: Toni Morrison's *Beloved*, Tragedy, and Moral Experience

In arguing that Dewey has a tragic sensibility I am not suggesting that he adequately grappled with what I take to be the tragedy at the heart of American democracy—the problem of racism. Unlike Josiah Royce, for example, who understood that the problem of racism warranted a book-length treatment, Dewey never addressed the issue in any of his major works as a central challenge to his conception of democracy. Obviously, he did not view racism as a congenital ailment of American democracy. If he did, he would have had to engage the problem philosophically precisely because racism understood as such would block the way to the realization of his conception of democracy. On one level, I understand West's criticism of Dewey as one that calls attention to his failure to address substantively "the blue note" of American history and its centrality to who we, as Americans, take ourselves to be. But it doesn't follow from this criticism that Dewey lacked a tragic vision. It simply means—and this is deeply disturbing given the normative force of his work on democracy—that Dewey does not offer a significant philosophical analysis of race in the United States.

In the last few pages of this essay, I hope to reconstruct the view of tragedy I've attributed to Dewey in light of the brutal realities and choices that animate Toni Morrison's novel *Beloved*. My aim in reading the novel in this way is two-fold: (1) to sketch in a somewhat preliminary way an example of a pragmatic view of tragedy that begins with the tragic choices made available by the reality of white supremacy in the United States, and (2) to insist that our reflections on democracy in the United States begin with a fundamental engagement with the historical legacies of racism that potentially prevent democracy's realization. I want to urge us to look the facts of our racial experiences squarely in the face, see the tragedy therein, and go about intelligently guided experimentation to provide a better future for our children. Morrison's magisterial novel is, in my view, the best place to begin such a project.

Even though the novel is set in Cincinnati during Reconstruction, *Beloved* is a story about the psychical and physical devastation of slavery and the challenge of forging a self in its aftermath. As Valerie Smith notes, "the characters have been so profoundly affected by the experience of slavery that time cannot separate them from its horrors or undo its effects." Sethe and Paul D work tirelessly to hold back the past, but are constantly haunted—literally in Sethe's case— by the consequences and memories of slavery. In some ways, the novel makes the Nietzschean point that to live without forgetting is utterly impossible. As Nietzsche says, "There is a degree of insomnia, of rumination, of historical awareness, which injures and finally destroys a living thing, whether a man, a people, or a culture."[74] Indeed, we are confronted in the novel with Sethe literally being consumed by an embodied past. We are also told that "this is not a story to pass on." *Beloved*, in my view, constitutes a profound insistence that the past does not count exclusively. But this knowledge and the possibilities of action that mark the epiphany of the novel are the fruit of the tragic choice at the heart of the story.

Sethe's choice to attempt to kill all of her children to keep them safe from slavery reflected her lived experiences at the Sweet Home plantation. She desired nothing more than to protect her children from the terror of slavery. To be sure, she wanted to protect them from physical violence, but more importantly, she wanted to safeguard them from assaults on their souls. Slavery and, by extension, white folks, on Sethe's view, "could take your whole self for anything that came to mind. Not just work, kill, or maim you, but dirty you. Dirty you so bad you wouldn't like yourself anymore. Dirty you so bad you forgot who you were and couldn't think it up" (215). Sethe's intimate knowledge of this experience led her to insist that her children would never experience such evil. Her back of cherry blossoms, Schoolteacher's list of human and animal characteristics, and her violated insides served as constant reminders—historical burdens as it were—of slavery's assault on the soul.

But Sethe's historical burdens or, for that matter, any of the characters' in the novel are not presented simply to describe the horrible nature of slavery. Morrison's novel, as many critics have suggested, rewrites the traditional slave narrative by reconstructing what those stories silenced: the interior self of the slave. The descriptions of the past function, in some ways, to disclose the impulses and habits formed in the context of experiences that carry the characters in one way or another. Sethe's choice then is informed, in part, by a disposition shaped in the brutal context of Sweet Home. However, it is Sethe's freedom that ultimately transforms her choice from a melodramatic depiction of the evil of slavery to a tragic vision of the construction of a self in the aftermath of slavery. As Terry Otten writes:

> In projecting the inner life of her heroine, Morrison rescues the authentic self, making Sethe the victim of her own divided nature and thereby making her capable of choice and, ultimately, of achieving tragic stature. Sethe's crossing the river into freedom marks the climactic victory of the slave narrative and the beginning of the potential for tragic action.[75]

In explaining her choice to Paul D, Sethe reveals how freedom makes it possible to love unconditionally and to claim responsibility for her children. Sethe says to Paul D, "Look like I loved em more after I got here. Or maybe I couldn't love em proper in Kentucky because they wasn't mine to love. But when I got here, when I jumped off the wagon—there was nobody in the world I couldn't love if I wanted to" (162). As Otten rightly notes, it is this ability and obligation to choose that marks the dividing line between melodrama and tragedy.[76] It sets apart Sethe's act of infanticide from all of the other acts that are mentioned in the novel. Sethe declares to Paul D, after she describes how freedom afforded her the opportunity to make a shift for her baby, "Well all I'm saying is that's a selfish pleasure I never had before. I couldn't let all that go back to where it was, and I couldn't let her nor any of em live under schoolteacher. That was out" (163).

In my view, Sethe's choice is one of competing values and incompatible, but morally justifiable, courses of action. I don't have the space here to vindicate this claim, but I want to suggest that it may be useful to read the novel in this way precisely because it reveals a pragmatic view of tragedy, which takes seriously the blue note of American history. Otten has convincingly argued that *Beloved* "is more essentially Sophoclean than Euripidean." Morrison, who readily acknowledges the influence of Greek tragedy on her work, says that "this is not

Medea who kills her children because she's mad at some dude, and she's going to get back at him. Here is something that is *huge* and *very* intimate."[77] As Otten argues:

> The novel sustains tragic focus in its depiction of conflict within character, in its obsession with the presentness of the past, in its movement—however circuitous— toward reenactment, in its ritualistic elements, and in its ultimate ambiguity mirroring the "victory in defeat, defeat in victory" that ends high tragedy.

The Sophoclean dimension of *Beloved* links it to the pragmatic view of tragedy I have attributed to Dewey. But, more importantly, it is the way Morrison handles Baby Suggs's response to Sethe's "rough" choice and renders Denver's actions to save her mother from the ghost of history which reveals a *distinctly pragmatic* sense of the tragic.

Baby Suggs, holy, initially offers a stunningly powerful conception of self-love which urges bodies and souls torn by the horrors of slavery to lay down the "heavy knives of defense against misery, regret, gall and hurt" (86), to see beyond the opaqueness of their brutal pasts, and to allow themselves to imagine a future. This required, in Baby Suggs's view, what Valerie Smith describes as the sanctification of the black body. They needed to love that which had been reduced to a mere instrument of labor and see the spiritual worth that resided in them: "More than your eyes or feet. More than lungs that have yet to draw free air. More than your life holding womb and your life-giving private parts, here me now, love your heart" (89).

But, as Carol Schmudde notes, Baby Suggs's message is rendered ambiguous by Morrison's narrative technique. For Baby Suggs, after witnessing the consequences of Sethe's choice, "repudiates her own message, finding it inadequate to express or explain the tragic action which lies at the heart of the novel."[78] As Morrison writes:

> Those white things have taken all I had or dreamed, she said, and broke my heart-strings too. There is no bad luck in the world but whitefolks. . . . Baby Suggs, holy, believed she had lied. There was no grace—imaginary or real—and no sunlit dance in the Clearing could change that. Her faith, her love, her imagination and her great big old heart began to collapse twenty-eight days after her daughter-in-law arrived. (89)

Baby Suggs suffered from a debilitating form of despair, what Morrison describes as marrow weariness. This is a form of existential fatigue, which cuts not simply to the bone but through it straight to the marrow. I want to suggest that this is Baby Suggs's response to the problem of evil as poignantly evidenced in the moral dilemma posed by Sethe's choice. As Stamp Paid says, "God puzzled her and she was too ashamed of Him to say so" (177).

Baby Suggs's response to Stamp Paid's arguments to return to the Clearing and "say the word" reveal that her faith had been completely shaken. For her it was not simply a matter of God's failure to relieve the suffering of black folks, but rather, it was the reality—her lived experience—of white folks coming into her yard. That reality and the choice it exacted made her tired. Stamp Paid, faced with a similar form of existential fatigue, "now, too late, understood her":

> The heart that pumped out love, the mouth that spoke the word, didn't count. They came in her yard anyway and she could not approve or condemn Sethe's choice. One or the other might have saved her, but beaten up by the claims of both, she went to bed. (180)

Baby Suggs's reaction to Sethe's tragic choice is one of resignation. There is no grace, real or imaginary. There is only the fact that white people can treat black folk anyway they choose. And, it seems that, for her, the only appropriate response to such a reality is resignation. But, again, Morrison's narrative technique complicates such a conclusion. For, as Denver gathers up the courage to reenter the community to save her mother from an embodied past, Baby Suggs's words provide her with the practical wisdom to risk herself. Ironically, this comes on the heels of an exchange (remembered by Denver) between Sethe and Baby Suggs in which Baby Suggs declares, "Lay down your sword. This ain't a battle, it's a rout" (244). This appears to be a note of resignation, and Denver can't leave the porch. But then she hears clearly the words of Baby Suggs:

> You mean I never told you nothing about Carolina? About your daddy? You don't remember about how come I walk the way I do and about your mother's feet, not to speak of her back? I never told you all that? Is that why you can't walk down the steps? My Jesus my.
> But you said there was no defense.
> There ain't.
> Then what do I do?
> Know it, but go on out the yard. Go on. (244)

Here the past is thought of instrumentally: as the fruit of our undertakings that shapes our characters and informs our choices. To be sure, Baby Suggs invokes the past to call Denver's attention to the pervasiveness of evil in the world—to the stream of experiences that make up the history of 124. But she does this not to elicit resignation, but to urge Denver to act intelligently in the world. Baby Suggs says, "Know it, but go on out the yard." The "it" refers to the pain and suffering that is constitutive of black experiences in the United States. It refers to those unspeakable things unspoken, the sublime of the black experience. I am reminded here of James Baldwin's description in *The Fire Next Time:*

> This past, the Negro's past, of rope, fire, torture, castration, infanticide, rape; death and humiliation; fear by day and night, fear as deep as the marrow of the bone; doubt that he was worthy of life, since everyone around him denied it; . . . rage, hatred, and murder, hatred for white men so deep that it often turned against him and his own, and made all love, all trust, all joy impossible—this past, this endless struggle to achieve and reveal and confirm a human identity, human authority, yet contains, for all its horror, something very beautiful.[79]

Baby Suggs's words, like Baldwin's, direct our attention to the perils of evil that inform the world of action. Nevertheless, she exhorts Denver to act.

Baby Suggs tells Denver, in effect, that she must come to terms with the death and suffering that is her past—she must come to terms with Sethe's choice—but she must also understand this history and the tragedy therein as part of the exigencies of life—dare I say the beauty of life? Tragedy is understood then as an ineliminable part of what it means to be a black agent in this world. On my reading, Baby Suggs's practical wisdom rewrites William James's formulation at the end of "The Will to Believe":

> Act for the best, hope for the best, and take what comes. . . . If death ends all, we cannot meet death better.
> Know it, but go on out the yard. Go on.

Morrison's novel doesn't end with guaranteed satisfactory outcomes. At the end of the story, we are faced with broken human beings trying to piece together a life with one another. No grace still, real or imagined. We have an emphasis on the possibility of a future, represented in Denver, and a need to forget in order to make a future possible for Sethe. This emphasis on the future extends the novel's insight beyond that of the individual. For, like Dewey, what is at stake here is not only what kind of persons we will become, but what kind of world is in the making. In the end, I believe Morrison's novel brilliantly makes the point of a pragmatic view of tragedy: we must look the tragedy of our moral experiences squarely in the face, and with little certainty as to the outcomes, we must, *humbly,* act to make a better world for ourselves and our children. This requires of us an intimate knowledge of the tragic choices that constitute our living, because that knowledge will help us act intelligently and will help us see how fragile we truly are.

Conclusion

I have attempted in this essay to demonstrate that John Dewey's philosophy presupposes a tragic vision. I have suggested that his concept of tragedy should be understood as one in which competing and conflicting values are characteristic of any situation properly called moral. On my view, although I do not argue the case here, Dewey naturalizes Hegel's view of tragedy. Dewey sees conflict and uncertainty as a constitutive and ineliminable feature of our moral experience. For him, there are no guaranteed, satisfactory outcomes when we choose between conflicting values. We still learn from tragedy that crude reductions of the complexity of our moral lives can lead to an exclusive attachment to one value and a disregard for another.[80] But this doesn't result, for Dewey, in a kind of Hegelian conclusion about synthesis; instead, Dewey commends his view of intelligently guided experimentation in a world shot through with contingency.

We seek to secure our world then not by way of quests for certainty but rather, by practical means, exposing our vulnerability as fragile, finite creatures to the perils of evil. In light of this, Dewey's philosophy of action can be rendered in slogan-like fashion: There is so much in the world we cannot control, we ought to control that which we can intelligently, and, even if we do so successfully, the hazardous character of our world remains only modestly modified, much less eliminated. Intelligence, on this view, must be understood within the context of a generally humble orientation to the universe. In relation to all that is, we are so small and our world is less grand. But, as Oliver Wendell Holmes noted, "it is our world—the good in it is ours, just as is the bad."

Yet Dewey failed in some significant way to address the evils of white supremacy in his work. To be sure, Dewey's influence looms large among African Americans who have struggled to end racism in the United States.[81] But Dewey never substantively engaged the problem of racism in any of his major work. My reading of Toni Morrison's novel *Beloved* is an attempt to reconstruct the tragic vision I've attributed to Dewey, for the reality of white supremacy has always haunted American democracy. Even more poignantly, it has been the tragic choices in regards to race that we've made as a nation—the butchering of precious ideals as William James put it—that ironically have made possible our present way of life. Slave narratives, for example, sought melodramatically to disclose the evil at the heart of American democracy. Morrison's reconstruction of those stories has provided a glimpse into the tragic choices made and the consequences endured in light of that evil. However, America's past does not count exclusively. It provides us with the knowledge to engage intelligently the problems that prevent democracy's realization. That past humbly orients us to the world of action, by countering immodest claims of America's greatness and of the nation's inevitable triumph with the brutal reality of broken black bodies and souls. *Beloved* is a story which insists that our reflections on the future of American democracy begin with the remarkable irony at its root. And, for me, this is the lesson the novel renders to Dewey: if we are to think seriously about American democracy, we must come to terms with the tragedy of race.

NOTES

1. This essay is the result of many conversations with Cornel West. We have been arguing over Dewey and tragedy for close to seven years. I am truly in his debt. I would also like to thank Jeffrey Stout, Tom Dum, David Wills, Jeffrey Ferguson, Uday Mehta, and Don Koch for their insight for comments on drafts of this essay. I am also deeply indebted to the work of my friend and former student, Melvin Rogers. His brilliant master's thesis helped clarify my thinking on Dewey and the tragic. See Melvin Rogers, "John Dewey and the Theory of Democratic Deliberation" (M.Phil. dissertation, Cambridge University, 2000). I also want to thank Sara Skokan, who is presently pursuing her doctorate in religion at Columbia University. She helped

me comb through much of Dewey's corpus. Much of what follows relies on her hard work and is informed by her insightful commentary.

2.   John Dewey, *Human Nature and Conduct* (New York: Modern Library, 1930), p. 200.

3.   G. W. F. Hegel, *The Philosophy of Fine Art,* trans. P. B. Osmaston (London: G. Bell and Sons, 1920), vol. IV, reprinted in *Hegel on Tragedy,* ed. A. and H. Paolucci (New York: Harper & Row, 1975), pp. 68, 71. Also quoted in Martha Nussbaum, *The Fragility of Goodness: Luck and Ethics in Greek Tragedy and Philosophy,* updated edition (London: Cambridge University Press, 2001), p. 67. There are close affinities between the view of tragedy I am attributing to Dewey and the view of Nussbaum.

4.   Nussbaum, *Fragility of Goodness,* p. 67.

5.   Sidney Hook, *Pragmatism and the Tragic Sense of Life* (New York: Basic Books, 1974), p. 5.

6.   William James, *Pragmatism* (Indianapolis: Hackett, 1981), p. 132.

7.   Hook, *Pragmatism,* p. 13.

8.   William James, "The Moral Philosopher and the Moral Life," in *The Will to Believe and Other Essays in Popular Philosophy* (New York: Dover, 1956), pp. 202–203.

9.   Ibid., p. 209.

10.   John Dewey, *Quest for Certainty: A Study of the Relation of Knowledge and Action* (New York: Capricorn Books, 1960), p. 266.

11.   Dewey, *Human Nature and Conduct,* pp. 10–11.

12.   Richard Bernstein, "Community in the Pragmatic Tradition," in *The Revival of Pragmatism: New Essays on Social Thought, Law, and Culture* (Durham: Duke University Press, 1998), p. 149.

13.   Dewey, *The Quest for Certainty,* p. 3.

14.   Ibid.

15.   Ibid., p. 7.

16.   Ibid., p. 17.

17.   John Kekes, *Facing Evil* (Princeton: Princeton University Press, 1990), p. 5.

18.   Dewey, *The Quest for Certainty,* p. 8.

19.   For a more detailed account of Dewey's use of Darwin, see James Campbell's *Understanding John Dewey: Nature and Cooperative Intelligence* (Chicago: Open Court Press, 1995), chap. 2.

20.   John Dewey, *The Influence of Darwin on Philosophy and Other Essays* (New York: Prometheus, 1997), p. 17. Dewey also writes in *A Common Faith* that "Men have never fully used the powers they possess to advance the good in life, because they have waited upon some power external to themselves and to nature to do the work they are responsible for doing. Dependence upon an external power is the counterpart of surrender of human endeavor. Nor is emphasis on exercising our powers for good an egoistical or a sentimentally optimistic recourse. It is not the first, for it does not isolate man, either individually or collectively, from nature. It is not the second, because it makes no assumption beyond that of the need and responsibility of human endeavor, and beyond the conviction that, if human desire and endeavor were enlisted in behalf of natural ends, conditions would be bettered. It involves no expectation of a millennium of good"; Dewey, *A Common Faith* (New Haven: Yale University Press, 1934), p. 46.

21.   John Dewey, "The Need for the Recovery of Philosophy," MW 10:45.

22.   John Dewey, "The Development of American Pragmatism," in *Philosophy and Civilization* (New York: Peter Smith Edition, 1968), pp. 24–25.

23.   See Richard Rorty's *Philosophy and Social Hope* (London: Penguin, 1999), pp. 51–52. Dewey invokes here the idea of natural piety. In *A Common Faith*, he writes "Natural piety is not of necessity either a fatalistic acquiescence in natural happenings or a romantic idealization of the world. It may rest upon a just sense of nature as the whole of which we are parts, while it also recognizes that we are parts that are marked by intelligence and purpose, having the capacity to strive by their aid to bring conditions into greater consonance with what is humanly desirable" (24). He writes at the end of *A Common Faith*, "We who now live are parts of a humanity that extends into the remote past, a humanity that has interacted with nature. The things in civilization we most prize are not of ourselves. They exist by grace of the doings and sufferings of the continuous human community in which we are a link. Ours is the responsibility of conserving, transmitting, rectifying, and expanding the heritage of values we have received that those who come after us may receive it more solid and secure, more widely accessible and more generously shared than we have received it" (86).

24.   Dewey, *The Influence of Darwin on Philosophy*, p. 15.

25.   Dewey, *Quest for Certainty*, p. 307.

26.   Dewey, *Reconstruction in Philosophy* (Boston: Beacon Press, 1948), p. 147.

27.   See Gregory F. Pappas's "Dewey's Ethics: Morality as Experience," in *Reading Dewey: Interpretations for a Postmodern Generation*, ed. Larry A. Hickman (Bloomington: Indiana University Press, 1998). Pappas writes in note 10 that "When a felt moral perplexity controls and pervades the development of the situation as a whole, we can designate the situation as a moral one" (118). Pappas's article is one of the best sketches of Dewey's ethics that I am aware of.

28.   Dewey, *Ethics* (1932, LW 7:164).

29.   Ibid., pp. 164–65.

30.   Dewey, "Three Independent Factors in Morals" (1929–30, LW 5:280).

31.   Ibid.

32.   Ibid.

33.   Martha Nussbaum makes a similar point in her reading of the *Antigone*. She writes, "One and the same action or person will frequently possess more than one of the attributes picked out by these words—since in many cases they go together harmoniously. But they can be present separately from one another; and, even when co-present, they are distinct in their nature and in the responses they require. Many friends will turn out to be just and pious people; but what is it to be friend is distinct from what it is to be just, or pious. The ordinary expectation would therefore be that in some imaginable circumstances the values named by these labels will make conflicting demands. Friendship or love may require an injustice; the just course of action may lead to impiety; the pursuit of honor may require an injury to friendship. Nor would each single value be assumed to be conflict-free: for the injustice of the city can conflict, as this Chorus will acknowledge, with the justice of the world below; and piety towards one god may entail offenses against another. In general, then, to see clearly the nature of each

of these features would be to understand its distinctness from each other, its possibilities of combination with and opposition to each other, and, too, its oppositions within itself" (54).

34. Dewey, "Three Independent Factors in Morals," p. 280.
35. Hilary Putnam, *Renewing Philosophy* (Cambridge, Mass.: Harvard University Press, 1992), p. 190.
36. Ibid., p. 194.
37. LW 5:279–80, emphasis added.
38. Dewey, *Human Nature and Conduct*, 150. Also see Melvin Rogers, "John Dewey and the Theory of Democracy Deliberation" (M.Phil. dissertation, Cambridge University, 2000), chaps. 2 and 3.
39. William James, "The Will to Believe," in *The Will to Believe* (originally published in 1897; Cambridge, Mass.: Harvard University Press, 1975), p. 33. Also quoted in Putnam's *Renewing Philosophy*, p. 195.
40. Arthur Schopenhauer, *The World as Will and Representation* (New York: Dover, 1969), vol. 2, p. 573.
41. Ibid., p. 584.
42. Schopenhauer, "On the Suffering of the World," in *Essays and Aphorisms*, trans. R. J. Hollingdale (London: Penguin Books, 1970), p. 48.
43. Charles Sanders Peirce, for example, wrote that there were three types of pessimists: "The first type is often found in exquisite and noble natures of great force of original intellect whose own lives are dreadful histories of torment due to some physical malady. Leopardi is a famous example. We cannot but believe, against their earnest protests, that if such men had had ordinary health, life would have worn for them the same colour as for the rest of us. Meantime, one meets two few pessimists of this type to affect the question. The second is the misanthropical type, the type that makes itself heard. It suffices to call to mind the conduct of the famous pessimists of this kind, Diogenes the Cynic, Schopenhauer, Carlyle, and their kin with Shakespeare's Timon of Athens, to recognize them as diseased minds. The third is the philanthropical type, people whose lively sympathies, easily excited, become roused to anger at what they consider to be the stupid injustices of life. Being easily interested in everything, without being overloaded with exact thought of any kind, they are excellent raw material for litterateurs: witness Voltaire. No individual remotely approaching the calibre of a Leibnitz is to be found among them." *Collected Papers of Charles S. Peirce*, vol. 6, ed. Charles Hartshorne and Paul Weiss (Cambridge, Mass.: Harvard University Press, 1935), pp. 330–31.
44. Dewey, "The Need for the Recovery of Philosophy," p. 45.
45. Dewey, *Reconstruction in Philosophy* (Boston: Beacon Press, 1948), p. 178.
46. Ibid., p. 179.
47. William James, *Pragmatism* (Indianapolis: Hackett, 1981), p. 128.
48. Dewey, *The Later Works*, vol. 1, pp. 45, 42, 93.
49. *Experience and Nature*, p. 421.
50. See James Campbell's insightful discussion of Dewey's meliorism in his *Understanding John Dewey* (Chicago: Open Court, 1995), p. 260.
51. Dewey, *Middle Works*, vol. 5, p. 371. Also quoted in Campbell, *Understanding John Dewey*, p. 260.

52.   Dewey, *Experience and Nature* (New York: Dover, 1958), pp. 418–19.

53.   Cornel West, "Pragmatism and the Sense of the Tragic," in *Keeping Faith: Philosophy and Race in America* (New York: Routledge, 1993), p. 108. West recognizes Hook's argument for a pragmatic sense of the tragic. However, he believes it "remains far from the depths of other tragic democratic thinkers like Herman Melville, F. O. Matthiessen, and Reinhold Niebuhr" (108).

54.   Ibid., p. 110.

55.   Ibid., p. 113.

56.   Ibid., p. 116.

57.   Ibid., p. 117.

58.   Of course, Royce doesn't end here. He accepts "the sorrow of possessing ideals" and rejects Schopenhauer's conclusion that nonexistence ought to be preferred over a life of suffering. Royce maintained that although life is one of endless battles it is nevertheless not a complete failure. Self-sacrifice, giving oneself over to a great cause, helping and comforting those in need are moments in which we can feel ourselves "in perfect union and harmony with the whole of conscious life." West rightly notes that Royce refused to give in to pessimism and argued that we must "dare to hope for an answer." For Royce, evil also sounds a clarion call for us to struggle against it; and the goal of conscious union of every conscious being with the whole of conscious life sustains the strenuous mood which makes that struggle worthwhile. In response to Schopenhauer's and, by extension, Lincoln's challenge, Royce wrote, "As for Schopenhauer's objection that the unrest predominates, we admit the fact. Schopenhauer's inference is that the will to live ought to be quenched. We reply that this is a matter not thus to be decided. As we first chose our goal by independent volition, so now we may choose how much hindrance of our endless efforts to reach the goal will be regarded as compensated by our occasional successes. Not the comparison of two sums is desired, but the verdict of volition upon the worth of two sets of experiences. Which will you choose? The last question is simply unanswerable, except by a direct act of will. Here are the facts: A goal, viz., self-forgetfulness in the contemplation and creation of the fullest and clearest universal conscious life; a struggle to reach this goal, a struggle with blind nature, with selfishness within, with hatred without; this struggle alternating with periods of triumph; the process of alternating struggle and occasional triumph an endless process. How like you this life? It is the best that you are apt to find. Do you accept it? Every man has to deal with these queries quite by himself, even as with his own eyes he must see colors. It is our province merely to suggest the ultimate questions"; Royce, "Pessimism and Modern Thought," in *The Basic Writings of Josiah Royce*, ed. John J. McDermott (Chicago: University of Chicago Press, 1969), pp. 271–72.

59.   West, "Pragmatism and the Sense of the Tragic," p. 114.

60.   Dewey, *Quest for Certainty*, p. 300.

61.   Ibid., p. 301.

62.   *Reconstruction in Philosophy*, p. 178.

63.   I am reluctant to concede to Richard Rorty that Dewey's use of experience is best discarded. Although I recognize the merit of Rorty's worry, I still believe that there is something quite useful in Dewey's idea of nondiscursive

experience (particularly as a way to talk about racial terror). See Richard Shusterman's "Dewey on Experience: Foundation or Reconstruction?" in Casey Haskins and David I. Seiple, eds., *Dewey Reconfigured: Essays on Deweyan Pragmatism* (Albany: State University of New York Press, 1999).

64. As Hillary Putnam writes in *Renewing Philosophy,* "For Dewey, the democracy that we have is not something to be spurned, but also not something to be satisfied with. The democracy that we have is an emblem of what could be. What could be is a society which develops the capacities of all its men and women to think for themselves, to participate in the design and testing of social policies, and to judge results" (199).

65. Cornel West, *The American Evasion of Philosophy: A Genealogy of Pragmatism* (Madison: University of Wisconsin Press, 1989), p. 228.

66. Cornel West, "Subversive Joy and Revolutionary Patience in Black Christianity," in *The Cornel West Reader* (New York: Basic Civitas Books, 1999), p. 438.

67. Rorty, *Philosophy and Social Hope,* p. xxix.

68. Ibid.

69. Dewey, *Quest for Certainty,* p. 300.

70. In these moments West's understanding of the self appears Kierkegaardian. The question then arises: Is Kierkegaard's conception of the self reconcilable with Dewey's?

71. Dewey writes in *The Influence of Darwin on Philosophy* that "[o]ld ideas give way slowly; for they are more than abstract logical forms and categories. They are habits, predispositions, deeply engrained attitudes of aversion and preference. Moreover, the conviction persists . . . that all the questions that the human mind has asked are questions that can be answered in terms of the alternatives that the questions themselves present. But in fact intellectual progress usually occurs through sheer abandonment of questions together with both of the alternatives they assume—an abandonment that results from their decreasing vitality and a change of urgent interests. We do not solve them: we get over them" (19).

72. Dewey, *A Common Faith,* p. 82. Dewey still must confront the challenge of George Santayana—his interest in human solitude and his insistence on the importance of the comic. See Henry Levinson's brilliant book *Santayana, Pragmatism, and the Spiritual Life* (Chapel Hill: University of North Carolina Press, 1992).

73. Arthur Schopenhauer, *The World as Will and Representation,* trans. E. J. Payne (New York: Dover, 1969), vol. 1, pp. 252–53. Also quoted in Nussbaum, *The Fragility of Goodness,* p. 79.

74. Friedrich Nietzsche, *On the Advantage and Disadvantage of History for Life,* trans. Peter Preuss (Indianapolis: Hackett, 1980), p. 10.

75. Terry Otten, "Transfiguring the Narrative: *Beloved*—from Melodrama to Tragedy," in *Critical Essays on Toni Morrison's* Beloved (New York: G. K. Hall, 1998), p. 287.

76. Ibid., p. 291.

77. Amanda Smith, "Toni Morrison (PW Interviews)," *Publisher's Weekly,* 21 August 1987, p. 51. Also quoted in Otten, "Transfiguring the Narrative," p. 288.

78. Carol Schmudde, "Knowing When to Stop: A Reading of Toni Morrison's *Beloved,*" *CLA Journal* 37, no. 2 (December 1993): 121.

79.   James Baldwin, *The Fire Next Time* (New York: Vintage, 1963), p. 98.

80.   Nussbaum, *Fragility of Goodness,* pp. 80–81.

81.   See George Hutchinson, "Pragmatism and Americanization," chap. 1 in *The Harlem Renaissance in Black and White* (Cambridge, Mass.: Harvard University Press, 1995).

Part Two.   *Pragmatism*
                        and Means

7 Booker T. Washington: A Pragmatist at Work

Bill E. Lawson

> I do not care to venture here an opinion about the nature of knowledge in general but it will be pretty clear to any one who reflects upon the matter that the only kind of knowledge that has any sort of value for a race that is trying to get on its feet is knowledge that has some definite relation to the daily lives of the men and women who are seeking it.
>
> —Booker T. Washington

> When a people are smarting under the wrongs and injustices inflicted from many quarters, it is but natural that they should look about for some individual on whom to lay the blame for their seeming misfortunes, and in this case I seem to be the one. It is not a responsibility, which I have sought, but since it has come to me, I am willing to do my duty as best I can.
>
> —Booker T. Washington, 1903

Booker T. Washington died in 1915, and even before his death there was much disagreement among African Americans as to how to view his strategy for improving the plight of poor blacks and the relationship between whites and blacks in the South. Some thought that Washington was the greatest black man who ever lived. He had risen from the shacks of slavery to have dinner with the president in the White House and tea with the queen of England. He had pushed the value of hard work and individual responsibility. His school the Tuskegee Institute was the model for education around the world. He was truly committed to the betterment of black people.

His detractors, on the other hand, saw Washington as a detriment to black progress. While applauding his focus on education, they chided him for his seeming acquiescence to the stereotypes that whites held of blacks. His reluctance to push for social equality and his arrogance in dealing with other members of his race was especially disliked. Washington was seen as being too accommodating to the attitudes of white racists.

In the years since his death, there have been many assessments of Washington's life and work.[1] What prompted my thinking about Washington and pragmatism were the following comments about him in a review of *Better Day*

Coming: Blacks and Equality, 1890–2000 by Adam Fairclough. Reviewer Diane McWhorter writes of Fairclough's assessment of Washington:

> [Ida B.] Wells's brief militant epoch gave way to the accommodationism of Booker T. Washington, who built a white approved power base at Alabama's Tuskegee Institute on the premise that blacks should pursue excellence within the confines of second-class citizenship. Fairclough offers a revisionist view of Washington as a pragmatist rather than as an Uncle Tom, and there is no question that incremental uplift was a sound goal for his poor Deep South constituents, indoctrinated in the culture of slavery. But that argument cannot overwhelm Washington's spiteful record of undermining full-equality radicals like W. E. B. Dubois.[2]

McWhorter seems to have the view of pragmatism that implies that "whatever works" is correct. This was not Washington's position. Indeed, Fairclough goes to great lengths to show that Washington was not a pragmatist in the "whatever works" camp. In his view, Washington was a man driven by a sense of justice and compassion for black people.

In this essay I defend the position that Washington was indeed a pragmatist. He was, I contend, a pragmatist in the truest sense of the tradition of pragmatism. If Washington had a failing it was his straying from the pragmatist tradition in the later stages of his life. The claim is not that Washington was a social and political theorist. He often said that he was a man of action not words. He saw himself as a person who did things, not a person who talked or thought about what needed to be done. Washington's pragmatism was pragmatism of action rooted in the social context of the moment but coupled with a larger social agenda.

To call Washington a pragmatist or better yet pragmatic is not new. Noted scholar Harold Cruse and others have called him pragmatic.[3] Indeed, it is not surprising to see in any number of texts Washington being called pragmatic. What one finds lacking in the pragmatic mantle is some clear understanding of what the writer means when he or she calls him pragmatic. Washington was pragmatic, and he was a true pragmatist.

What I propose is that Washington's pragmatism was rooted in the philosophical tradition of John Dewey. The claim is not that Washington was a theorist of pragmatic thought but that his approach to resolving the problem of race embodied the basic elements of pragmatism: solving basic life problems. Washington's pragmatism must be seen and understood by looking at an overview of his project for improving race relations rather than looking at what is taken to be his personal failings.

Two Examples of Pragmatic Thinking

Booker T. Washington was born in slavery in 1856. His early life is told in his best-selling autobiography, *Up from Slavery*. In 1881 Washington was asked to take over as the principal of a "colored" school in Tuskegee, Alabama.

His job was not an easy one. There were only a few dilapidated buildings and no real faculty. Washington was not dissuaded. He took on the task with his usual optimism and energy. By 1895 Tuskegee was one of the premier black schools in America. Yet it was Washington's speech at the Cotton State exhibition that brought him to national prominence.[4] In this famous speech Washington urged that blacks and whites work together to solve the racial discord that existed. It would take a concerted effort on the part of both parties to ease and eventually resolve racial prejudice. Blacks and whites both had talents that could make the country great. The problem was getting both sides to recognize what needed to be done. Washington thought that the race problem could be solved with concerted efforts from both races. Bringing the races together was Washington's task, a task rooted in the American tradition of pragmatism.

To understand Washington as a pragmatist thinker, consider the following example: In 1892 Homer Plessy, a fair-skinned black man, bought a railroad ticket and boarded a train. The conductor asked Plessy if he was "colored." Plessy answered yes. The conductor instructed Plessy to move to the colored car. Plessy refused and was arrested. What makes this story even more interesting is that Plessy's arrest was part of a plan by the Comité des Citoyens (Citizens Committee) to challenge the increasing Louisiana laws regarding racial mixing. Louisiana was not alone in its treatment of black citizens. The Comité decided that the pragmatic thing to do was to challenge the seating restrictions in court. All across the South, people of African descent were being subjected to discriminatory treatment based on race. Blacks were refused service in restaurants, hotels, and other places of public accommodation. If a black person was refused a hotel room because the rooms were not rented to "niggers," he or she had to seek shelter some place else. There were a number of actions the person could perform. He or she could sleep on the street. They could find a black church and ask to spend the night in its sanctuary. This way of securing night lodging was often done by black travelers. One could try another inn. Any one of these actions in the "everyday" sense of pragmatism, doing whatever works to resolve a difficulty, would be seen as acceptable. "Pragmatic" in the everyday sense is taken to mean practical, realistic, and nonideological. To say that a person is pragmatic or a pragmatist is to say that he or she is practical and/or realistic; the person is doing what is necessary given the situation. The person is doing what he or she thinks is practical given an assessment of the social situation.

This is often the manner in which scholars have assessed Washington. He was seen as looking at the situation and then saying or behaving in a "pragmatic" manner: that is, he said or did what was practical for the particular moment. So his speech at the Atlanta exposition can be seen as his attempt to act in the moment, as he said what he thought needed to be said given the social situation. Washington, on this view, was not an opportunist but was more concerned with behaving in a way that was realistic given what he thought to be the social situation. Thus, his accommodations to southern whites are seen as pragmatic. How else could he behave and counsel blacks to behave in the South in the 1880s? One must remember the social setting of the time. The politics of the South were increasingly antiblack. Most blacks lived in squalor and received very little formal education. To speak out for black rights was often dangerous. Washington's behavior, given this view, was reflective of his working in the social moment. He was just being practical, that is, pragmatic.

Moreover, Washington had a larger agenda. He was trying to make a better life for all citizens of the United States, both black and white. Thus his thinking about the social reality of both blacks and whites was more encompassing than often thought. Washington was concerned with the ending of racist practices that prevented blacks from living full and meaningful lives in the United States. He realized that to solve the problem of race relations would require a clear assessment of the social context in which the problems were set. For example, the behavior of the train conductor and the innkeeper was part of a much larger legal and social structure that blacks encountered in all parts of the United States. What was the best "pragmatic" action to deal with the racist legal and social policies that affected the lives of both blacks and whites in the United States? Although Booker T. Washington was concerned with inability of blacks to get a ride unmolested on trains or to get a night's lodging, he was more concerned with changing the legal and social practices which degraded blacks. His pragmatism was a social and political pragmatism. The issue for what can be called a "social pragmatist" was how to deal with the racist practices that made the Comité's "pragmatic" decisions necessary. Washington knew that he had to be creative, and it is on this point that his approach can be seen as masterful.

What makes Washington's work as a pragmatist provocative is that he was faced with the problem of how to attack the prevailing legal and social racism, that is, the question: How do we better race relations in a country that has had a 250-year history of racism toward blacks? There are at least two ways. One way is to attack the behavior. This was the position of Du Bois and his followers. Blacks are citizens of the United States and should be accorded respect as such. They should be allowed in places of public accommodation and allowed to exercise the political franchise. The goal is to force whites to behave in a certain manner toward blacks. Since we cannot legalize behavior, we can, however, force whites to treat blacks with a modicum of respect by permitting blacks to vote, ride on public transportation, or eat in a public restaurant. Blacks had to push for their political and social rights, and to do less would be immoral.[5]

Washington, on the other hand, felt that if the attitude of whites about blacks did not change it would be difficult to get a change in behavior. Whatever behavior changes that did take place would be short-lived and done so with a grudge. Washington thought that given the racial history it was necessary to work to change attitudes. In explaining his emphasis on industrial education he asserted

> Now, in regard to what I have said about the relations of the two races, there should be no unmanly cowering or stooping to satisfy unreasonable whims of Southern white men, but it is charity and wisdom to keep in mind the two hun-

dred years schooling in prejudice against the Negro which the ex-slaveholders are called upon to conquer. A certain class of white Southerners objects to the general education of the colored man on the ground that when he is educated he ceases to do manual labor, and there is no evading the fact that much aid is withheld from Negro education in the South by the states on these grounds. Just here the great mission of industrial education coupled with the mental comes in. It "kills two birds with one stone," viz.: secures the cooperation of the whites, and does the best possible thing for the black man.[6]

Industrial education as the focal point of black education had been in the public debate long before Washington started Tuskegee.[7] The idea of industrial education had its roots in Europe:

Stemming from the educational theories of Europeans such as Pestalozzi and Fellenberg the sentiment for agricultural and industrial education found congenial soil in the Yankee traditions of morality, thrift and industry, economic independence, and material success and enjoyed its first considerable vogue in the United States during the second quarter of the nineteenth century. After the Civil War, under the impact of industrialization, it was transformed from a reformist fad into a widely practiced form of education. Yet it always remained an all-inclusive concept, elusive of narrow definition as to both its content and purpose. Some thought of it as a pedagogical technique of acquiring simple manual skills and dealing with concrete objects as aids in teaching. Many thought of mental discipline that would come from manual training and learning trades. Large numbers advocated manual labor schools in which youths would acquire an economically useful trade or mechanical skill and could earn part or all of their way through school. Related to this was the idea that modern society needed skilled factory workers and scientific farmers. And on a more advanced level industrial education was thought to include technological and engineering schools. Teaching of domestic science was introduced at an early date. Most of the theorizing had strong moral overtones about inculcating habits of thrift and morality and a feeling for the "dignity of labor." By some, industrial education was viewed as a means for helping the laboring classes to rise in the world, while others viewed it as a type of instruction suitable for adjusting them to their subordinate social role.[8]

Yet in the United States it becomes for blacks the line of demarcation for the education of the black masses. What type of education was best for blacks coming out of slavery? The debate over the appropriate education set the tone for much of our understanding of Washington. James D. Anderson argues that former slaves attempted to create an educational system that would extend and support their emancipation.[9] In his view, Washington is a puppet of Samuel Chapman Armstrong, the founder of Hampton Institute:

Armstrong developed a pedagogy and ideology designed to avoid such confrontations and to maintain within the South a social consensus that did not challenge traditional inequalities of wealth and power. In time these two ideologies and programs of black education collided, and Armstrong's prized pupil, Booker T. Washington, was at the center of the confrontation. Washington founded Tuskegee Normal and Industrial Institute in 1881, and by the turn of the century, the

"Hampton-Tuskegee Idea" represented the ideological antithesis of the educational and social movement begun by ex-slaves.[10]

Anderson's thesis raises a number of interesting questions, only two of which will be addressed here: First, was Washington merely a puppet of Armstrong? And second, what other options were open to Washington?

Historian Kevern Verney addresses these questions in his discussion of Washington just being pulled along by persons and circumstances over which he had no control:

> The attention that both Washington's contemporaries and later historians have devoted to his life and career belies the accuracy of this ineffectual stereotype. The work of a marionette would hardly warrant such extensive debate. An essential attribute of greatness, the potential for which Washington surely possessed, must be the ability to transcend difficulties rather than succumb to them. In the words of one biographer, whatever his dreams and failures Washington was a man of tremendous force, which he exerted on black and while America at a time when both were still capable of changing under the thrusts of strong, determined individual leaders.[11]

Washington was not a mere puppet. For him it was clear that the attitudes of whites about blacks and the attitudes of blacks about whites had to be changed in order for there to be lasting peaceful relationships between the races. As a pragmatic thinker, Washington understood that the plan of action had to fit the moment while keeping his goal of inclusion in sight. This is why he worked behind the political scene to change laws and support candidates sympathetic to the cause of blacks. It did not matter what political stripe the person wore. The task was to create an environment that moved the status of blacks forward:

> Washington has frequently been judged severely because of the assumption that a set of more positive, untried, policies was open to him. In this context, an examination of alternative, albeit untested, initiatives that may have been available to the Tuskegean is a useful exercise. Whether such strategies would, or would not have been more effective than those actually chosen by Washington is, by definition, impossible to judge, precisely because they remain untried. Nonetheless, identifying alternative action that might have been open to him and that might have offered some hope of success, even in the context of the repressive racial atmosphere of his era, still serves a purpose. If nothing else, it cast doubt on the validity of the view that the Tuskegean pursued every realistic option available to him, and that he could have done no more.[12]

Nevertheless, Washington was not obligated to try every possible realistic option. His view of the world was rooted in the late-1890s view of the self-made man. His connection with the leading white industrialists of the day was consistent with this view. Politics, economics, and social policies must be rooted in one's understanding of the social moment. Still, Washington was able to transcend the moment.

What is important to remember here is that there was no general rule for dealing with the problem of racial antagonism. This is the main underpinning when one reads Washington as a pragmatist. Washington understood the complexity of the "race problem." One had to assess the social situation and arrive at a creative solution to this problem. One could not be inflexible in their approach to the problem of race. One could not be permanently wedded to a particular approach, nor could one become mired in the "what if." This is pragmatism at its best.

What was the problem Washington faced? He tells us in his description of the need for Tuskegee and its task:

> First, it must be borne in mind that we have in the South a peculiar and unprecedented state of things. It is of the utmost importance that our energy be given to meeting conditions that exist right about us rather than conditions that existed centuries ago or that exist in countries a thousand miles away. What are the cardinal needs among the colored people in the South, most of whom are to be found on the plantations? Roughly, these needs may be stated as food, clothing, shelter, education, proper habits, and a settlement of race relations. The seven millions of colored people of the South cannot be reached directly by any missionary agency, but they can be reached by sending out among them strong selected young men and women, with the proper training of head, hand, and heart, who will live among these masses and show them how to lift themselves up.
>
> The problem that the Tuskegee Institute keeps before itself constantly is how to prepare these leaders. From the outset, in connection with religious and academic training, it has emphasized industrial or hand training as a means of finding the way out of present conditions. First, we have found the industrial teaching useful in giving the student a chance to work out a portion of his expenses while in school. Second, the school furnishes labor that has an economic value, and at the same time gives the student a chance to acquire knowledge and a skill while performing the labor. Most of all, we find the industrial system valuable in teaching economy, thrift, and the dignity of labor, and in giving moral backbone to students. The fact that a student goes out into the world conscious of his power to build a house or a wagon, or to make a harness, gives him a certain confidence and moral independence that he would not possess without such training.[13]

Tuskegee was to be Washington's staging point for a large-scale effort. From Tuskegee he would send forth teachers to help raise the economic and social status of blacks. This was the task that Washington set for himself. Ultimately he was committed to integrating the masses of blacks into the full social and political fabric of the United States. He never wavered from this pursuit. Yet Washington knew that his task was a difficult one and must be thought out with great care. The first thing a pragmatist must understand is the nature of the problem. Second, the pragmatist thinker must be creative.

Washington's Pragmatism at Work

In 1880 a former Confederate colonel figured that he could win a seat in the Alabama state legislature if he could secure the "Negro" vote. He went to Lewis Adams, a former slave, and struck a deal. In return for the black vote the colonel would support a bill for a school in Tuskegee. Both parties kept their part of the bargain, and the Alabama legislature "appropriated $2,000 a year for the establishment of a normal and industrial school for Negroes in the town of Tuskegee."[14] When Washington got to Tuskegee he found the "institute" landless, buildingless, teacherless, and studentless:

> Once at Tuskegee, Washington found the institute to be only an idea:
> A $2,000 appropriation for teachers' salaries, and two shacks that were hardly more than chicken coops. He realized that his work was cut out for him if he ever hoped to have Tuskegee approach Hampton in any sense of the word.
> One of three routes would have been open to anyone less resourceful than Washington: He could have thrown up his hands, quit the scene, and returned to Hampton where there was already adequate equipment and a viable program within whose context a great deal of opportunity for service existed; he could have resigned himself to make do and struggle hopelessly on against the odds until his ambition and physical strength burned to cinders; or he could have staged a confrontation with the Commission and blown the whole idea to bits. But Washington was resourceful.[15]

Washington had foresight and was able to keep his focus on his larger goal. He knew that he had to buy land to accommodate the school. He used his wits to get money for a down payment on land. Since its land was covered with trees, he had to convince many of the incoming students to do manual labor. These incoming students saw themselves above manual labor, but Washington would hear none of it. There is a story about Washington's telling the students that they were going to have a "chopping bee." To their surprise it was just a way to get them to chop down trees to clear the land.[16]

The land issue and lack of students and teachers were not the only problems facing Washington. There were hostile whites, hostile blacks, no money, and he was starting a school that was not affiliated with any particular religion. Yet he understood that for Tuskegee to survive it needed the support of the white and black community.

It is interesting to note that in his work *My Larger Education*,[17] Washington titles chapter 2, the chapter that discusses his early work at Tuskegee, "Building a School around a Problem":

> One of the first questions that I had to answer myself after beginning my work at Tuskegee was how I was to deal with public opinion on the race question. . . .
> Of course all of these different views about the kind of education that the Negro ought or ought not to have were deeply tinged with racial and sectional feelings. The rule of the "carpet bag" government had just come to an end in Alabama. The masses of the white people were very bitter against the Negroes as a result of the excitement and agitation of the Reconstruction period.
> On the other hand, the colored people—who had recently lost, to a very large extent, their place in the politics of the state—were greatly discouraged and disheartened. Many of them feared they were going to be drawn back into slavery. At this time also there was still a great deal of bitterness between the North and the South in regard to anything that concerned political matters.

I found myself, as it were, at the angle where these opposing forces met. I saw that, in carrying out the work that I had planned, I was likely to be opposed or criticized at some point by each of these parties. On the other hand, I saw just as clearly that in order to succeed I must in some way secure the support and sympathy of each of them.

I knew that Northern people believed, as the South at that time did not believe, in the power of education to inspire, to uplift and to regenerate the masses of the people. . . . Northern people would be willing and glad to give their support to any school or other agency that proposed to do this in a really fundamental way.

It was, at the same time, plain to me that no effort put forth in behalf of the members of my own race who were in the South was going to succeed unless it finally won the sympathy and support of the best white people in the South.

Finally I had faith in the good common sense of the masses of my own race. . . .

Still it was often a puzzling and a trying problem to determine how best to win and hold the respect of all three of these classes of people, each of which looked with such different eyes and from such widely different points of view at what I was attempting to do. One thing which gave me faith at the outset and increased my confidence as I went on was the insight which I early gained into the actual relations of the races in the South. I observed, in the first place, that as the result of two hundred and fifty years of slavery the two races had come together in intimate ways that people outside of the South could not understand, and of which the white people and colored people themselves were perhaps not fully conscious. More than that, I perceived that the two races need each other.[18]

Washington had to be cognizant of the social conditions that needed to be addressed in the dealings between the races and within the races. This list would include white attitudes about blacks, black attitudes about whites, white attitudes about race relations, black attitudes about race relations, legal restrictions on blacks at the moment, white attitudes about these restrictions, and social interaction between the races. To work around these problems required him to be creative. One of his most creative ventures was to make Tuskegee an important institution in and for the community. He realized that if the school did not aid the community, both blacks and whites, it was doomed to failure. He encouraged students to work in the community and used the woodworking and brickmaking facilities at Tuskegee for the benefit of local whites and blacks. All of this was in accordance with Washington's view of changing both attitudes and behavior. Historian Robert Factor gives the following assessment of Washington's early work at Tuskegee, which illustrates Washington's views on the value of knowledge:

In its first three years, Tuskegee Institute vindicated Washington's approach in the only way acceptable to him. It worked. Tuskegee proved that a school could substantially affect a community, that the cash nexus between the races was stronger than the prejudices that sundered them, and that Southern leaders would accept education of the right kind. Whites, accustomed to service from Negroes, had shown themselves willing to pay for the training of skilled colored hands. Mutually beneficial economic intercourse was possible between the races, so long as the Negro had something useful to offer.[19]

Faith in the Ability of Persons to Work Out Problems

One of the constant themes of Washington's program was his insistence on the ability of blacks and whites in the South to work out their problems. He argued that intelligent southern whites knew that the education of blacks would help both races. It was the ignorant whites who failed to appreciate the value of black education. Washington thought that with industrial education he had the magic bullet for race relations in the South. This was the thrust of his speech at Atlanta, which he reiterated later in *Up from Slavery:*

> I am often asked to express myself more freely than I do upon the political condition and the political future of my race. These recollections of my experiences in Atlanta give me the opportunity to do so briefly. My own belief is, although I have never before said so in so many words, that the time will come when the Negro in the South will be accorded all the political rights which his ability, character, and material possessions entitle him to. I think, though, that the opportunity to freely exercise such political rights will not come in any large degree through outside or artificial forcing, but will be accorded to the Negro by the Southern white people themselves, and that they will protect him in the exercise of those rights.[20]

Washington was ever hopeful that blacks and whites in the South could solve the "race problem." He believed to his death that whites and blacks could work it out to the satisfaction of both groups. To him this meant that blacks would be fully participating members of the Republic. It is this aim that guided Washington. As his biographer Samuel Spencer wrote:

> His strategy was just as realistic as his estimate of the situation. "I do not deny," he wrote, "that I was frequently tempted during the early years of my work, to join in the denunciation of the evils and injustice that I saw about me. But when I thought the matter over, I saw that such a course would accomplish no good and that it would do a great deal of harm." Washington believed that his alternative approach was not only constructive but aggressive. "I felt that the millions of Negroes needed something more than to be reminded of their sufferings and of their political rights, that they needed to do more than defend themselves," he explained. For obvious reasons the average Southern Negro could take no part in agitation or protest: he could only vaguely hope that he or his children might eventually benefit from efforts carried on in his behalf by men far removed from his day-to-day existence. But Washington fired the imagination of even the poorest tenant farmer by offering him an active role in a creative, dynamic program which affected him personally and directly. By setting tangible goals and demonstrating how they could be reached, he pointed the way to a better life for the Negro in his own home and community. Furthermore, a wealth of evidence existed to show that the program got results which were understandable and real.[21]

Remember that Washington saw knowledge as valuable only if it helped change people's lives. There was too much theorizing about the race problem. What was needed was action, actions that took into account the social history and the current situation of all concerned. This belief coupled with his faith in and under-standing of the ability of persons to solve their problems is the hallmark of pragmatism.

Pragmatism beyond Tuskegee

From 1895 till his death, Washington was a major player on the national and local scenes. His political involvement and his work with northern philan-thropists deserve attention. Here a lengthy quote from historian August Meier is telling:

Although overtly Washington minimized the importance of the franchise and civil rights, covertly he was deeply involved in political affairs and in efforts to pre-vent disfranchisement and other forms of discrimination.

For example, he lobbied against the Hardwick disfranchisement bill in Georgia in 1899. While his public ambiguities permitted Southern whites to think that he accepted disfranchisement if they chose to, through the same ambiguities and by private communications Washington tried to keep Negroes thinking otherwise. In 1903 when the Atlanta editor Clark Howell implied that Washington opposed Negro officeholding, he did not openly contradict him, but asked T. Thomas For-tune to editorialize in the *Age* that Howell had no grounds for placing Washington in such a position, for it was "well understood that he, while from the first depre-cating the Negro's making political agitation and officeholding the most prominent and fundamental part of his career, has not gone any farther." Again, while Wash-ington opposed proposals to enforce the representation provisions of the four-teenth amendment (because he felt that the South would accept reduction in repre-sentation and thus stamp disfranchisement with the seal of constitutionality), he was secretly engaged in attacking the disfranchisement constitutions by court ac-tion. As early as 1900 he was asking certain philanthropists for money to fight the electoral provisions of the Louisiana constitution. Subsequently, he worked secretly through the financial secretary of the Afro-American Council's legal bureau, per-sonally spending a great deal of money and energy fighting the Louisiana test case. At the time of the Alabama Constitutional Convention in 1901 he used his influ-ence with important whites in an attempt to prevent discriminatory provisions that would apply to Negroes only. He was later deeply involved in testing the Ala-bama disfranchisement laws in the federal courts in 1903 and 1904. So circum-spect was he in this instance that his secretary, Emmett I. Scott, and the New York lawyer Wilford Smith corresponded about the cases under pseudonyms and repre-sented the sums involved in code. Washington was also interested in efforts to pre-vent or undermine disfranchisement in other states. For example, in Maryland, where disfranchisement later failed, he had a Catholic lawyer, F. L. McGhee of St. Paul, approach the Catholic hierarchy in an attempt to secure its opposition to disfranchisement and urged the Episcopal divine George Freeman Bragg of Balti-more to use his influence among important whites. Washington contributed money generously to the test cases and other efforts, though, except in the border states, they were unsuccessful. In 1903 and 1904 he personally "spent at least four thousand dollars in cash, out of my own pocket in advancing the rights of the black man."[22]

Meier notes that one should pay attention to Washington's effort against railroad seating segregation.[23] Then there was his influence with President Theodore Roosevelt. He counseled the president on appointments and always sought to help the appointment of persons sympathetic to the cause of blacks:[24]

> Comparable to Washington's influence in politics was his position with the philanthropists. He wielded an enormous influence in appropriations made by Carnegie, Rosenwald, the General Education Board, and the Phelps-Stokes and Jeanes funds. Negro schools that received Carnegie libraries received them at Washington's suggestion, and even applied for them upon his advice. Contributors sought his advice on the worthiness of schools; college administrators asked his advice on personnel. His weight was especially appreciated by the liberal arts colleges. Washington accepted a place on the boards of trustees of Howard University in 1907 and of Fisk University in 1909.
> In the case of Fisk he proved exceedingly helpful in attracting philanthropic contributions. So complete was Washington's control over educational philanthropy that John Hope, president of Atlanta Baptist College, and a member of the anti-Bookerite Niagara Movement, found the doors of the foundations entirely closed to him. Only through the intercession of his friend Robert Russa Moton, a member of the Hampton circle and Washington's successor at Tuskegee, was Hope able to obtain Washington's necessary endorsement of his school to philanthropists such as Carnegie.[25]

Hope later felt remorse at having asked Washington. He did not want his followers to see him as "selling out" to him.[26] Such was Washington's power and amenity.

It must be remembered that Washington had to hold off both southern whites and northern black intellectuals. Again, he was able to be creative and walk the fine line between these diverse groups.

Washington for the Twenty-First Century

Nothing here is meant to excuse or minimize Washington's personal action during his lifetime: his "darkie" stories, his failure to address the lynching program forthrightly, his failure to comment on the Brownsville incident, or his heavy-handed approach to other black leaders. As Verney correctly notes, there were times when Washington's leadership could have been more dynamic.[27]

There is a slang term in use at this moment in history that seems apt when applied to Washington. The term is *playa*. Originally the term meant a man or woman who had a significant other and was at the same time having numerous sexual affairs with other persons. Over time the term has been used to describe someone who is good at what they do. The person who plays a sport well is an excellent example. While there are many good basketball players, Michael Jordan was a playa. He was very good at what he did. In any field of endeavor there are playas. Washington was a playa. During his lifetime he was able to garner support and funds to maintain his vision of education and racial uplift. He was able to get northern white philanthropists and southern white bigots to support him. He was able to start a number of schools in the South and some in the North based on his Tuskegee model. He worked behind the scenes to get bills passed and officeholders elected who would support black issues. He was able to influence the appointment of people to public office on both the state and national levels. Washington was also able to draw on the varied skills and race loyalty of black women. Indeed, his ability to focus on the larger grant-giving donors rests on the success of the important and more common fund-raising activities of his wives and other black women committed to the stability and growth of the Tuskegee project.

There is a flip side to the playa's life. Persons who cannot perform as well tend to dislike the playa. It is important to note that those persons who do feel as if they are not getting as much attention or respect tend to dislike the playa and work to discredit him. This is called *playa hatin'*.[28] There were many black men who resented Washington's ability to play the game. Washington's biographer Louis Harlan gives the following assessment of Washington's detractors by one of his admirers:

> The interesting feature of the occasion to me, a Washington admirer wrote, "was of a number of people here who, from their applause indicated a feeling of hostility to Mr. W. In studying these malcontents I felt that I could account for each of them by reason of interest in rival institutions, Howard, Atlanta, &c, and others under the not very elegant term of 'sore-heads' who have succeeded wonderfully in doing nothing for themselves and hence have a grievance against any man who is doing something."[29]

Washington saw his main black opposition coming from northern black male intellectuals, who disliked Washington's program and the fact that he had influence beyond what they thought he deserved. Washington noted in his discussion of the Intellectual and the Talented Tenth that

> The truth is, I suspect, as I have already suggested, that "The Intellectuals" live too much in the past. They know books but they do not know men. They know a great deal about the slavery controversy, for example, but they know almost nothing about the Negro. Especially are they ignorant in regard to the actual needs of the masses of the coloured people in the South today.[30]

This echoes the quote at the beginning of this essay. Washington thought that knowledge had to have some practical application. It was nice to have theories, but one must show how the theory related to the everyday life of poor black men and women. If these intellectuals had some workable practices, they would be working at them rather than criticizing him. In the end Washington's views live on, even if not acknowledged by some of his adherents.

Scholar Harold Cruse realized that in the 1960s black militants became disenchanted with the integrationist slant of the civil rights movement. Yet he noted that black power is nothing but the economic and political philosophy of Booker T. Washington given a 1960s militant shot in the arm and brought up to date. Unfortunately, Du Bois had poisoned the well against Washington:

> Du Bois was more successful than he thought in pointing out and even magnifying the defects in Washington's work and philosophy. His attacks on the Tuskegean were so poignant and poetic that they outlasted the considerable positive aspects of Washington's works, and survived to be misused generations later as liturgical rejections of any thought to the self-examination that reason sometimes prescribes.[31]

Those familiar with the history of social contact between Washington and Du Bois will note that there was great animosity between the two. Du Bois's critique of Washington has to be taken with a grain of salt. Nevertheless, in the 1960s Washington was seen as the poster boy for racial integration and accommodation. While Fanon, Du Bois, and Malcolm X were the writers of choice for black militants, most of them probably only read the Atlanta speech and Du Bois's critique of Washington in *The Souls of Black Folks.* Indeed, it was years after I started college that I realized that Washington's speech was not entitled "the Atlanta Compromise."[32] A careful reading of Washington's works shows a man dedicated to the betterment of the condition of black people in the United States. Cruse correctly assesses that Washington had already espoused much of what black power advocates claimed they wanted to achieve. Buy black, support black professionals, and learn black history. Make the black community self-sufficient.

Still, scholars have not seen Washington in the best of light. Philosopher Bernard Boxill views Washington as playing solely on the self-interest of whites. Boxill describes Washington's position in terms of the race/class debate. Is it race or class that defines the problems of blacks in the United States? Boxill thinks that for Washington it is class, and this is why Washington made his appeals to the self-interests of whites:

> While Booker T. Washington certainly thought that his reforms were just, it was not their justice that he urged on the public, presumably on the assumption that he would otherwise not be heeded. What he emphasized to the public was that his reforms would lead to overall prosperity. This reliance on the public's self-interest rather than its moral sense is also clear in the rhetoric of the separatist wing of the class school, though there is a difference in the way it appeals to that self-interest; whereas the integrationist wing appeals to the majority's self-interest by trying to persuade it of the increased profits and economic advantages reform will bring, the separatist wing appeals to the majority's self-interest by threatening to harm it unless it implements the reforms demanded.
>
> In insisting on the dominance of self-interest over morality, the class school does not mean to imply that moral considerations play no role in human affairs. It does, however, suggest that this role is subsidiary and only supportive. In particular, the class school suggests that, whatever the validity of moral considerations, they will generally have little motivating force unless the relations it recommends obtain. Thus its integrationist wing implies that until blacks acquire skills and com-

petence, and by steady productive work contribute to the markets of the world, they will not respect themselves or be respected by the majority; its separatist wing implies that, until blacks can credibly threaten the white majority, they will not respect themselves or be respected by the majority.[33]

If Boxill had read Washington as a pragmatist, he would have seen that his comments miss their mark. Washington was committed to a mutual working out of the race problem. He understood that white attitudes prevented many of the political and social gains blacks wanted. The goal was to incorporate blacks into the economic system in a meaningful manner. Given his understanding of race relations, Washington had to cleverly maneuver to present his plan of successfully incorporating blacks into the economic framework. His appeal was not solely to the self-interest of whites, but relied on his belief that blacks and whites could mutually solve the problems of racism. This was not a new position. Meier, relating the history of racial interaction, notes that Washington's view echoed that of Frederick Douglass:

> Using the very argument that Booker T. Washington was to make famous half a century later both Frederick Douglass and the highly important Rochester Convention of 1853 held that economic progress, based on mutual self-help and racial cooperation, was a practical program for racial elevation and the achievement of citizenship rights, for when Negroes became valuable to society they would be respected; and therefore for the present they needed trade schools more than liberal arts colleges.[34]

Even with this reading of Washington, scholars still tend to overlook his importance as a symbol of pragmatic action. Philosopher Cornel West, for example, in *The American Evasion of Philosophy*,[35] does not even discuss Washington. This, I think, is a mistake. If my reading of Washington is correct, he is the embodiment of the pragmatist tradition. As West notes:

> American pragmatism is a diverse and heterogeneous tradition. But its common denominator consists of future-oriented instrumentalism that tries to deploy thought as a weapon to enable more effective action. Its basic impulse is a plebeian radicalism that fuels an antipatrician rebelliousness for the moral aim of enriching individuals and expanding democracy. This rebelliousness, rooted in the anticolonial heritage of the country, is severely restricted by ethnocentrism and patriotism cognizant of the exclusion of people of color, certain immigrants, and women yet fearful of the subversive demands these excluded people might make and enact.[36]

Washington was thoughtful and future oriented. He understood, better still, that there must be a fusion between theory and practice. One had to do more than theorize about the problem. One had to act and act with faith, understanding, and creativity. In part, his pragmatic spirit reveals the soul of a rebel committed to making American democracy work for all of its citizens. Still, one can understand the oversight of Washington and West's inclusion of Du Bois. Du Bois appeals to the theorist side of West. Du Bois theorized about race, whereas Washington worked to improve the lot of southern blacks combining pragmatic theory with practice.

Conclusion

It must be remembered that for all of Washington's influence, it was very likely impossible for one person to do what Du Bois and others claimed that he did or could have done for the situation of blacks at the end of the nineteenth and the beginning of the twentieth centuries. The segregation train was well on its way when Washington appeared on the scene. He could not stop it or change its direction by himself. Whether he aided the racist tide will always be a matter of debate.

If my reading of Washington as a pragmatist is correct, we can look anew on his programs for racial uplift and see his maneuvers for what they were, the tradition of American pragmatism in action. This will lead us to conclude that Washington was not merely the fawning accommodationist that has become the popular claim. He worked for the betterment of black people in one of the worst periods of black existence since slavery. He maintained a faith that humans could resolve their differences through cooperative interaction. The question is whether moral inquiry attempts to make statements about what is moral or whether the task of moral inquiry is to make judgments leading to action. Are we asking "What is morality, i.e., rights, obligations, etc.?" or "How ought we to respond to the difficulties we face?" Washington was not a theorist, pragmatic or otherwise, but he was concerned about responding to the problems of the "Negro" by doing, actually accomplishing something. His life's work could serve as an instrument to provoke further exploration about actual needs and getting results rather than stating and justifying moral ideals. He understood the social context in which the problem was set and tried to resolve the quagmire of bad race relations with creativity. This is all that we can ask of any person.

In sum, our job, like that of Booker T. Washington, is to suggest moral judgments connected with action, judgments that are a stimulus to others and ourselves to act to get the issues of race relations resolved as much as humanly possible, while respecting the humanity of each individual.

NOTES

1. See, for example, Hugh Hawkins, ed., *Booker T. Washington and His Critics* (Lexington, Mass.: D. C. Heath and Company, 1974); Kevern Verney, *The Art of the Possible* (New York: Garland, 2001); Raymond W. Smock, *Booker T. Washington in Perspective* (Jackson: University Press of Mississippi, 1989).
2. NYTimes.com review, "Overcoming Repeatedly," 29 July 2001.
3. Harold Cruse, *Plural but Equal* (New York: William Morrow, 1987).
4. Booker T. Washington, *Up from Slavery* (Norwood, Mass.: Norwood Press, 1900), pp. 217–37.
5. Bernard Boxill, "Self Respect and Protest," in Leonard Harris, ed., *Philoso-*

phy Born of Struggle (Dubuque: Kendall/Hunt Publishing Company, 1983), pp. 190–98.

6. Booker T. Washington, "The Educational Outlook in the South," in Howard Brotz, ed., *Negro Social and Political Thought 1850–1920* (New York: Basic Books, 1966), p. 354.

7. August Meier, *Negro Thought in America, 1880–1915* (Ann Arbor: University of Michigan Press, 1946), p. 85.

8. Ibid., p. 86.

9. James D. Anderson, *The Education of Blacks in the South, 1860–1935* (Chapel Hill: University of North Carolina Press, 1988).

10. Ibid., p. 33.

11. Verney, *Art of the Possible*, p. 45.

12. Ibid., p. 46.

13. As originally published in *The Atlantic Monthly* (September 1896), p. 323.

14. Emmett J. Scott and Lyman Beecher Stowe, *Booker T. Washington: Builder of a Civilization* (New York: Doubleday, 1916), p. 3.

15. Ethelbert W. Haskins, *The Crisis in Afro-American Leadership* (Buffalo: Prometheus Books, 1988), p. 80.

16. Scott and Stowe, *Booker T. Washington*, p. 6.

17. Booker T. Washington, *My Larger Education* (Garden City, N.Y.: Doubleday, 1911).

18. Ibid., pp. 21–24.

19. Robert Factor, *The Black Response to America* (Reading, Mass.: Addison-Wesley, 1970), p. 151.

20. Washington, *Up from Slavery*, p. 234.

21. Samuel R. Spencer, Jr., "The Achievement of Booker T. Washington," in Hawkins, *Booker T. Washington and His Critics*, pp. 170–71.

22. Meier, *Negro Thought in America*, pp. 110–11.

23. Ibid., p. 113.

24. Ibid., p. 112.

25. Ibid., p. 114.

26. Leroy Davis, *A Clashing of the Soul* (Athens: University of Georgia Press, 1998), p. 193.

27. Verney, *Art of the Possible*, p. 46.

28. Geneva Smitherman, *Black Talk* (New York: Houghton Mifflin, 2000), p. 232.

29. Louis Harlan, *Booker T. Washington: The Wizard of Tuskegee, 1901–1915* (New York: Oxford University Press, 1983), p. 38.

30. Washington, *My Larger Education*, p. 127.

31. Haskins, *Crisis in Afro-American Leadership*, p. 107.

32. W. E. B. Du Bois, "Of Mr. Washington and Others," in *The Souls of Black Folks* (New York: New American Library, 1969), p. 80.

33. Bernard Boxill, "The Underclass and the Race/Class Issue," in Bill E. Lawson, ed., *The Underclass Question* (Philadelphia: Temple University Press, 1992), pp. 26–27.

34. Meier, *Negro Thought in America*, p. 86.

35. Cornel West, *The American Evasion of Philosophy: A Genealogy of Pragmatism* (Madison: University of Wisconsin Press, 1989).

36. Ibid., p. 5.

8   Should We Conserve
the Notion of Race?

David E. McClean

Geneticists have told us that race does not exist, that it has no "reality." I do not agree that race has no "reality" because I see no reason to overprivilege the scientific account of race's status—no more reason to limit the discussion of race to the scientist's vocabulary than to limit the question of whether we should make more bombs or grow more corn to that vocabulary (because the answer to the question has more to do with what is relevant to *who* we are than *what* we are). Race, while a legitimate subject for scientific study, has taken on a meaning and a life far greater than the mere scientific pronouncement of its death can do much about. It has become an entrenched cultural, social, and political matter, eclipsing, in many respects, its scientific allure. On the other hand, it makes little sense to *ignore* the scientific pronouncement, and almost no one versed in the literature does, even racial conservationists (those who wish to retain race as a social category). Indeed, it makes no more sense to ignore the scientific pronouncement about race than to ignore the scientific conclusion that disease is caused by germs, genetic anomalies, and poisons in the environment, rather than by evil spirits. I will argue that the implications of the scientific pronouncement, along with other sociohistoric factors that surround the history of the idea of race, can be read differently than many racial conservationists have tended to read it. On my alternative reading, race serves no useful or salutary purpose, particularly in a liberal or cosmopolitan civilization that has certain philosophical and political commitments concerning that in which the moral worth of individuals and communities consist.

I do not believe that the concept of race should be scorned (it is not completely analogous to evil spirits), but in the face of the scientific evidence the questions and answers that attend the question of racial conservation should probably be, and at the hands of some scholars have been, rephrased. As intimated, race has far more to do with culture and politics than with natural science, and culture and politics are largely contextual affairs—they concern some "us," however erratic the borders that surround that "us" might appear. So, given the geneticist's conclusion, it seems reasonable to frame the question of the conservation of race (i.e., should we conserve the notion of race?) in terms of "our" particular axiological commitments and aspirations as evidenced by our public rhetoric and the instruments and narratives that we agree establish our important social and political institutions, and regulate and frame our communal ones. On my reading, this accords with certain pragmatist preferences. The pragmatist, like some of her Continental counterparts, prefers to ask questions about *who* we think we are and about whether a concept, ideology, practice, or even myth (1) contributes to that self-conception, (2) detracts from it, or (3) is not very relevant to it.[1] Put differently, the pragmatist wants to plumb the contextual "cash value" of social ideas. Given these criteria, I want to argue that the idea of race is no longer very useful, no longer very salutary for our axiological project, notwithstanding the modern racial conservationists' belief that it is.

I am, of course, aware of the possible charge of *petitio* here, that I am not permitting the "we" or "our" to be construed as or limited to a *racial* community (or other type of community constructed around different specific and narrow predicates, such as ethnicity or affinity) and already imply at the outset that it can't be, that the axiology to which I refer is and should be based on a much larger social and political framework. I have no foundationalist answer to this charge, and in fact such "we's" and "ours" may very well be built around all sorts of predicates, and are so built all over the world. I am taking certain things for granted here, namely, that pluralism and democratic practices are first-order social goods—for "us." My "we" is larger than any racial or other narrow predicate because it has been amply demonstrated that communities that are based upon such narrow predicates rest within axiological or values frameworks that do not necessarily lend themselves to the pluralism and democratic practices that we in the West claim to hold in the highest regard. So the contextual "we" to which I refer is the political community that provides the general normative and political framework of our (racialized, sexualized, classified, professionalized, etc.) lives, a framework that we strive diligently to perfect and more or less protect, one that provides enough overlapping consensus to evoke solidarity and what John Rawls calls "fraternity" among diverse agents and populations. On this account, it is the particular nation-state in which we live, that is, America as well as other similarly situated, liberal democratic states. It is only too obvious that there can be different axiological "we's" that can form such a framework (tribes, theocracies, monarchies, religions, even guilds). I also acknowledge, and in fact presuppose here, that no such large "we" is devoid of small communities, each having its own idiom, and each taking stances of assent and dissent within that larger "we." This, too, seems obvious. Such idioms and such dissent are what, as we might say in the West, "makes a horse race"—but are what in other political configurations make for outcomes far more unfortunate than such a cliché can properly capture.

Race: Definiendum or Dogma?

All racial typologies have had mischievous careers,[2] whether Kant's, Blumenbach's, Linnaeus's, Coon's, Agassiz's, or Du Bois's, to name but several. To one degree or another, they have all fizzled out in the presence of the modern genetic pronouncement that there is no scientifically valid concept of race, no genetically tenable basis for racial distinctions. What there are, we find, are clines—gradual changes, across space, in certain characteristics exhibited by members of populations—and collections of phenotypic characteristics that have been inbred within a geographically more or less segregated population (and which can be and have been just as easily bred out). While there are clearly differences in appearance between certain geographically separated populations whose members evolved in relative conjugal isolation, the phenotypic expressions by which these are and have been divided into races are arbitrary. Nevertheless, for reasons both malicious (Nazi eugenics) and not (Du Bois's "vindication" anthropology), some people have wondered whether there may nevertheless be resulting differences that make a difference. That is, they have wondered about such questions as "Is group X smarter than group Y?" or "Is group X more prone to incivility?" What we have found is that intellectual heft is nicely and randomly distributed around the globe, right along with incivility.[3] We have found that the facts that the refrigerator wasn't invented in Nubia and that paper wasn't invented in Britannia are contingent facts and not genetic manifestations *simpliciter* of the people of Nubia and Britannia—that the inventions of the refrigerator and paper are based on cultural *values* and choices given existing technological advancements that have nothing to do with a race to the top of some preordained, universally valorizable cultural summit (because there is no such summit).

Without providing a long discussion regarding the incoherence of racial typologies, I will simply utilize one exemplar, taken from the previous list, who wrestled with these confusions: that of W. E. B. Du Bois. Du Bois gave us a composite concept of race in his famous address/essay *The Conservation of Races*. Race for Du Bois had several and disparately weighted features that provide its definition. In that essay he understood race as a collection of contingent but somewhat stable and replicated social practices, originating roughly within a specified geographical area in conjunction with what we today call certain recurring phenotypic expressions. On his account, to be a member of a particular race meant a mixture of these components in a way that will reliably identify a person as such a member. To put it another way, the defining elements of a race are (1) common blood, (2) common language, (3) shared history, (4) shared traditions, and (5) striving together toward the fulfillment of shared ideals of life, so much so that human history is more properly described as the history of races. Further, for Du Bois, each race has its own special genius and its own gifts to contribute to humankind that only it can contribute (this is Du Bois's racial teleology).

I agree with those who argue that Du Bois did not intend to limit race to "common blood." Tommy Lott, for example, provides an interesting and useful analysis of Du Bois's use of racial types and common blood that goes well beyond *The Conservation of Races* to make this point.[4] Yet I do not see a tenable way to *fully* unlink common blood from, say, a common language or common traditions in Du Bois's account, in part because Du Bois could not drop the idea of common blood (expressed as morphological characteristics) as part and parcel *of* the definition of race within his vindication project: that is, he used physical characteristics as "an essential feature of his project to correct the systematic erasure of black people from history."[5] Should one assent to the idea that race begins with or must be understood in terms of a *Real*[6] or *scientific* definiendum, one would be able to follow Du Bois to his conclusion that while this is so, the important features of race are sociocultural and not biological. But as there is no such Real scientific definiendum called race, there is nothing for sociocultural practices to hook on to. So, with the benefit of hindsight and modern genetics, we can say that in terms of Du Bois's vindication project, while necessarily referring to physical characteristics, he could have argued not that the Negro race, in its various shades and forms, has done and will do great things, but rather that "*people who looked like us,* whom whites call Negroes and denigrate as barbarians, established great civilizations in Egypt," etc. This would have done the trick. No racial categories required.

But as Du Bois assumed the contextual framework and categories of race-talk, of talking about races as though they were Real, he was stuck laboring inside the belief that there are in fact essential biological categories into which sociocultural practices can be parsed, a notion that of course begs for the labeling of those categories. To put it another way, race was a kind of "substance" to which sociocultural "predicates" were supposed to have attached. But notwithstanding Du Bois's own objections to emphasizing biology over those sociocultural predicates, it is hard to see what that substance was supposed to be in Du Bois's account if not essential morphological types. It is difficult to see how those predicates hook up to biology, and, in the final analysis, it seems that Du Bois himself couldn't see how either.[7] Clearly, Du Bois got stuck speaking the language of race even though it was conceptually possible for him to have made his case without it, without *interpositioning* a category called *race* in front of *human* in his serious anthropology or his vindication project. As we look back at his work it is easy for us to see that he could have done without it. Although Du Bois may have ultimately wanted to "define" race away from biology and toward sociocultural practices and achievements, it was in a way an attempt to define a *nondefiniendum*—an interpositioned category that, violating the basic warning of Ockham's razor, caused more trouble than it was worth. Of course, Du Bois is no more to be faulted for falling into this dogmatic trap than the other race theorists of his time. The dogma was simply not exposed as such, and it is difficult to see how it could have been, given the political and social climate in which Du Bois was laboring, and especially given the scientific knowledge and tools available (notwithstanding Franz Boas's contributions).[8] Or, as Peirce might have put it apropos Du Bois, race was among the "things which it does not occur to us *can* be questioned."[9]

We can now turn to another aspect of Du Bois's account of race. Given Du Bois's vindication project, when I raise the hood, so to speak, on Du Bois's conception of race the salient motor that seems to drive it is racial teleology, that each race has something special (spiritual) to offer humanity. The pragmatist has trouble with this notion. That is to say, we think that it is notoriously difficult to understand the ideals of any more or less coherent population—for example, a nation-state—as though the ideals are essential features of the members of the population. Rather, its ideals will be shaped, over time, by its intercourse with other populations with different contingent ideals and practices. No population may be said to have immutable or fixed ideals, although it will certainly have ideals. Further, the idea that a coherent population—what Du Bois would call a race, for example (even if "defined" nonbiologically)—has a particular spiritual or metaphysical gift to bestow upon civilization is one that, if not understood metaphorically or propagandistically, smacks of bad metaphysics. Is a recounting of the anthropological facts about a culturally distinguishable people to tell a story of that people that is to be understood as a chapter in a larger book that tells the greater teleological story of humankind in general? Although this may constitute useful rhetoric to be employed to foment a needed sense of purpose in a people, on many important levels it may also be described as a species of jingoism. To argue that a race (or a nation, or nation-state, or tribe) is destined to (supposed to, predisposed to) contribute a "missing" component to human culture is to argue something quite fantastic. It would be at the very least the hypostatization of goals and practices. There can in fact be no missing components since there is in fact nothing that humans are destined to be.[10]

There are no elements that make up Du Bois's concept of race that are not contingent. Obviously, phenotypic expressions are contingent upon the selection of sex partners, and while the selection of sex partners from within one's own cultural community has proven to be more probable than the selection of sex partners from outside, there is no reason that the odds will long remain in the favor of in-group mating, not in an era of globalization; but Du Bois himself seemed aware of this in his own time, within the context of America, where Africans, Native populations, Europeans, and others intermarried and/or mated across racial boundaries, and still do (Du Bois himself was of mixed ancestry). In addition, the geographical locations of groups are contingent upon political maps, which are themselves fluid, as well as upon patterns of migration.

It is true, however, that *belief* that each of the defining elements of race referenced above is far less contingent (or is in fact culturally necessary or culturally critical) than most pragmatists might be able to accept is a powerfully conservative device—a device that might so slow the rate of change as to cast the illusion of permanence around cultural practices or self-conceptions. Norms and cultural practices are frequently thought of as reflecting something about the way the world really is in itself, or something immutable concerning human nature. Even a pragmatist is forced to acknowledge the retarding power of cultural conservatism, as well as some of its benefits (such as resoluteness of moral purpose among the members of the population—important in times of crisis— or a feeling of belonging in a seemingly nihilistic universe, etc.). But whether or not such conservatism leads to salutary or harmful states of affairs, few pragmatists are likely to accept the notion that the cultural status quo should escape critique, regardless of what conservatives may believe about the status of their cultures or about the world. This, I think, was as true for John Dewey as it is for Richard Rorty, who have rather different views about the manner in which cultural practices are or should be established. Yet, as we shall see, it is in some way the cultural conservative voice that contemporary race conservationists employ in their efforts to maintain the legitimacy of socially constructed racial types in spite of the incoherence and unsavory history of the idea of race.

The Prevailing Social Constructivist Conclusion

The preceding and cursory analysis of Du Bois's view of race was intended only to begin to demonstrate the problems presented when the notion of race is conserved, even when an attempt is made to define race nonessentially. I selected Du Bois not to make light of his analysis or goals but because, in my view, Du Bois was extremely sensitive to the critical importance of properly interpreting the data compiled during various anthropological inquiries into race and culture that were going on during his career, as well as to the dangers that quick and erroneous conclusions regarding those data would present in the realm of politics and social intercourse between so-called racial groups. There were some who did attempt to use the "science" of race as justification to perpetuate various myths of racial hierarchy that were, needless to say, unfavorable as regards people of African origin (as "African origin" was generally understood at the time, that is, as merely the birthplace of black people rather than the entire species).

But even if Du Bois's conclusions regarding race are not tenable, it does not mean that the notion of race can be so easily dismissed, since to *believe* in race and to inject racial thinking into the construction of important institutions and communal social practices is to make race real even though it does not correspond to a natural kind, that is, is not Real. This is done easily, when race is thought of as socially constructed. As I have said, I am not one to suppose that what is real need be adjudicated as such by the methods or standards of the natural sciences alone. When we attempt to do that, to allow such reductionist adjudication, we wind up throwing out the baby with the bathwater—we wind up chucking much of culture. Anything that tends to govern behavior—class, professional categories, etc.—and that may serve as an organizing or a unifying principle *is* real.[11] Even though I think Du Bois's account of race is untenable the idea of race nevertheless does some taxonomic work, just like believing in an afterlife or natural law does some psychological or ethical work. This, also, is obvious. But one thing seems clear: that something "does some work" is an insufficient reason to move it beyond the pale of scrutiny, revision, or rejection. Whether a pervasive cultural notion should be embraced or rejected should, on my account, depend considerably upon whether it contributes to, detracts from, or is relevant to the achievement of larger social and political aspirations as well as, I would add, jibes with the moral beliefs that we, by a consensus reflectively and democratically formed, have come to hold as central to the kind of people we wish to become.

Given the tests I find it most useful to apply, the tests of how race (*or any other social construct*) contributes or detracts from who we want to be, and given how I understand "we," I am in the camp that thinks that whatever work race does, it has compiled more minuses than pluses on its score card. It has served as the basis for invidious social strife and murder; it has divided families, poisoned the flowering of possible and actual friendships and love relationships; it has imbued certain cultures with a false sense of absolute superiority and others with the bitter taste of imputed inferiority. It divides neighborhoods and cities down factitious lines of demarcation. It has been used to defer dreams and stultify plans, hopes, and prospects. It has been used to limit the life opportunities of countless millions of children by distorting their self-images. In short, it has done the same kind of damage as (less complex) cultural inflations, such as nationalism and tribalism, but with less to show for itself in terms of salutary productions than the basic notion of nation or tribe has been able to show.

Looking at race as a social construct says very little about whether it should stay one as a matter of practice, and arguments along social constructivist lines tend to be, at times, merely descriptive, leaving us, as Du Bois was, stuck within a problematic discourse. I think that the following observations, by Linda Martín Alcoff, will help me to make this point:

> Anti-essentialisms have corroded the sense of visible difference as the "sign" of a deeper, more fundamental difference. . . . However, at the same time, and in a striking parallel to the earlier modernist contradictions regarding the significance of race, in the very midst of our contemporary skepticism toward race as a natural kind stands the compelling social reality that race, or racialized identities have as much political, sociological, and economic salience as they ever had. As [David Theo] Goldberg puts it, liberal Western societies maintain the paradoxical position whereby "Race is irrelevant, but all is race." The legitimacy and moral relevance of racial concepts is officially denied even while race continues to determine job prospects, career possibilities, available places to live [etc.].[12]

Alcoff then goes on to state that

> Race is socially constructed, historically malleable, culturally contextual, and produced through learned perceptual practice. Whether or not it is valid to use racial concepts, and whether or not their use will have positive or negative political effects, depends on the context. . . . [This position]—what I will call a contextualism about race—is clearly the best option both politically and as a metaphysical description. . . . One can hold without contradiction that racialized identities are produced, sustained, and sometimes transformed through social beliefs and practices and yet that race is real, as real as anything else, in lived experience, with operative effects in the social world.[13]

These observations boil down to the following: (1) The idea of race as Real is pretty much dead, but (2) the damage race has done still remains, although notwithstanding that damage, (3) race, as a social construct, could be something we might choose to keep around.

While one may be unable to fashion a logically unassailable, noncontextual argument that the concept of race should go, one can, *as a participant in the context in which racial discourse is extant,* try to persuade others to take a look at why the concept of race should go given *precisely that context.* One can try to persuade others as feminists tried to persuade male chauvinists that people are not precluded from running for the Senate or becoming military generals simply because they have vaginas. It may be the case that the work race is supposed to do remains of value to some people, people who prefer to emphasize the pluses rather than the minuses of racial typologies, whatever they might be, but given its historical uses it seems quite reasonable to suggest that race should be relegated to, at best, the realm of quirky private preferences. Its "cash value," the ingredient that it is supposed to add to our salutary democratic projects and intimate relationships, is hard to discern, even though its role in our self-descriptions isn't. But there is not much one can do, by dint of logical rigor, to force someone to stop taking complexion and hair type, for example, as important conditioners of their own identities and/or how they will be recognized. But one can recommend to those who believe that race is important to the construction of their self-conceptions that they try to rethink why they need it. One can try to persuade others to do away with them by showing them how life might be without them. If they get the point of David Theo Goldberg's observation, as I think we all do, one might try to persuade those who cling to the idea of race to nevertheless understand the layers of racialized reality that operate in their lives so that they might better see the difference between those *levels* upon which racialization is inescapable—for now—and those that they can peel back and discard.

Some might argue that stripping our "core selves" of cultural furniture like race is to ask that we give up the features of ourselves that are most important, that make us interesting individuals and, as groups, unique subsets of humanity, and that add flavor to human social intercourse. They might further argue that whether or not one's being racialized causes others discomfort or "gets in the way" is not the problem of the self-racialized subject, but is the respondent's problem. These seem like fair points, but in some ways they dodge the issue. I am critiquing this choice to be racialized in view of what we now know about (i.e., the present discourse concerning) race. I am asking how and why it is, in a world where the foundations of racialized thinking are under assault, one might still *choose* to be taken seriously as a racialized subject. I am wondering how racialization can long remain outside of the bag of personal eccentricities—how racialized people can long remain off the list of social eccentrics (just as male chauvinists have become, more or less, eccentrics). We are clearly not there yet, but I think that's probably where we are headed, and should be.

Goldberg's observation, as quoted by Alcoff, that "Race is irrelevant, yet all is race" presupposes that we continue to see problems of social justice that have a racial prehistory as "racial problems" or problems of "racism," rather than as simply "stupid, unpardonable bias unacceptable to a civilization like ours." Shifting our descriptions of these sorts of injustices away from racial language and categories—to, in a sense, change the subject—is, I think, critical to deflating race itself, to removing the cloud of race from around our social intercourse and politics. In my view, this is an experiment that we have, as a society, yet to attempt. Because we have not attempted it, the pedestrian view that is still rife with notions of racial essentialism is not likely to go any time soon. And it is at the level of the daily social actors, these pedestrians that make up Alcoff's "context," that race thinking continues to do the most damage. To hark back to Wittgenstein, if we all indeed do live in a house of language, it is hard to see why we should not take the language game of race more seriously as one begging for therapeutic critique.

Lucius Outlaw's Racial Conservation

There are some who might argue that to shift from talking about "racism" to "stupid, unpardonable bias unacceptable to a civilization like ours" is to make a potent response to past or present race-based injustices impossible, or at least more difficult (take the American context as an example). I do not agree. I think that racism can easily be redescribed as the practice of illegitimate morphological parsing, or some similar phrase. This is consistent with my previously stated views regarding Du Bois's vindication project. I see no reason why, for example, Title VII of the Civil Rights Act of 1964 could not be rewritten to remove the word "racism" (and so "race") every place it appears and replace it with something like "morphological parsing" or "the practice of morphological parsing." "Race" itself would become "morphology." This, in my view, does not take very much imagination. I cannot see why every moral critique of racism is not best reconceived and redescribed as a moral critique of illegitimate parsing. In doing so, we drop "race" without dropping the redress of past or present injustices. (Bear in mind that Title VII captures nearly all the other human predicates on the basis of which discrimination and bigotry have hounded people in America [so far]—color, religion, sex, and national origin. As Title VII already addresses color, it already explicitly acknowledges morphology if conceived in its broadest sense.) This is perhaps fodder for a rather sweeping legal and public policy discussion with significant statutory implications. Unfortunately, that discussion cannot be developed here.

Further, there are those who would argue that to *completely* exorcize race as part of one's identity is sort of akin to inflicting a social handicap upon oneself, particularly where racialized thinking and racism have been serious historical problems. It is to replace *Realpolitik* with naïveté. On this account, not to be aware that one lives in a racialized society with a racialized history will ultimately prove problematic since it will create certain expectations that cannot be realized (such as fair treatment in a variety of contexts). One had better acknowledge one's ascribed racial identity, one's blackness or whiteness (etc.), since one is racialized *from the outside in,* whether or not one finds one's racial assignment agreeable, and this has certain concrete implications. Further, it is often argued that to bristle at one's racial assignment is to attempt to step outside of the history of race and racism or is an attempt to scorn or deride race-based institutions, or even race-based remedies to past race-based injustice, as mentioned. I often hear this from other Americans of African descent. I think that some of these criticisms have merit, and certainly the concerns that drive them do. But it is often the case that in the heated public discourse concerning race certain distinctions are lost that would allow for greater understanding of both the nature of the rejection of racial assignments by many of those who do the rejecting as well as the understandable suspicion on the part of some who see that rejection as, possibly, bad faith and a lack of historical sensibility.

I want to go back to my suggestion that there are certain layers of racial ascription that can be peeled back and discarded. Usually the rejection of racial assignments is a rejection of those assignments at *only one moral level,* or one layer, and is not intended to be a *total* rejection of racial assignments on *all* (e.g., sociopolitical) levels. An American of Chinese descent, for example, may take a cosmopolitan view of race as something that says very little about who she is in view of her private life choices, projects, interests, personal yearnings, and actual choice of associates. While her "tinted" skin and "almond-shaped" eyes may be acknowledged as an aspect of her *social* identity or taxonomy that may conjure notions of possible national or geographic origins, on a more personal level she may in fact merely see her morphology (and certain cultural practices) as having only a personal *aesthetic* significance, as one might view being a redhead or naturally muscular, and not significant because it marks her as a *kind* of human being. On the other hand, she may at the same time possess a level-headedness to match her cosmopolitanism. She may recognize that people who look like her share a history of *struggle* in the United States that has created certain bonds, social conditions, and cultural habits and practices, and that to consciously turn her back on that history may be problematic as it may, inter alia, lead her to exist in a psychologically deluded and sociopolitically dangerous state of mind (as long as the types of slights and oppression that shaped that history remain extant or as long as there is a probability of their return). Therefore, her acceptance of that history and of her "Asianness" as more than aesthetic features is a way to embrace and revalorize the features of herself that have been most denigrated by Euro-American society.

I can see no reason why approaching racialization (for as long as we are stuck with the idea of race) in this more nuanced way should prove problematic. But note, given what I have argued, that the revalorization discussed can be accomplished without any reference to a "yellow race." Yet there are those who do not think that revalorization can take place without such references. The philosopher Lucius Outlaw argues that race informs and shapes the life-worlds of many people accustomed to seeing themselves in important ways as members of racial groups.[14] I view Outlaw's analysis regarding race as part and parcel of the general postmodernist move toward contextualization and certain robust communitarian preferences.[15] This postmodernist move, while doing in my opinion some important cultural and philosophical work, has also led to what can be characterized as context fetishization, to disparate groups hypervalorizing the specific and peculiar markers of their identities over and against those of others, to a defense of one's context (community, religious perspective, political ideology, race) "weapon in hand," as Stanley Fish's version of communitarianism seems to trumpet.[16]

While Outlaw does not believe that racial identities should be invidiously hypervalorized in this way, and he believes that such hypervalorization is avoidable, he would probably disagree with my conclusion that *racial* identities should be deflated (or should be abandoned), since he would probably argue, inter alia, that my deflation of race is too much of a nod to the intellectual and cultural privileging of the Enlightenment project, is part and parcel of a worldview that valorizes totalizing rationalistic axiologies that leave little room for "nonrational" bases of communal solidarity and communally derived sources of meaning. To the contrary, my quarrel is not with cultural and ethnic participation, which I think both useful and emotionally fulfilling, but specifically with the notion that race should be one of the important fixtures of that participation. What I think Outlaw needs to address is why he thinks the charge of harboring a vulgar modernist sensibility (particularly stinging to people, like me, schooled to understand Enlightenment excesses) should stick concerning those who challenge race in the various ways it is being challenged today.

I would like to explore more directly Outlaw's reasons for this and his general championing of the conservation of races, and offer some criticisms of his position. In his *On Race and Philosophy,* Outlaw makes the following statements (pp. 10 and 11):

I   Why, then, endow raciality and ethnicity with highly honorific philosophical significance? The answer, simply put: *because we must* . . .

II   But it has not come to pass that physical and cultural differences among groups of peoples in terms of which they continue to be identified, and to identify themselves, as races and ethnies have either ceased to exist or ceased to be taken as highly important in the organization of society . . .

III   Of course, some protest that such identities are inappropriate, in part because the notions of the racial or ethnic group involved in them lack science-certified empirical confirmation or philosophically certified logical precision. However, it strikes me that these protesters, while well-intentioned, are nonetheless misguided, for they have forgotten a very important injunction from Aristotle that for any given science or systematic attempt to achieve certified knowledge one should seek no more precision than the subject matter allows . . .

IV   On the basis of a revised philosophical anthropology that draws on an enhanced social ontology mindful of social collectivities, then, perhaps those who philosophize would not mislead themselves in thinking that the elimination of antagonisms tied to invidious valorizations of raciality and ethnicity can be facilitated by "lexical surgery" that removes "race" from usage and replaces it, instead, with references to, say, "communities of meaning" as offered by Kwame Anthony Appiah . . . or as he has proposed more recently, to "ethnic identities," since he claims there is no such thing as race. . . . I worry that efforts of this kind may well come to have unintended effects that are too much of a kind with racial and ethnic cleansing in terms of their impacts on raciality and ethnicity as important means through which we construct and validate ourselves.

I think these four excerpts fairly portray some of Outlaw's principal concerns regarding the deflation of race.

As regards (I), Outlaw is referring to some of the problems that attend a Eurocentric flattening or homogenizing of cultural difference in the name of universal reason (which was itself—that is, universal reason—given a "highly honorific" status)—the kind of homogenization that attends positivism and scientism, for example. He argues for the legitimacy of consulting communal (racial/ethnic) sensibilities, rationalities, and perspectives in the course of philosophical inquiry. He goes on to make this point over and again in *On Race and Philosophy*. Indeed, as Outlaw points out, this coupling of the valorization of universal reason with Eurocentric chauvinism was a weapon used to deride the cultural and intellectual productions of non-European peoples and to serve as a justification for their subjugation wherever such subjugation was possible. Outlaw, rightly, seeks to unmask. He shifts the attention from universal reason, the mask worn by Eurocentric chauvinists who offered themselves as the cultural standard for the whole world, toward and in favor of culturally based and culturally informed philosophical and intellectual approaches not necessarily based on or privileging the laws of logic and Western scientific methods. The mask removed, it is easy to see that chauvinism for what it is/was. Outlaw's unmasking is an attempt to push back European culture, and in particular some of the more robust, science-mad, and Eurocentric metanarrative productions of the Enlightenment and modernity, in an effort to make space for and revalorize the cultural and intellectual productions of non-European peoples as important to the existential life-worlds that give them *meaning*. He is attempting to privilege first and foremost and to hold in regard the internal consensuses of non-European cultures as to what is relevant to those cultures, regardless of and in some sense in spite of the gravitational pull of modernity.

I have little quarrel with these goals, for the intellectual paths that a culture takes will depend on what is *relevant* to that culture, not what universal reason dictates, and what is relevant to a culture, or to use Outlaw's word, to *ethnies*, need not be determined or vetted entirely by the dictates of so-called pure reason, although my concerns about the effects of the Enlightenment project are, I believe, somewhat less than Outlaw's. Where I do not follow Outlaw is in his claim that raciality/ethnicity "must" be given "highly honorific philosophical significance." It seems enough that we have learned, with the help of people like Wittgenstein, Nietzsche, and James, that one can only philosophize from where one is, that one begins thinking about the world with a bag full of biases, values, and preconditions; that one, to recall Hegel's more lucid historicism, is a son of his times. Why these biases, values, and preconditions should be "highly honor-ific" is not only curious, but may also be dangerous if one's philosophizing is arbitrarily prevented from overcoming or deconstructing at least some of these biases, values, and preconditions. A proper response to the Enlightenment's excesses and totalizations cannot be to lock ourselves, more or less, into the mono-logical intellectual and cultural productions of a *Volk*. I take one of the primary goals, and serious obligations, of the intellectual life to be such attempts to over-come the bounds of metaphorically "static" contexts to the extent possible as situated beings. I cannot conceive of a philosophical life chained (and I use that word quite deliberately) by such robust racial or *völkisch* loyalties that philoso-phy and inquiry turn into arbitrarily truncated activities or discourses.

In any event, "Enlightenment-style" reason need not be totalizing and is un-likely to be put away as an important tool, *among other tools,* in figuring out our world and negotiating ourselves through it. "Reason" is not and never was the problem, and if it is we are all in trouble since I have no idea how we can proceed without it. Reason is just that creative and problem-solving capacity that all sane human beings possess, Hegel's *Idea* notwithstanding. Rather, the problem has always been the privileging of logical and scientific approaches in *all* types of inquiry, the creation of a totalizing rationalism, as though meaning and value are or can be limited to the determinations and products of such approaches. Pragmatism's holism, from Dewey on, has had a response to this that seems to have worked pretty well in addressing the cult of Reason, and without a call for "highly honorific" philosophical significance attached to race and ethnicity, but rather with a call to understand that the nature of scientific and philosophical inquiry is, in general, of a piece with other types of social practices and of a society's aspirations.

Critical or philosophical inquiry should avoid placing, to the fullest extent practicable, any cultural practice (and race-seeing is one such practice) in the category of "highly honorific" (which is precisely where the Enlightenment, ironically, placed science and rationalism) inasmuch as such inquiry must often destabilize cultural practices by asking the culture rude questions so that it may look at and critique itself, perhaps leading to new and "better" cultural practices ("better" in view of its own axiological and moral commitments and of its own experiences with trying to achieve and sometimes change them). *This does not mean that cultural critique must itself be totalizing, eviscerating core values and beliefs in one large critical sweep.* The process of inquiry, of critiquing cultural practices, is usually best done piecemeal, akin to the way Neurath describes the manner in which philosophical conceptual schemes are changed.[17]

It is incoherent to, at the same time, (1) assent to the demise of race as Real, (2) profess that race nevertheless has sociocultural reality, *and* argue that (3) as a sociocultural reality race is beyond serious rational critique. Whereas (1) and (2) are together coherent (if arguable), the conjunction of (3) is not. It de-feats the whole point of serious cultural critique and social criticism. Although sociocultural practices are protected from *merely* logical or scientific analysis, they are not unassailable from the axiological rationality that drives the culture itself or from simple critical inquiry. That Outlaw, as a philosopher, either does not see merit in this distinction or seems to want to claim otherwise leads one to ask some rather critical questions. Are all critical assessments of cultural productions, race included, manifestations of the Enlightenment disease? Have the Enlightenment and reason become bogeymen, or might it not be best to simply avoid its excesses and to bracket and discard some of the more idiotic, pseudo-scientific claims of some of its heroes?

In (II), Outlaw asserts that racial/ethnic bonds continue to hold communities together, and that physical features are caught up in the formation of those bonds. In (III) Outlaw asserts to those who would do away with racial/ethnic groups by dint of logical reasoning that they are violating the Aristotelian principle that we must determine whether the subject of an inquiry is a *techne* or an *episteme*—that race/ethnies are more appropriately analyzed as morals and politics are examined, that is, with appropriate reference to the needs, character, and purposes of individuals and communities.[18] These, of course, cannot be divined by recourse to bare epistemic (read, scientific) reasoning. In (IV) Outlaw accuses those who are attempting an eliminativist attack on race of something of a kind with mass murder. Although I take Outlaw's remarks as figurative, the sharp rhetorical flourish of "ethnic cleansing" is noted. For the invocation of "ethnic cleansing" tips off the reader to just how much Outlaw is committed to robust racially and ethnically based identities—so much so that, as I have suggested, he seems to view them as almost inviolable, as having almost inalienable rights to exist as they are and to be protected from eroding assaults from the outside, and especially by those who use Eurocentered notions of reason and scientific method.

The answer to some of my perplexity in reading Outlaw's arguments for the conservation of race may be found in this: One may note that in (I) through (IV) Outlaw always pairs race with ethnicity (which is why I have explained Outlaw's account with reference to "racial/ethnic" imperatives above). I think this is problematic and an important but useful flaw in his argument, one which allows him to rhetorically conserve the moral legitimacy of race by frequently pairing race and culture in an effort to suggest that one cannot do without the other. On his account, to criticize the idea of race seems akin to criticizing ethnies or cultures *themselves*. But, of course, it isn't.

We recall that for many years race was understood to be precisely Real. Its demise as Real is based precisely upon the advancements made in scientific inquiry, and it is precisely what can be inferred by the logic of that inquiry (which we all generally accept) that leads to the conclusion that one of the two legs of racial thinking (races as natural kinds) has been lopped off (leaving behind only, perhaps, race as a social construction). Anthony Appiah's (and others', Naomi Zack's, for example) critiques of race as a social construct, the only remaining leg, generally *begin* here. It is a beginning that accepts but does not overprivilege good, solid scientific arguments and allows for the formulation of *cultural critiques* on the basis of reasonable inferences and possible implications drawn *from* those arguments. Appiah and others do not offer *scientific* arguments for the elimination of the social construct leg upon which race stands. They simply begin with the question, *in view of those arguments,* Why should one keep racial thinking around? Their arguments take for granted that race is at best a *violable* construct, just like any other.

Unquestionably, racial thinking has led to certain cultural productions, certain memes, certain literatures and has been tied up, seemingly inextricably, with ethnic identities. These can be thought of as the output of a certain metaphysical view of the world, as certain artifacts of that view, that is, the view that races are Real. It has its cognates. At one time, we believed that sickness was caused by evil spirits, as mentioned earlier, and the treatment for disease was delivered by incantations and prayers by shamans. But in a society that holds to the rudiments of germ pathology—the fruit of epistemic thought and solid, scientific arguments—it is hard to argue that shamans and medicine men should continue to be given the same stature that they once had, even if they have contributions to make in holistic healing. To ignore germ theory itself, to hold on to the artifacts of outdated metaphysical views as though no change had occurred, would be more than puzzling. It would be ridiculous. So, too, is a view that any cultural or social construct, even when enshrouded in the embrace of a particular culture or ethnie, is beyond critique. If critiques of cultures or ethnies are to be taken as forms of intellectual imperialism, I am not quite sure where that leaves philosophers and intellectuals, or any other thinking person in the modern world. Outlaw, I know, does not generally view culture critique to be intellectual imperialism (he engages in it himself, and well). This is why I remain perplexed by his line of reasoning as regards the conservation of race.

Clearly, race need not be thought of, even as a construct, as critical to the survival of a culture or an ethnic group. Many persons around the globe value their cultural practices and productions with hardly any thought to something called race. Outlaw is right in suggesting that it is inappropriate to charge collections of cultural behaviors and values as collections of "errors" according to epistemic standards. One cannot say that French or Italian cultures are "erroneous," since to do so is to commit a category mistake. And one certainly cannot call into question, *all at once,* the totality of one's cultural practices and values. Yet one can call *some* of them into question when the evidence suggests it is time to do so. To not do so may well be a mark of reactionism. What Outlaw has to account for, in my view, is why race, as a construct, as part and parcel of cultural practice, "must" remain a category and a value within a culture or ethnie. This is precisely what he does not do. Few people puzzle about the existence of culture, of ethnic groups, and of the attachments people feel to them. But many people who understand the status of race in the sciences and the history of race as a social construct do wonder what race actually adds to identity, and in that regard Appiah is quite right in his general critique of race. Appiah is not engaged in lexical excision, as Outlaw argues, when he questions the concept of race and the continued use of the word. He is quite aware that belligerent cultural conflicts, even those that concern morphology, will not disappear by removing

156 *David E. McClean*

race from the lexicon. But he does labor under the belief that by continuing to announce the death of race as a Real basis for human segregation and division, as well as demonstrating the truly enormous complexities that attend ethnic and cultural identity, people may be persuaded to rethink some of their biases and bigotries—some of the objects of their "highly honorific" commitments. This seems entirely reasonable.

Culture is ubiquitous, a sine qua non of the human condition. Race is not or need not be. It is simply not true that *racial identity* is and has always been "taken as highly important in the organization of society." What *have* people taken as highly important, then? What is indeed true in (II) is that ethnic identification has been important in such organization, and still is. But again, Outlaw's hitching race to ethnicity is a move that preserves or enhances the moral legitimacy of racial identification. What works in the favor of his argument is that such hitching forces *images* of ethnic groups into our heads and in such images we *picture* a people's physicality (as in my example of the Asian woman), and we may believe that physicality so essential to their forms of life that it seems inconceivable that the two can be separated. When we think of Chinese or Bajan culture and when we view Chinese or Bajan individuals as members of ethnic groups we move to *picture thinking*. Indeed, Outlaw would be right in noting that physicality is often integral to Chinese and Bajan ethnic identities. He wants to argue that it should remain so. He views nosy questions about why physicality should matter at all as rude, the first salvo in a philosophical war of "ethnic cleansing."

But why should sincere intellectuals shrink from asking these rude questions —even the Chinese and Bajan intellectuals who exist within Chinese and Bajan cultures? It is hard to see why intellectuals should shrink from asking rude questions about any aspect of human culture, whether it be race, religious fundamentalist dogma, Western materialism, patriarchy, untouchables, wife burning, the sacrifice of virgins, temple prostitution, fossil fuel consumption, vivisection, female circumcision, foot binding, the infallibility of the Pope, or any other "valued" bit of cultural practice or metaphysics. I can't figure out why such critique should incite the use of terms like "ethnic cleansing."

The fact that racial identities actually continue to shape the life-worlds of people is precisely because of the mythologies and dogmas that have surrounded race for the past two hundred–plus years. We have been stuck with race, whether we wanted to be or not. Race was a lens by which we came to view ourselves as determined beings. But the geneticist's pronouncement of the metaphysically fictitious status of race, for many, meant the bursting of the constraints of an illusion. Many viewed the demise of race-as-Real to be potentially *liberating*. For us, race is a nonsalutary encumbrance, an incoherent sociocultural idea. Yet if one were to be persuaded by Outlaw's arguments, one would conclude that it is precisely the constraints and determinations of race that should be *preferred*, so long as we can avoid the risks of bringing some of its nasty baggage along. Is this some kind of stalemate? Does the debate simply hinge on a choice? Do we simply say that one person's chains are another's wings? If that be so, then it may simply be that no line of reasoning will serve to undo racial commitments; one would only choose to be determined by race, or choose not to be.

Regarding Outlaw's belief (against the facts of the history of the race concept) that race can be preserved without invidious result, I have serious doubts about whether it makes sense to take the chance to see if he is right or wrong, especially when racial valorization is increasingly thought to be untenable and we are so close to finding ways to educate "pedestrians" (and especially our children) to do away with it altogether. Since, in my view, the question of whether we should keep or get rid of race presents the rare opportunity to dispose of a troublesome basis for social division and strife, I am not willing to place much confidence in that assertion. I have no doubt that Outlaw *himself* could pull it off. But what gets done with race on the street is out of Outlaw's (or anyone else's) hands. Given my fears here, although race may remain a potent social category for the foreseeable future, the cost-benefit analysis that has been performed on race leads me to seriously question why anyone would *want to* hold on to it, especially given that it is difficult to see any real psychological or social harms that attend its deflation. I don't see how one would be cut adrift existentially, how one would cease loving one's dialect and language, the foods and music and values and tales and spirituality of one's ethnic group, the fact that one is still a son or daughter of Scotland or India *if, in the very next instant, racial thinking and raciation, in every form and manifestation, would disappear forever.*

Since we are, after all, talking about a social construct, something that we may keep or get rid of given the reaching of a certain consensus, we need to ask some hard questions about what the mystery ingredient is—call it "R"—that race is supposed to bring to the table in establishing the kind of cosmopolitan-democratic order that we claim to want. Is "R" a sense of physical pride? If it is, why should one take pride in phenotypic or physical expressions? Is "R" a sense of shared history? What's wrong with just shared history? Is shared history enough to constitute a race? If so, then is not, as critics have pointed out, being an American or a Spaniard to belong to a race of people? Does "R" serve as a rampart that protects diversity and pluralism? But again, there are all kinds of pluralisms that will *always* exist as long as individuals and communities exist. Is there a fear of a monochromatic "beige" society? Whatever rush we get out of a broad morphological spectrum within the human species (green eyes, rosy nipples, wooly or flaxen hair) is certainly replaceable (if it ever comes to that) by new ways of expressing our salutary or other morally inert differences even if the ends of the spectrum were bred away through blithe procreative disregard.

If I am right, then in fact there is no "R," and race adds nothing worth preserving, with the possible exception of weak taxonomic distinctions no different than the size of feet or the frequency of overbite. It does nothing, in a civilization like ours, to help us achieve the kinds of social goals we wish, but it may serve a great purpose in a society *unlike* ours, with different social and cultural aspirations. So if it is held on to as a social construct (and, as Outlaw prefers, it may be) rather than as a fact of natural science, which it is not, the greatest burden of justification should rest upon those who refuse to let it go rather than those who would see it deflated or exorcized—whether they are inside or outside of the academy.

NOTES

1. Here a critic could argue that the "who" we wish to be could just as easily be despotic as democratic. Indeed, it could be. Is this mere relativism? I assent, with Richard Rorty, to the Habermasian *conclusion* that such "whos" as these (i.e., despots) will be less likely to emerge as we approach an ideal condition wherein increasingly open and honest discourse is permitted by whatever regime is in power. This agreement has less to do with obedience to the call of reason than with what seems to be a tendency in creatures like us to watch out for our own necks, however long it may take us to fashion better ways to do so. Monarchies were once thought to be a good way, but our acquaintance with a spate of Caligulas and George III's over the ages has made us rethink that notion and experiment with alternative regimes. As a species, we now have some experience with despots and we are coming to learn that permitting the conditions wherein despots become appealing alternatives will sooner or later make preserving our necks difficult. But one can be assured that some of us will forget, and indeed frequently do forget, our lessons—that we will one day welcome them back under different guises using "principled" and "well-reasoned" arguments. I am reasonably certain that there is no definitive philosophical response to such political realities, none that will trump the "wisdom" of a culture that leads it to conclude that all this democracy and freedom stuff simply goes too far. I do know that the lack of such a response has nothing to do with my willingness to die to keep despotism out of my political culture or with my fervent desire to strengthen and broaden liberal democratic practices and cosmopolitan sensibilities.

2. For a foundational understanding of racial typologies as developing out of the eighteenth century, see Milford Wolpoff and Rachel Caspari, *Race and Human Evolution* (New York: Simon & Schuster, 1997).

3. According to the United Nations' 1999 *Global Report on Crime and Justice*, "There is remarkable agreement around the world concerning the comparative seriousness of crimes. All major and minor types of crimes: burglary, robbery, assault, car theft, are recognized all over the world, no matter what region. No matter what part of the world, over a five year period, two out of three of the inhabitants of big cities are victimized by crime at least once." As for intelligence, what is meant by "intelligence" depends upon contextual factors, such as what cognitive skills are actually valued. These factors vary from culture to culture and from period to period. See the *Journal of the*

American Academy of Child Adolescent Psychiatry 38, no. 4 (April 1999): 487–88.

4.   Tommy Lott, "Du Bois's Anthropological Notion of Race," in Robert Bernasconi, ed., *Race* (Malden, Mass.: Blackwell, 2001), p. 59.

5.   Ibid., p. 71.

6.   I use "Real" (vs. "real") to mean something that the natural sciences would consider to be a proper subject of study, for example, a natural kind.

7.   In *Dusk of Dawn* Du Bois tells us regarding Africa and Africans: "The mark of their heritage is upon me in color and hair. These are obvious things, but of little meaning in themselves; only important as they stand for real and more subtle differences from other men. Whether they do or not, I do not know nor does science know today"; in *Du Bois: Writings* (New York: Library of America, 1986), p. 639. The philosopher Kwame Anthony Appiah says that "Du Bois takes race for granted and seeks to revalue one pole of the opposition of white to black. The received concept is a hierarchy, a vertical structure, and Du Bois wishes to rotate the axis, to give race a 'horizontal' reading. Challenge the assumption that there can be an axis, however oriented in the space of values, and the project fails for loss of presuppositions. In his later writings, Du Bois—whose life's work was, in a sense, an attempt at just this impossible project—was unable to escape the notion of race he explicitly rejected"; Kwame Anthony Appiah, *In My Father's House: Africa in the Philosophy of Culture* (Oxford: Oxford University Press, 1992), p. 46.

8.   Boas, an anthropologist working at the turn of the last century, concluded after significant study that there are no pure races and that no race is innately superior to another.

9.   C. S. Peirce, "Some Consequences of Four Incapacities," in *Charles S. Peirce: Selected Writings (Values in a Universe of Chance)*, ed. Philip P. Wiener (Toronto: General Publishing Company, 1958), p. 40.

10.   Lott (73) points out that Du Bois, for some interesting reasons having to do with a shifting view of the course and status of modernity itself, later attempted to distance himself from the notion of racial teleology.

11.   I am reminded of Foucault's preface to *The Order of Things:* "This book first arose out of a passage in Borges, out of the laughter that shattered, as I read the passage, all the familiar landmarks of my thought—our thought, the thought that bears the stamp of our age and our geography—breaking up all the ordered surfaces and all the planes with which we are accustomed to tame the wild profusion of existing things, and continuing long afterwards to disturb and threaten with collapse our age-old distinction between the Same and the Other. This passage quotes a 'certain Chinese encyclopaedia' in which it is written that 'animals are divided into: (a) belonging to the Emperor, (b) embalmed, (c) tame, (d) sucking pigs, (e) sirens, (f) fabulous, (g) stray dogs, (h) included in the present classification. . . .' In the wonderment of this taxonomy, the thing we apprehend in one great leap, the thing that, by means of the fable, is demonstrated as the exotic charm of another system of thought, is the limitation of our own, the stark impossibility of thinking that"; Michel Foucault, *The Order of Things: An Archaeology of the Human Sciences* (New York: Vintage, 1970), p. xv.

12.   Linda Martín Alcoff, "Toward a Phenomenology of Racial Embodiment," in Bernasconi, *Race*, p. 267.

13.   Ibid., p. 270.
14.   Lucius T. Outlaw, *On Race and Philosophy* (New York: Routledge, 1996).
15.   Outlaw's communitarianism is clear when he quotes Du Bois with apparent agreement concerning the need for "combined race action" (155) and when he tells us that what is critically important concerning the conservation of race is that such conservation is about (156) "the end in view, . . . in this case the historical development and well-being of a relatively distinct group of people who suffer oppression at the hands of persons of another group." He then ends the discussion in the chapter with the following: "Thus must the race be mobilized and organized. . . . Thus must the race of African peoples—all races—be 'conserved.' For many persons—and I place myself in this group—the continued existence of discernable race and ethnie-based communities of meaning is highly desirable *even if, in the very next instant, racism and perverted, invidious ethnocentrism in every form and manifestation would disappear forever.*" It is terribly unclear why *race* is provided as a sine qua non for communities of meaning. One of the other odd things here is that Outlaw seems to take racial communities as a kind of natural, organic given, yet he argues for their conservation with fervor, as though they are things that must be vigorously defended. As a deflationist, whenever I hear such vigor my suspicions get aroused—my antennae go up. What seems at stake for Outlaw, as for Du Bois, is the "unfinished project" of the advancement and vindication of a *particular* race. That vindication cannot take place in his view, or so it seems, if the notion of race is razed. Although he references "all races" it is difficult for me to imagine that Outlaw was motivated to write *On Race and Philosophy* with primary regard to the need for Asians and Caucasians to lock arms racially and show the world their stuff.
16.   Stanley Fish, *The Trouble with Principle* (Cambridge, Mass.: Harvard University Press, 1999), p. 14.
17.   Quine's essay "Identity, Ostension and Hypostasis" is helpful here: "Yet we must not leap to the fatalistic conclusion that we are stuck with the conceptual scheme that we grew up in. We can change it bit by bit, plank by plank, though meanwhile there is nothing to carry us along but the evolving conceptual scheme itself. The philosopher's task was well compared by Neurath to that of a mariner who must rebuild his ship on the open sea"; Willard Van Orman Quine, *From a Logical Point of View: Nine Logico-Philosophical Essays,* 2nd ed. (Cambridge, Mass.: Harvard University Press, 1953), p. 78.
18.   I assume that the reference is to Book I of the *Nicomachean Ethics:* "For a well-schooled man is one who searches for that degree of precision in each kind of study which the nature of the subject at hand admits: it is obviously just as foolish to accept arguments of probability from a mathematician as to demand strict demonstrations from an orator." I do not think that the critics of race as social construct are guilty of an error with any family resemblance to this admonition.

9   Pragmatism and Race

Paul C. Taylor

Introduction

What can pragmatism contribute to the study of race? That is to say, how can being a pragmatist, or thinking like one, in the classical, philosophical sense, help one think more clearly and productively about race, racial discourse, and racialized states of affairs? For autobiographical reasons, I enter this question, and the study of race, through an interest in what's sometimes called the African American condition. That focus will to some degree persist in what follows, in my choice of sources and interlocutors, in my choice of problems and examples. But I do not mean to suggest that race-talk just is a way of talking only about black folk or about black-white relations, any more than I mean to suggest that a black person's race is in some absolute sense more important than her class, gender, sexual orientation, or national background, *or* that the U.S. model of race-thinking can stand in for race-thinking everywhere. My sense is that race-thinking can join other accounts of social differentiation—relying on class, gender, and so on—in illuminating the social landscapes of places that have been shaped by the ideologies and institutions of, for example, white supremacy. I think also that one might come to see this beneficial use of race-thinking by considering certain practices and theories that relate to and arise from the experiences of black people in the United States. And I'm sure that the U.S. inheritance, refinement, and exportation of modern racialism across global networks, both under colonialism and under late capitalism, makes U.S. race-thinking a less parochial subject than it might otherwise be.

But these caveats and convictions about the uses and limits of race-thinking just demand that I reformulate the question with which I began: how does pragmatism highlight or uncover the alleged advantages of race-thinking, and how does it help us avoid the obvious disadvantages? I've already mentioned my interest in something called the African American condition. Obviously, there's little sense in speaking of such a condition if there is no sense in speaking of African Americans as a group or, perhaps, as a population, which is to say as a collective that, unlike a true group, may not be conscious of its unity (think of the sortal efforts of epidemiologists). One way to make sense of the idea of an

African American collective identity is to say that black folk constitute a race. It is, of course, not the only way, but it is an important, useful, and defensible way. My aim here is to show that this way of thinking becomes available when one starts to think like a pragmatist.

If one declines to think like a pragmatist, it is possible and not terribly difficult to accept the idea of an African American collective, which is to say to accept the burden of explaining it, while rejecting the notion of race. One might argue that there are no races, that race-thinking is unjustifiable, while conceding that this particular cognitive error has been causally efficacious, helping to create and maintain sociopolitical practices, some exclusionary, some not, that have profoundly shaped the contemporary world. Continuing in this vein one might say that these exclusionary practices have had disproportionate and distinctive effects on the people we call African Americans, with the result that African American individuals end up similarly situated vis-à-vis the mechanisms of white supremacy. This is a way to explain the unity of black folk, and to deflate it, without appealing to the confuted idea of race; it is a way to explain how there can be groups that traverse some of the same paths across the social landscape as races would, while insisting that, strictly speaking, there are no races. This is, in other words, an argument for putting the word "race" in scare quotes for reasons other than observing the use-mention distinction—as opposed, on the one hand, to leaving it unadorned, and, on the other, to denying it any role in our discursive practices.

In this essay I'll embrace the second part of the argument for scare quotes, while rejecting the first. I'll embrace the appeal to the asymmetrically constitutive operations of white supremacy, while rejecting the eliminativist claim that there are no races. I want to take the idea of collectivity somewhat more seriously than scare quotes allow; I want to offer (a glimpse of) a pragmatist metaphysic of race—rather than a nominalist rhetoric of "race"—as a way of accounting for, or explicating, the degree to which it makes sense to speak of an African American anything.

What Pragmatism Means

Pragmatism, like most "-isms," has taken so many forms that the label by itself fails to impart much information. Since I insist on applying the label to my approach, I should tell you how I'll use it. I think of pragmatism in an essentially Deweyan way, or, more precisely, in two Deweyan ways: in terms of the narrow view that Dewey sometimes called instrumentalism, and in terms of the wider view that sometimes goes by the name of naturalism. I'll take a moment to unpack these views, not because I propose to do anything particularly novel in the process, but because it's important to lay the groundwork upon which, or to establish the parameters within which, I'll begin to construct a pragmatic account of race.

Narrow Pragmatism

In the narrow, instrumentalist sense, pragmatism is the view that Dewey equated with this claim: "knowledge is instrumental to the enrichment of immediate experience through the control over action that it exercises."[1] A complex and somewhat evasive epistemology lurks behind this claim, but I don't propose to lay much stress on it. My interest lies in the way this *narrow pragmatic thesis* expresses two familiar ideas.

The first idea, call it *practicalism,* is that the condition of knowing involves being poised to intervene productively in the world's proceedings. As Nicholas Rescher says of pragmatism, this view is concerned with the teleology of human cognition, and it considers "the successful conduct of the affairs of life" as an ineliminable part of this teleology.[2] Think of the old saw about science being a matter of securing the capacity to predict and control events, and you'll see why Dewey describes knowledge as something that *enriches* experience. From this perspective, knowing how things stand involves—but is *not* equivalent to[3]—being in a position to interact harmoniously and fruitfully with them. Knowledge is an instrument, and knowing is a practice and skill that helps us get along better in the world.

The second familiar idea behind the narrow pragmatic thesis, call it *contextualism,* is that inquiry, or the pursuit of knowledge, is value-laden and situational. In speaking of immediate experience (remember: "knowledge is instrumental to the enrichment of immediate experience . . ."), or of experience prior to inquiry, Dewey had in mind the now common point that we come to any inquiry, experiment, or question with aims, interests, desires, presumptions, and habits, and that these have some bearing on the answer that we get from the world or from our interlocutor. Thinking, we are too accustomed to saying, is relative; knowledge is pursued and produced somewhere, somewhen, and by someone, and these variable factors are not inconsequential.

It's worth saying a bit more about just how these variable, situational factors are not inconsequential. First of all, for Dewey they lead directly to a kind of ontological and methodological *pluralism.* Attending to the context of inquiry helps us decide which theoretical vocabulary is most appropriate to the situation, and to choose between theoretical vocabularies is also to choose between sets of entities and forces. *Why did the gazelle jump?* seems like a pretty straightforward question; but finding out who's asking it and why, and what other information they have at their disposal, is an essential step in answering the question appropriately. The hunter or the toddler at the zoo may prefer an explanation in terms of the entities called beliefs and desires—*because someone scared it,* say—to a story about twitching muscle fibers and neural signals. The student of bovidae physiology, by contrast, may have precisely the opposite preferences. Philosophers have long wrestled with the impulse to anoint one or another of these ontological levels as The Real level, the place where the ontological action is. Dewey resisted this reductionist impulse. He insisted that there are different levels, different reals, valid for different purposes, and he made this contextualist pluralism an integral part of his pragmatism.

In addition to these procedural-cum-ontological consequences, contextual factors may also have what we might call *ideological* consequences, in at least two of the many Marxian senses of "ideology" (one drawing Marx out in the direction of Althusser, the other in the direction of Sartre). As individuals, we are more or less likely to see certain things in certain ways, sometimes because of the habits of cognition and perception into which we've been socialized, sometimes because of our deep and abiding interest in things *being* a certain way—a way, as it might be, that preserves our place in a power structure, or that undermines someone else's. Knowing this, we may wish to find some way of supplementing individual contributions to the process of inquiry, or of bringing individual interests and commitments to light (especially if, as it might be, these interests are opaque even to the agent in question). This is why Dewey insisted on the cooperative and self-corrective character of intelligent inquiry, and on the role of philosophy as, in his words, a criticism of the influential beliefs that underlie culture.

Broad Pragmatism

I'll approach pragmatism not just from the standpoint of an instrumentalist epistemology, but also from the perspective of a broader, metaphilosophical view. Like the narrower view, this metaphilosophy can be broken down into a few now familiar ideas. I'll refer to these as naturalism, experimentalism, and sodalism.

NATURALISM

By "naturalism" I mean to indicate a view with both metaphysical and methodological aspects. Metaphysically speaking, naturalism consists of the negative point that there are no intrinsically non-natural entities. The non-natural, or, perhaps better, the *super*-natural, is a place of anomic whim, where spirits or gods or properly endowed humans can abrogate the usual phenomenal patterns. A naturalist rejects this view and insists that the world is through and through a place of nomological regularities. Put another way, a way that highlights the methodological aspect of the view, the Deweyan naturalist holds that nothing is in principle inexplicable or inaccessible to the methods of science, even if, as it might be, we lack the cognitive or perceptual endowment that's necessary for finding the right explanations. For this Deweyan methodological naturalist, the basic pattern of explanation and inquiry used for science can usefully be generalized to other realms of human activity, including, as Dewey put it, the "social and humane subjects." This is not, as some have thought, an uncritical valorization of the scientific method and enterprise; it is, rather, an appeal to an ideal of science as a critical, cooperative, and self-corrective method for turning up resources to enrich human life. As it happens, the science that shaped Dewey most deeply, or that ran parallel to his deepest convictions, was biology. The historicist and ecological sensibility manifested by evolutionary theory tracked Dewey's own interest in treating objects of inquiry as products of change, within systems, over time. So a Deweyan methodological naturalism also demands a historicist and contextual sensibility.

EXPERIMENTALISM

The second element in my broad notion of pragmatism is experimentalism. I use this label to indicate the view that, under the irremediable conditions of human finitude, all we can do is act, though more or less intelligently, and take our chances with the outcomes. Conduct is always dogged by the possibility of error, and though we try to minimize this possibility through the application of intelligence, we can never shake it. That's what it is to be human. Dewey often criticized the philosophic fascination with necessity and certainty, with transcultural and suprahistorical standards, a fascination that he traced to the desire for metaphysical guarantees (which he in turn traced to antiquated notions of knowledge and experience and to something akin to existential dread). We wish to be reassured that things are as we think they are, or as we would like them to be, and that the way things are is stable and fixed. Pragmatic experimentalism rejects this quest for certainty and accepts instead the irreducible possibility of error, the radical contingency of things, and the need to act, to hypothesize and experiment, even in the absence of guarantees.

SODALISM

The third element in my broad notion of pragmatism is sodalism. I've adopted this term from the word "sodality," which in one of its senses means a fellowship, society, or association of any kind. I've chosen this admittedly inelegant word because I have in mind a view that takes association, in its many forms, as a basic feature of the human condition, and because all of the other words I might use to point to this perspective—communalism, socialism, holism—have connotations that are not relevant for my purposes.

What I call pragmatic sodalism is concerned with the fact of human association in two respects. First of all, the broad sense of pragmatism takes philosophy to be an instrument for social improvement. Dewey's commitment to this view can be seen in his condemnation of philosophy that privileges abstract technical problems over the problems of everyday people. It can be seen in his depiction of philosophy as a kind of vision, as a practice of putting forward imaginative prophecies, which is to say hypotheses, of how the world might look if we comport ourselves differently. And it can be seen in his characterization of philosophy as a kind of criticism, in the definition I mentioned in the discussion of contextualism.

True to the romantic and counter-Enlightenment roots of pragmatism, sodalism also has a chastened perspective on the value of methodological versions of individualism. In his political philosophy Dewey sought to temper liberalism's zeal for individualism with arguments in the mode of both genealogy and philosophical psychology. He argued, for example, that while it made sense in an age of lingering absolute monarchies and burgeoning market economies to demand, above all else, individual freedom from state interference, in an era of what we'd now call globalization, of world-spanning communications technologies, capitalist ambitions, and ecological dynamics, the greater danger may lie in leaving the accumulated consequences of millions of individual decisions (or many fewer corporate decisions) unchecked. On this view social problems may not become apparent, to say nothing of being solvable, until we ascend from the level of individual agency to the level of collective consequences, at which the patterns of social practice that "conjoint behavior" produces become more readily discernible.

Pragmatism and Racialism

With this picture of pragmatism in place, we can see what would count as a pragmatic account of race. First, as a species of *practicalism* it would approach race theory as a practical endeavor, as an undertaking that helps us deal with, to paraphrase Dewey, the problems of people. This focus on practice and on concrete outcomes militates against useless theorizing, but not in the way that we find in stereotypes of William James's theory of truth. The point is not that if you don't like it it's false, but that theories are devices for navigating the world—beliefs, Peirce said, are rules for action—and that a theory that doesn't help you navigate in its specific domain probably ought to give way to another mode of approach. Telling me that there are no races, even while populations mostly coterminous with the ones we used to think of as races can still be systematically distinguished by appeal to all sorts of social measures, is probably not an approach that helps me get around in a world shaped by white supremacy.

Second, as an application of *contextualism,* pragmatic racialism would approach race-thinking, and accounts of race-thinking, as in conversation with their places and times, as the product of interaction among humans and between humans and their environments, and as situation-specific stories about social life. It would, in other words, concede that the concept of race depends on a particular cultural history for its very existence, and that specific applications or developments of the concept depend on particular local histories and conditions. This contextual variability might seem to provide a *reductio* to any kind of racialism, but pragmatic racialism, as a variety of contextualist pluralism and in its third aspect as an instance of *experimentalism,* would deny that races must appear on every ontological level in order to exist, and that "race" must refer to something transhistorical and (ontologically) objective in order to successfully refer. The experimentalist embrace of contingency also entails an insistence on the need to act, to be willing to intervene in ongoing processes and initiate change for the sake of improving existing conditions.

Fourth, as a variety of *naturalism,* pragmatic racialism would reject out of hand the kind of super-naturalism that attends some varieties of racial essentialism. It would hold that we must account for the commonalities that unite members of a race, if there are any, without violating our usual patterns of observation and inference, and without suspending our commitment to the rest of what we count as knowledge. Further, a naturalistic racialism would hold that as students of the phenomenon of race-thinking, we miss much of its complexity unless we treat it, as Dewey sometimes said of other things, as a historical growth, as something that has come into being under specific but variable conditions.

Finally, as a *sodalistic* perspective, pragmatic racialism is anti-individualist. Individualists about race make a variety of claims. Some say that racism is no longer a factor in U.S. social life because very few people still act in consciously discriminatory ways. Some say that racism is most saliently a matter of interpersonal interactions, of individual fear and ignorance, rather than, say, a matter of systematically skewed outcomes of institutional operations. And some say that racial identity is a matter of individual choice: that you can choose your race, unilaterally opting out of the structures of identification and ascription, of interpellation, that have shaped the lives and life chances of people in this country since the seventeenth century. A pragmatic racialism rejects the demand to reduce all collective action to the intentions of individuals and to assess all social phenomena from the standpoint of the individual. Instead, it accepts populations as in some respects, for some purposes, basic entities, which means locating individuals on the broader social terrain, and identifying individual perspectives as necessarily partial windows onto the relevant terrain. To take just one example, one that I'll return to: I might decide that I don't want to be black, but, to use Du Bois's famous "test" from *Dusk of Dawn,* if I were on a train in the state of Georgia in 1940, looking the way I do, I'd have to ride in the Jim Crow car, with all the black people. I'm not in a good position to interact with the world, to resist it even, unless I recognize what's likely to happen to me; and racial categories are an efficient and effective way of summing up my prospects under the conditions of white supremacy—as well as a point of entry into existing lines of antiracist organizing. So my pragmatism encourages me to add that I'd have to ride Jim Crow with all the *other* black people—not because we give racism the last word about who we are, but because effectively responding to racism requires realistically assessing *how things are,* and because centuries of antiracist work have made racial categories available as resources for mobilizing against racist assaults.

What Race Means

That's all very nice, the eliminativist might say, *but you still haven't told me why I should remove the scare quotes from "race."* In the introduction we saw that someone who rejects the concept of race could accept that race-thinking has created and maintained sociopolitical practices that have shaped the social world. Such a person might assent to K. Anthony Appiah's claim that there are in the United States today three or four "sociocultural objects" that we mislead-ingly identify as races.[4] Each of these "objects" consists of people who occupy similar social locations: the constituents of these objects are sorted into them by others and so can expect similar modes of treatment under similar condi-tions (he calls this the ascription of a racial identity), and they may see them-selves as constituents of, and so sort themselves into, these objects (he calls this identification with a racial identity).

If even the eliminativist can concede all that, why do I insist on talking about these objects as races? For five reasons: First, *race-talk is a way of assigning deeper meaning to human bodies and bloodlines.* Much more than the insistence on hierarchies and heritable traits, the inference from, say, skin color to less readily discernible characteristics (even where these are produced by environ-mental causes) has consistently distinguished race-thinking over the centuries. In the contemporary United States (as elsewhere, though differently) the proba-bilities that govern many facts about individual people are indexed to their bodies—whether they have dark skin or light, single-fold or double-fold eye-lids, kinky hair or straight, and so on—and to their heritage—whether their ancestors would have been sent to an internment camp during World War II, or made to ride Jim Crow in 1940s Georgia, or removed to a reservation in the mid-nineteenth century. In comparing similarly situated black and white people, for example, it's easy to see that the likelihood of encountering certain events, conditions, or modes of treatment varies pretty directly with body and bloodline. Considering these facts under the rubric of race keeps the nature of the phenomenon in question fully before us: the distribution of social goods has for a long time been indexed to what we once thought of as the markers of race, and those historical inequities—rates of home ownership and infant mortality, levels of net financial worth, and more—have ramified with the passage of time. At the same time, some contemporary inequities—like racial profiling, housing discrimination, and adoption preferences—have come to mirror the historical inequities. A reconstituted notion of race can discourage us from examining these conditions only in terms, say, of class (or, more troublingly, of individual initiative or the luck of the genetic lottery), which obscures the histories of un-just takings and rigged distributions.

Second, *race-talk highlights the often poor fit between self-identification and social-ascription/interpellation.* That is, in the same way that invoking the con-cept of race signals the assignment of deeper meaning to human bodies and bloodlines, it signals the individual's *embedment* in larger structures that shape her career in the world. On familiar and problematic versions of racialism, those structures are related to racial essences; for critical, pragmatic racialism they derive, more and less directly, from the operations of the mechanisms of white supremacy. Holding on to the idea of race may help highlight the fact that in-dividuals may not unilaterally opt out of the practices of racial identification. I may say that I don't consider myself black, but it's just a fact of my social loca-tion that I'm more likely—than some other person with the same income and education but whose physiognomic features prevent him, as mine do not, from satisfying our commonsense criteria for membership in the black race—to be harassed by police or to have a family member who's been to jail or never been to college, or to have quite little in the way of net financial assets. Race-talk affirms that we are embedded in broader social structures not of our own making, and that our experiences of and in these structures can be relatively independent of our wishes and stubbornly correlated with—even if never, by anyone, consciously linked to—such things as skin color and hair texture.

Third, *race-talk highlights the relationship between sex and the patterned distribution of social goods.* A sense of one's own attractiveness, or the encouragement that helps in developing such a sense, is a social good, as, I suppose, is access to a wide selection of potential mates. In the United States these goods are quite inequitably distributed. This is less the case than it once was but still remains in evidence—consider, for example, the persistence of the light-skinned, straight-haired "video vixen" in hiphop videos, or the popularity of eyelid surgery among Asian American men and women.[5] The evidence may be even more telling, providing greater insight into our somaesthetic preferences, the continued insularity of our racial groups, and the sustained normativity of whiteness, if we consider relative rates of intermarriage. According to census figures, the members of every racial group except the "American Indian/Eskimo/Aleut" group are much more likely to marry within their groups than outside them, and nonwhites who marry outside their groups are much more likely to marry white people than anyone else. Holding on to race-talk stresses the role that sedimented perceptions of human difference play in our conceptions of the erotic, the beautiful, and the romantically appropriate, and it gives us another opportunity to see, in the patterns that emerge from our erotic, romantic, and aesthetic choices, the color-coded tracks into which we sort ourselves socially.

Fourth, *race-talk makes an additional level of sociological abstraction available to us, a level above talk of ethnicity or national origin.* There are profound differences between African immigrants and the people we call African Americans, as there are between black Jamaicans and black residents of the United States. But all of these people are black people, which is to say that under certain circumstances they will be similarly situated vis-à-vis the mechanisms of U.S. social and political life. I'm thinking here, once more, of rates of intermarriage, as well as of the well-publicized encounters between African and Haitian immigrants and the New York Police Department. If we collapse race to ethnicity, then there's no vocabulary for describing the patterned similarities in the conditions of these quite different people. One might also take up here the question of the logic and genealogy of the concept of ethnicity, a concept that rises to prominence in U.S. sociological discourse as a way of backing away from the idea of distinct and hierarchically ranked white races—that is, European ethnic groups. But that's a discussion for another time.

Finally, as a matter of philosophic procedure, *we haven't been given a good argument for abandoning race-talk.* Yes, the physical anthropologists tell us that they'd prefer not to talk about race, and for perfectly good reasons. And yes, many philosophers have buttressed these arguments with some of their own. So allow me to tell you why these criticisms of race-thinking don't sway me—at least, not the way they sway many people.

Race: For and Against

Critics of race-thinking quite reasonably attend to the substantial dangers of the practice, but in their haste to do so they often overlook some similarly substantial virtues. My sense is that a pragmatist approach highlights the virtues while remaining mindful of, and avoiding, the vices, all in a way that leaves us poised to engage productively with our social environments. In order to make this case I have to get clear on the relevant dangers and opportunities, on the different arguments they inspire, and on the limitations of those arguments.

The most familiar and easiest way of interpreting race-talk is by appeal to the regime of what we might call classical racialism. This is a name for the view of human variation, solidified in the modern West, that motivated and rationalized both European colonialism and the transatlantic slave trade. Classical racialists like, say, Kant, hold that races are groups of people whose character, customs, worth, and potential are determined by some shared inner essence, that this essence is inherited and happens also to determine specific physiological similarities, and that it is possible to rank these different groups on a scale of value by appeal to the clusters of traits that define them (either because a fixed degree of value just is one of the traits, or because the other traits determine the value).[6] Some people refer to this view simply as racialism, full stop; but I will insist on qualifying the term, mainly because I'll want to distinguish problematic varieties of racialism from defensible ones.

By now the dangers inherent in the classical racialist view ought to be familiar, and over the years they've called forth responses that are likely to be similarly familiar. During the last century or so we've seen a gradual devaluation of race as an instrument of biological science, an *antibiologism* that reflects our growing awareness of the complexity of human variation. Also, over the last forty years or so we've seen a variety of assaults on the idea that race is somehow independent of or prior to other registers of social location and identity, like gender, class, national origin, and sexual orientation. This second development, call it the move to *intersectionality*, indicates our evolving awareness of the interconnectedness of the forces that shape our life chances and social identities. In addition, over the last twenty years or so we've seen more and more people reject the myths of racial purity and identify themselves as mixed-race individuals. This third development, call it the move to *identity pluralism*, usefully highlights the contingency and suppressed vagueness of race-thinking (or, anyway, of what we might call *English-style* race-thinking, to distinguish it from the Latin American varieties that never prized purity as highly). And, finally, over the last ten years or so we've seen renewed opposition to racial determinism, or the idea that race membership governs, or ought to govern, an individual's tastes, talents, values, beliefs, and ethical affiliations. This important fourth development, call it the *cosmopolitan option* (after the form of it with which I'll be concerned), in effect harmonizes the insights of the other three: it underscores the (at least potential) uniqueness of each individual, of each person who, to borrow the language of the aesthetic moralists, creates himself or herself at the interface between genetic endowment, the physical environment, and different registers of the environing social formations.

The virtues I claim for race-thinking are almost certainly less familiar, especially in light of our usual emphasis on the lessons of the four critical, antiessentialist developments of antibiologism, intersectionality, identity pluralism, and cosmopolitanism. Nevertheless, different members of the latest generation of what we might call critical race theorists—we might call it this if we grant the resultant homonymy with the school of legal studies that goes by the same name—have developed distinct positions by emphasizing one or another of the merits of race-thinking. (I mention here a focus on *critical* race theorists to signal that I'm setting aside the question of the persistence of *classical* race theory, in, for example, discussions of race and sports, or in the work of Michael Levin.)

Some critical race theorists claim that the merits of race-thinking are vastly outweighed by the errors it encourages. For such people, whom I've already labeled *eliminativists,* these errors come in two broad types: metaphysical—because "race" denotes a kind of biological population that doesn't, and can't exist, which is to say that there just *aren't* any races—and moral—because race-thinking undervalues individuality, or facilitates the distribution of social goods by appeal to morally irrelevant traits. On this view there may be some minimal value in race-thinking, perhaps because sometimes, under current but rapidly changing conditions, it is politically useful, or psychologically expedient, or a useful index of the lingering effects of white supremacy. But, strictly speaking, races don't exist, and to act as if they do is more dangerous than not. I have in mind here people like Naomi Zack and Kwame Anthony Appiah, whom I've discussed elsewhere.[7]

Other theorists assimilate the quite real dangers of race-thinking to the more general difficulty of actualizing justice under Humean conditions and focus instead on what a revised racialism can tell us about humans as social animals. The people I have in mind here, call them *social naturalists,* strip race-thinking of its nineteenth-century associations (with biological essentialism and with rigid and naturalized sociopolitical hierarchies) and argue that we humans effectively sort ourselves into breeding populations. Culture may be the instrument of this process—that is, we inhabit different cultures, and it may be that they tell us who does and doesn't count as a potential mate—but it produces a situation in which human physiological variation runs in definite, if loose, patterns, and community sentiments systematically track these physiological differences. This loose description covers all at once a wide range of views, some of which have been offered by, for example, Lucius Outlaw and Philip Kitcher. (Assorted sociobiologists have adopted views that might fit into this category; but in light of the special concerns that animate this work and the special problems that arise from it, I'll leave it out of this account.) For these theorists race-thinking has the virtue of illuminating the social landscape, of giving a partial account of why there are somewhat physically distinct human groups, and of how physical distinctiveness figures into the broader patterns of group differentiation.

Yet another group of theorists argue that the quite real dangers of race-thinking are balanced by an opposed and equally real danger. Their view is that a rush to eliminativism will obscure the profound ways in which race-thinking has structured and continues to structure the social landscape. The theorists I have in mind here, including Michael Omi, Howard Winant, David Roediger, and to some extent David Theo Goldberg, subordinate metaphysical questions to sociopolitical analysis and genealogical inquiry; their aim is to track the vicissitudes of the race concept as a way of diagnosing current conditions. Let's refer to this view as *neutralism*, since its proponents tend to be ambivalent or agnostic about the metaphysical details while insisting on the value of race-thinking for politics and social theory. The neutralists follow the social naturalists in valuing race-thinking as a resource for social explanation, but they diverge by locating racial conditions entirely in the realm of social phenomena.

All three of these views emphasize aspects of our practices of racial identification that are essential for any adequate account. The eliminativists reinforce our skepticism about racial "science" and about the conditions under which what some have called strategic essentialism might be warranted. The neutralists encourage us to study the ways race-thinking shifts over time, and the relation between these shifts and current sociopolitical conditions. And the social naturalists counsel that we examine the human body's role in the construction of social solidarity and hierarchy. This last is particularly useful advice, since it points us in the direction of the peculiar connections between sex and race, between ethnicity and the erotic, connections that once provided a national justification for lynching and that recently encouraged a horde of journalists in both print and electronic media to, as one writer puts it, "philosophize on [actress Jennifer] Lopez's ass."[8]

As it happens, these views are also problematic, or at least partial, in certain ways. The social naturalists, for example, tend to say little about the specific human contexts, cultural, social, and political, in which distinct concepts of race take shape: all this threatens to become epiphenomenal. The neutralists, for their part, remain disturbingly coy about just what races are, a question that gets left to the empirical study of cultural practice, of how people in different places in fact comport themselves in the name of race. Although this move to the empirical is appropriate and important, especially in the study of a radically contingent social phenomenon, it is a little unsatisfying to be told just that race is a way of symbolizing social conflict by appeal to human bodies, and that the concept is otherwise vacuous. That is, it may be correct to say this, but there's probably something less abstract to say that's also correct, and that's available to us before we get to the level of sheer empirical inquiry.

The eliminativists, finally, seem locked into problematic ideas about the semantics of racial identification. The semantic thesis I have in mind holds that classical racialism originally and indefeasibly gave "race" its meaning, with the result that contemporary instances of race-talk must refer to the impossible populations of nineteenth-century race theory. Although this thesis usually goes unstated and undefended, presupposed by theorists eager to get on to other things, K. Anthony Appiah has gone to the trouble of actually arguing for it. I've complained elsewhere, in more detail than I can reproduce here, about Appiah's account, just as I've noted the great debt I owe him for making the position explicit and articulate.[9] I'll just briefly summarize his view and my worries about it.

Appiah's basic idea is that we don't quite know what we mean when we talk about race, that we rely on experts to work out and record the details, just as we do with such concepts as "proton" and, say, "acid." The experts on race did most of the work in the nineteenth century, when "race" took shape as a biological posit. Some people tried to define race differently, in terms drawn from social science—as Du Bois said early on, from history and sociology. But these alternative accounts, or aspirations to expertise, are circular: they require a biological story to identify the populations and agents that the social scientist should study. As Appiah says in one place, we have to have the race before we can study its history. And without the alternative account that history is supposed to help provide, the only way to pick out the race is by appeal to the old, flawed, biological reasoning.

There are two related problems with this semantic argument. First, it goes too quickly over the notion of circularity. Defining races historically needn't mean studying the history of a race; it might mean, as Du Bois at least sometimes saw, using the concept of race to pick out certain similarities in the social locations of individuals. Defining race in this way might involve a counterfactually specifiable susceptibility to certain modes of treatment, keyed to one's appearance and ancestry; or it might be a way of insisting that centuries of racist race-thinking have brought into being groups, or populations, that we should still call races. One has to argue for these possibilities, of course, as I think Du Bois does; but the point just now is that gesturing at an alleged circularity doesn't short-circuit the process of constructing that argument.

The second problem with the semantic argument is that the problematic appeal to circularity provides the only reason not to include people like Du Bois and Alain Locke in the history of race-thinking. Without that appeal, which is to say once we include people like Locke, it isn't nearly as clear that race-talk has to attempt (and fail) to refer to the impossible biological populations of the nineteenth century. In fact, it starts to look as if race-thinking might evolve, that classical racialism was only a stage in our ongoing and *improving* attempts to account for human variation. And if that's right, then it's hard to see why we should anchor this concept to the way it was used between, say, Jefferson's *Notes* (or, perhaps better, Morton's *Crania Americana*) and the immigration acts (and racial prerequisite cases) of the 1920s. Why should we say that race-thinking evolved from the egalitarian, environmentalist skepticism of Samuel Stanhope Smith (in his *Essay* of 1787) to its final form in the classical racialism of Morton and Josiah Strong, and that it declined thereafter? Why not say instead that it evolved from Smith through the deplorable days of Morton and Strong (because evolution isn't always an upward march) *to* the revised, sociohistorical racialism of Du Bois and Alain Locke?

Once we detach "race" from its formative modern contexts—just as we detach "light" and "cell" and "man" and "person" and "citizen" from theirs—we open the door to new questions. We're able to ask, in particular, what else "race" might mean, which is as much as asking whether adapting this old term to a new use, or reviving forgotten uses, serves any worthwhile purposes. And this, I take it, is a pragmatic question.

Conclusion

It is important to be clear about the difference that the move to critical pragmatism makes in the call to conserve the race concept. I am setting aside the classical racialist apparatus, with its essentialism and hierarchical thinking. I am also setting aside, with the claim that color determines conduct, the easy conflation of race, ethnicity, and nation: I am not claiming that race should be the center of anyone's politico-moral life, or that it somehow covertly fashions bonds of solidarity and culture. I am claiming that the vocabulary of race is a useful way of keeping track of a number of features of our conjoint social lives all at once—specifically, the features involved in the histories of systematically inequitable distributions, and in the continued patterning of social experiences and opportunity structures. It is a useful device because the concept has over the years come to connote registers of human experience—bodies, bloodlines, sex, and individual embedment—that might otherwise get obscured in social analyses, and because it can be used to abstract away from dimensions of experience—ethnicity, culture, and national origin—that receive adequate explanation in accounts that nevertheless fail to shed much light on specifically racial phenomena (involving the connections between bodies, bloodlines, and social location). Finally, I am not saying that the race concept is the only social theoretic concept that can illuminate our social landscape. The point is just that there are conditions under which race-thinking reveals to us aspects of the world that we are likely to miss without it.

NOTES

1. John Dewey, *Art as Experience* (1st published 1934; New York: Capricorn-Putnam, 1958), p. 290.
2. Nicholas Rescher, *Methodological Pragmatism* (New York: Blackwell, 1977), p. 24. Rescher identifies this as the central concern of pragmatism, which is a bit misleading at least in Dewey's case. For Dewey, an account of cognition was but part of a larger project of social reform.

3. One might interact harmoniously, as I've put it, by chance, without knowing anything. The "is" in "to know is to be in position to interact harmoniously" is the "is" of predication, not of identity. I would have more to say about the relation between knowledge and successful action (or a disposition to such action) if I were writing an essay in epistemology. But I'm not.

4. In K. Anthony Appiah, "Race, Culture, Identity: Misunderstood Connections," in K. Anthony Appiah and Amy Gutmann, eds., *Color Conscious* (Princeton: Princeton University Press, 1996), pp. 30–105.

5. Shiela McNulty, "Asians Bear the Knife for Western Look," *San Jose Mercury News,* 21 February 1995, p. A1; cited in Sander Gilman, *Making the Body Beautiful* (Princeton: Princeton University Press, 1999), p. 355, n. 70.

6. I have in mind here Appiah's distinction between intrinsic and extrinsic racism. See K. Anthony Appiah, *In My Father's House* (New York: Oxford University Press, 1992), pp. 14–15.

7. Paul C. Taylor, "Appiah's Unfinished Argument: Du Bois and the Reality of Race," *Social Theory and Practice* 26, no. 1 (spring 2000): 103–28.

8. O. V. R. Odiaga, "Sex and Celluloid: Hollywood and the History behind Jennifer Lopez's Butt," *Russell Simmons' Oneworld* (fall 1998): 98–99.

9. Taylor, "Appiah's Unfinished Argument."

10 Civil Smother: Folkways of Renewed Racism in the United States

Alfred E. Prettyman

Democracy . . . a name for a life of free and enriching communion . . . will have its consummation when social inquiry is indissolubly wedded to the art of full and moving communication.

—John Dewey, *The Public and Its Problems*

American pragmatism is a diverse and heterogeneous tradition. But its common denominator consists of a future-oriented instrumentalism that tries to deploy thought as a weapon to enable more effective action.

—Cornel West, *The American Evasion of Philosophy*

"Philosophy" . . . is not a narrowly specialized academic discipline, but rather a set of public tasks undertaken for the transformative purpose of human liberation and well-being by those who share an overlapping set of skills and techniques. The idea that philosophy involves and must be informed by such practical consultative and transformative work is as old as Socrates, Plato, and Aristotle in the Western intellectual tradition. Many non-Western traditions also acknowledge such roles for scholars, thinkers, and wise people.

—Judith M. Green, *Deep Democracy*

The villages of Comity-on-Hudson, in River County, New York, proudly announced, some three years ago, the opening of their first Learning Resources Center under the sponsorship of the county's 21st Century Collaborative. The Collaborative has been a prized project of a leading, long-serving, "liberal" county public servant. "21C," its affectionate acronym, chose to locate this center of information not in South Comity (accessible to many by foot) nor Central Comity or West Comity (where the greater number of parents seeking ways to help their children perform well in school live) but in the Upper Comity Elementary School. This Upper Comity school has the fewest poorly achieving students in the Comitys, is at quite challenging walking distance from the other Comitys, and cannot be reached by public transportation, since there is none.

When asked in a public forum why the first Learning Resources Center was opened in a location so distant from the African American, Haitian American, and Spanish American parents and students who needed it most, the esteemed public official deferred to a surrogate identified as the new county administrator for 21C. This familiar, tall brunette explained that it was important to work it through as a pilot project, see what kinds of problems arise, and fix them before replicating the Center elsewhere in the Comitys. Most people in the room seemed relieved that such a confrontational question had been answered reasonably. So in spite of a rising, female voice saying, "You haven't really answered that question. Don't you live in Upper Comity?" the public official deftly intervened with a negative sway of the head and a surprised, quizzical smile—as though trying to discern the identity of the voice while suggesting that the question was clearly misguided. She asked for the next question.

Although the esteemed public official did not live in Upper Comity, her administrator did—as the questioner and many others in the room well knew. The issue of accountability for the location of a publicly funded, vital community resource was evaded, for the moment, through the active and passive collusion of those in the room who were not significantly socially distant. The voices of those others in the room from whom most present felt some social distance were effectively smothered. (Social distance has to do with an individual's or a group of individuals' feelings of separation from other individuals of similar or different groups, whether large or small.)

Let us view this vignette through another lens: that of *politeness*. For those who believe that politeness of some kind is expected in all cultures—since the needs to feel valued and to have a sense of safety in communicating are common to cultures (Littlejohn 1999, p. 265)—this episode played itself out appropriately. The public official challenged on locating the first Learning Center in a place inaccessible to those needing it most deflected this *face-threatening act* (FTA) by referring it to her surrogate. When the surrogate's credibility was questioned, the public official intervened to deflect this FTA from her surrogate. In both instances the public official's deflections increased the social distance between the questioner and the public official.

Motivated by her concern for politeness, the public official acted to save her own face as well as that of her surrogate. Given her power, the public official incrementally increased her social distance from her questioners in such a way as to make them seem misguided, perhaps misbehaving. From her perspective she has treated with civility those whose questions sought to embarrass her.

But what of the face needs of the questioners? What of the legitimacy of their concerns? From the questioners' perspective their voices simply have been smothered.

This is not an uncommon failure in domestic intercultural communication. We see here a politician with a clear sense of her entitlement, her role rights (Lim 1994, p. 222). This, along with her self-identification with an in-group comprising a clear majority of her audience, gives her a sense of being able to act legitimately with little immediate concern for the face needs of those whose voices she has smothered. Her questioners are not relational partners; they are, in the context of this meeting certainly, an out-group. As such they are to be regarded warily—as the politician's surrogate does—regarded with detachment —as the politician herself does—and regarded by some with mistrust since they are "the others" (Ting-Toomey 1999, pp. 147–48). Those whose voices have been smothered are quite aware of this.

The social distance from which each regards the other is a major impediment to what Dewey calls "the art of full and moving communication" that makes possible "a life of free and enriching communion" in our democratic society, whatever its fundamental contradictions. As an interculturalist I am interested primarily in communication. This reflects my agreement with the observation that "the most commonplace activities of our lives—the things we take for granted—become great puzzles when we try to understand them. Communication is intertwined with all of human life, and any study of human life must touch this subject. Some scholars treat communication as central while others see it as more peripheral, but it is always there" (Littlejohn 1999, p. 2).

Communication is essential to both sustaining and diminishing social distance in our social relations. We must understand that for some, sustaining social distance is integral to their self-identity. They would find it difficult to accept the realization that the maintenance of social distance is an indicator of personal ethnocentricism of a greater or lesser degree (Ting-Toomey 1999, pp. 158–59).

In our personal relations social distance can be problematic. Littlejohn observes that "individuals involved in relationships are constantly managing boundaries between public and private, between those feelings and thoughts they are willing to share . . . and those they are not. Maintaining a closed boundary can lead to greater autonomy and safety, whereas opening the boundary can promote greater intimacy and sharing, at the cost of personal vulnerability" (Littlejohn 1999, p. 264).

It would seem paradoxical that a proclivity among certain of us citizens of the United States to rush chummily to "get on a first name basis," invited or not, with first acquaintances—an assumed sign of spontaneous, friendly openness— may become, disconcertingly, a self-enhancing gesture, one that really may do little to decrease social distance.

In some other societies the structure of language itself accommodates a baseline of social distance, reflecting a history of class consciousness that infiltrates the politeness of these forms of address. We do not have different forms of the pronoun *you* that distinguish formal from familiar address—as do *vous* and *tu* in French and *Sie* and *du* in German. Yet these formal modes of address do not necessarily impede decreasing social distance. Colleagues, collaborators may work together for years—in banking, in academia—and never, even when invited to, employ the familiar form of address in their very familiar relationship. This is often a matter of mutual respect, especially for one another's privacy and personal life. At times it can be a grateful acknowledgment that the relationship will not drift awkwardly, inappropriately toward the intimate.

Civil Smother 179

It is possible, however, to identify, generally, formal and informal modes of association and aversion that are markers of different degrees of social distance:

Continuum of Social Distance

Informal→   ←

      NR   NA   NI

P: . . . .

  Remote   Proximate   Associative   Intimate

Formal→   .   ←

P = Personal Interaction,   NR = Nearly Remote,
NA = Nearly Associative,   NI = Nearly Intimate.

The arrows are meant to indicate that movement may be in either direction along the dotted continuum. It also should be understood that it is possible for one's personal interaction to leapfrog along the continuum to decreased or increased social distance. And it is possible, as well, for strictly formal personal interactions to become transformed informal interactions, as any new friends or new lovers will readily attest. The most difficult move is breaking out of remote social distance. That difficulty might best be illustrated by encapsulated ethnocentrics: those who not only believe that their culture/convictions are the true and only right culture/convictions, but that those persons of any different culture/convictions are their enemies. One may break out of that cul-de-sac when an increasing number or variety of personal interactions brings one to the disposition of understanding that someone of a different culture or conviction need not be regarded as an enemy. Such a person may be no less ethnocentric, but no longer encapsulated. That person's formal social distance has lessened to become nearly remote, at the very least, and possibly nearly associative, if one is developing that collegially free and enriching communication that is the grounding of a truly associative relationship. The relationships that come of that kind of communication move one beyond an out-group proximate relationship to one based on mutual recognition. Moves by large groups toward associative relationships of this kind are clearly exemplified by the Catholics and Protestants of Northern Ireland in reaching the peace accord brokered by former U.S. Senator George Mitchell. Among such individual transformations few are as stunning as that of the Nation of Islam's Malcolm X, who preached that whites are devils until his hajj to Mecca, where he was overwhelmed by the vast presence of thousands of Muslims of all colors and stations in life with whom he joined in worship affirming their orthodox teaching of the true brotherhood of man. In embracing that disposition he then took unto himself the Suni Islam–derived name El-Hajj Malik El-Shabazz.

In-group and out-group association is something each of us can recognize no matter our ethnic, familial, national, or faith identity as individuals. We know what it means to be socially attached to other people with a strong sense of mutual commitment. Whether we spend much time with one another or not, we tend to prefer one another's company, have some interests in common, and tend to favor one another, especially when challenged by those who are not "one of us." The "spoils" of such association are taken for granted, require no conscious articulation.

But when the spoils we enjoy are gained in a manner that deliberately denies members of another group similar access to a clearly valuable service, position, or other good, should we not be morally diminished as members of the depriving group? Do we not then invite the enmity—at the very least—of those made less privileged by our exclusionary behavior? Writ large, is this not a question we must answer today as citizens of the nation claiming to be the leader of the world and the citadel of democracy?

Or have we no such moral obligations? Surely the claims of our particular democratic, civil society rest upon both ethical and social responsibilities (Dewey 1930, pp. 314–32). By what compass, through what qualities of personal choice might we reach a fair response to the moral challenge evaded by the Comity Village political leader and her cohorts?

Consider a different real-life vignette: the saga of Dave Stewart, an African American trying to become a general manager in that team sport referred to as "America's game," baseball. Two and a half years before, baseball commissioner Bud Selig ordered the inclusion of minorities as candidates for decision-making positions in baseball. This was good news to Stewart, no doubt, since he had, by then, spent four and a half years learning everything he had been advised to learn in order to become a general manager of a baseball club. For three years he was assistant general manager for the Toronto Blue Jays. Yet a man with no apprenticeship experience in general management of a baseball club was hired in November 2001 to be the new manager of the Blue Jays—passing over Stewart.

In like measure, at the request of the Los Angeles Dodgers owner, baseball commissioner and former baseball club owner Selig suspended his "order" that minorities be included among candidates for decision-making positions, because the Dodgers had someone already in their front office for their new general manager. This in turn also gets the Blue Jays owner Godfrey off the hook.

Writing of these developments in his *New York Times* 15 November 2001 column "On Baseball," Murray Chass observed,

> Here's what it comes down to for aspiring blacks and Latins whose racial and ethnic groups provide more than half of the major league player population: the Los Angeles Dodgers asked Selig a few months ago for permission not to interview minority candidates because they had someone, Dan Evans, in their front office whom they wanted to be their general manager. The Blues Jays had a black guy in their front office who wanted to be their general manger, but they kept interviewing white guys until they found one they liked.

Chass also questioned Selig's credibility for the example he has set "by having five white men in Major League Baseball's five highest-ranking positions below his. Look at a baseball publication with pictures of the top officials, and six white male faces smile out from the page."

In an attempt to mute any public outcry from his accommodation of his former fellow baseball owners, the baseball commissioner made the following statement: "For our own good, we need to do much better than we've been doing. This is a subject I have concern for about the industry."

Luckily he did not try to save face for the league by holding up to the public the single nonwhite general manager then in baseball, Kenny Williams of the Chicago White Socks. But his comment is notable in two ways: it is a clear admission, first of all, that baseball is a business, not a sport, and should be subject to United States antitrust regulation. Second, it is a clear example of an act of amplified negative behavior (the suspension of his order of nondiscrimination) being followed by statement of fairly unctuous amplified positive behavior (an expression of concern that the baseball industry is not doing better at being nondiscriminatory in the hiring of management talent). In his way commissioner of baseball Selig has given cover for the prejudicial or discriminatory behavior of his fellow industry partners through an expression of concern that is calculated to project a nonprejudiced public image. Another such calculated act was the owner's and commissioner's hiring of a minority general manager and manager to lead the Montreal Expos—a franchise they plan to eliminate by 2003—through the 2002 season.

Whether the behavior of the commissioner and club owners is best described according to Robert Merton's definition (Merton 1949, pp. 96–126) of *reluctant liberals*—those who are unprejudiced but will discriminate when it is in their interest to do so—or timid bigots—those who are prejudiced but afraid to show it—I leave to you. My question is, Who is being gulled here?

Is there any wonder that individual public servants and leaders of major businesses take the liberty of indulging in civil smothers when agencies of our national government continue to do so? In its infinite wisdom the National Park Service seems determined to create a new $9 million pavilion display of the Liberty Bell by covering over the historic site of George Washington's Philadelphia residence (the Robert Morris house) during his presidency, particularly the area where his slaves lived and worked. Dinitia Smith describes the situation in her *New York Times* article "Slave Site for a Symbol of Freedom" (20 April 2002, p. B7). Critics of the Park Service plan, who are

> [a] loose knit coalition of historians, led by Gary B. Nash, an expert on the American Revolution and Philadelphia history, and the Independence Hall Association, a citizen's group . . . have asked the Park Service to present a complete explanation of the Morris house's history in the area outside the new center, including a full-size floor plan outlined in stone, a description of the mansion and first person accounts from the eighteen century. They are also asking that the exhibition inside depict slavery more extensively.

Martha B. Aikens, the park superintendent, has refused these recommendations, saying that they would "create a design dissonance . . . potentially causing confusion for visitors." Can she really believe that the average U.S. citizen, young or old, tourist or not, is so witless? How confusing would it be for those curious about our history to appreciate that it was the abolitionist who made the Liberty

Bell a symbol of freedom, as Nash points out. She is willing to add one additional panel, which looks at slavery generally in the eighteenth-century context of Philadelphia.

Nash, author of the book *First City: Philadelphia and the Forging of Historical Memory* (2001), aptly summarizes what is at issue: "What we are talking about is historical memory. . . . You either cure historical amnesia, or you perpetuate it. This is a wonderful example of trying to perpetuate historical amnesia." Another smother.

Let us return to the villages of the Comitys in River County, New York. The behavior of the liberal politician representing all of the Comitys is not unlike that of the baseball commissioner or the park superintendent. During informal conversation following the forum in which she was challenged publicly, she ebulliently announced that she thought locating a Learning Resources Center in the Comity needing it most was "a terrific idea": "We just never thought of it."

Whether or not she is being disingenuous does not matter. Even if she isn't, the disjunction of her expressed egalitarian values in representing all of her constituents and her active promotion of locating a valuable public resource in a place fundamentally inaccessible to those who need it most seems prejudicial, if not witless. Was it, perhaps, her unacknowledged sense of social distance from them (is she a *reluctant liberal?*) or fundamentally aversive feelings toward them (is she a *timid bigot?*) that informed her discriminatory behavior?[1] Whichever it might be, it seems to me that her concern was to avoid recognizable discrimination by continuing to project a nonprejudiced public self-image. Her attempt to mollify the questioners whose challenge she smothered (clearly an act of amplified negative behavior in the eyes of her challengers) by acknowledging the reasonableness of their idea is a conscious act of amplified positive behavior intended to overshadow her smother. Otherwise, why was not the "great idea" acknowledged as such when the challenge first arose?[2]

Do understand that I am not suggesting that such persons as the park superintendent, baseball commissioner, and local liberal politician, who populate these real-life vignettes, behave this way in their every waking hour. I would not doubt they might point out close associations with minority colleagues as well as with those they might employ for personal services. But I do maintain that their behavior is emblematic of a pervasive incompetence in domestic intercultural communication among both leaders and ordinary citizens in the everyday society of these United States.

Undergirding this incompetence is a history of indulging in illusory rhetoric, in our educational institutions, in the marketplace, in the economic and social politics of this nation, even in our leisure pursuits. This is not the place to recount that history, but a few recognizable illustrations should be informative. Consider that trifle idea of the United States as a melting pot. Embedded in that simplistic confection is the notion that to become "American" is to assimilate. (Set aside, for the moment, the obvious national ethnocentricism, by which we anoint ourselves "American" to the exclusion of other members of the Americas.) Nothing could be farther from the reality of our political process for affirming citizenship. One is naturalized in becoming an American citizen. In exchange for committing oneself to the ideals of American constitutional government and its society, one is granted citizenship. There is no requirement that one give up one's original foreign, subjective culture—which is what assimilation calls for—but that one embrace the greater national objective culture by which we all have a shared identity. In other words, one is expected to become *acculturated* to this greater inclusive constitutional government and society. And with that very commitment the new citizen is guaranteed the right to continued participation in the particular shared activities, rituals, and language of their ethnic, national, or religious origin. This process of adapting to our national constitutional government and society while maintaining one's individual ethnic, national, or religious identity is the very essence of the meaning of acculturation.

Such dualistic identity has been a commonplace of our pluralistic society. It was as characteristic of the sustained First Immigration from the 1680s to 1803 and the sustained Second Immigration from the 1820s to 1924 (Higham 1984, pp. 18–28)—when a strict immigration law was enacted—as it is characteristic of immigration to the United States today. Ours is not the story of the tiger who leapt into the melting pot and was turned to butter. The populace of this "New Nation" has comprised a mosaic from its beginnings, although access to citizenship was not accorded to every member of that populace.

Consider briefly another misguided metaphor: the color-blind society. Color blindness is an optical illusion (*Mayo Clinic Health Letter,* March 2002, p. 8). For it to be descriptive of a social goal strikes me as utterly delusory. It is indicative of the befuddlement with which we cutely avoid the ineradicable reality that color is distinctive, distinguishing. I know of no one who considers color blindness a desirable quality when confronting a stop light. Similarly, why should any of us wish to indulge in such acts of misrecognition as this demeaning charade of not acknowledging and appreciating the distinctiveness of someone who does not look like you. To contend that color does not affect the way you are prepared to recognize and communicate with someone is, in fact, to acknowledge that it does.[3]

Such illusory rhetoric is accommodating of a disposition to avoid candor in our efforts to consummate that "life of free and enriching communion" which, for Dewey, gives democracy its name.

Let me rephrase the essential question I raised earlier: by what compass, through what qualities of personal choice, might we fairly respond to the moral challenges we face as members of this democratic society, in full acknowledgment of both our responsibilities and rights in interacting with our fellow citizens?

Alan Wolf tells us that "there is a moral majority in America. It just happens to be one that wants to make up its own mind." We live in a new era of moral freedom. "The twenty-first century will be the century of moral freedom. . . .

Moral freedom involves the sacred as well as the profane; it is freedom over the things that matter most." "The ultimate implication of the idea of moral freedom," he says, "is not that people are created in the image of a higher authority. It is instead that any form of higher authority has to tailor its commandments to the needs of real people" (Wolf 2001, pp. 197–200). As the subtitle of his book *Moral Freedom* suggests, it is a "search for values in a world of choice."

A complement to this descriptive and insightful social inquiry into ways in which moral choices have become unmoored from ethical and religious imperatives is an equally insightful and descriptive analysis of how our "Christian country has become the world's most [religiously] diverse nation"—as the subtitle to Diana L. Eck's book *A New Religious America* (2001) tells us. "These new voices have found a consonance of American ideals with their own faith":

> Buddhists have found the individual responsibility and the pioneering spirit of American life to be consonant with the spiritual pioneers, the Bodhisattvas, the freedom seekers of their own tradition. Jains have stressed the importance of their ancient doctrine of *anekantavada,* the manyness of perspectives on Truth, for the project of pluralism. Hindus have found in America's diversity good soil for the built-in theological diversity of their own tradition, and Muslims have found the constitutional values of religious freedom, human equality, and justice to be supportive of Islamic life. An orthodox Jewish scholar in Boston summed up his experience of America in a way that others might also agree with: What America means to an Orthodox Jew is that after centuries of being persecuted precisely because of the way he looks and he eats, he is for the first time in a place where it is perfectly all right for him to wear a black coat and to talk Yiddish, and to teach his children the *aleph-beth* before he teaches them the alphabet. He appreciates it because America gives him a chance to be himself without losing his humanity.

Our quest for full and free communication in the realization of our democracy must encompass all of these choices. It requires the development of dogged skills of listening, the kind of listening that is reflective of others rather than of ourselves and our inevitable, enculturated predispositions. It requires, as well, the candor that allows us to discuss the intercultural subterfuges by which we avoid the closing of social distances, and the admission of enculturated modes of personal aversion to people not like us. These are challenges that our liberal local politician representing the villages of Comity-on-Hudson of River County, New York, the baseball commissioner and his cohort owners, and the U.S. Park Service need to engage constructively if they are to function at a lesser social distance than the nearly remote.

To engage them calls upon what Cornel West describes as that "future-oriented instrumentalism" that, thoughtfully employed, can lead to more effective action. One need not be an academic philosopher to do this. To engage these challenges transformatively calls upon what Judith M. Green (1999) describes as "an overlapping set of skills and techniques."

Have you the stamina for such a commitment? Unless each of us tries, we, as members of this global village, may perish not from another's enmity or by another's sword, but from our collusive failure to find words that forge deeds.

NOTES

For this essay I have profited from the critical comments of my colleague William Crider, the organic/idealistic/pragmatic philosopher.

1. Merton's analysis of the relationship between prejudice and discrimination also identifies two other categories of people: all-weather liberals who are not prejudiced and do not discriminate, and active bigots who are prejudiced and quite willing to discriminate.

2. This explanation is based on response amplification theory. This theory as well as aversive racism theory considers the racial views of white Americans to be internally inconsistent. But for aversive racism theory "the contradiction is not between two types of feelings but between an individual's values and feelings." "Although one accepts the egalitarian values espoused by our society, one has negative feelings about African Americans that are unacknowledged or of which one is unaware. Aversive racists see themselves as liberals who disavow racism. Nevertheless, they experience discomfort and perhaps fear around African Americans. These feelings lead to anxiety and avoidance of African Americans. Aversive racists are believed to be concerned with avoiding recognizable discrimination to maintain a non-prejudiced self-image" (Stephan and Stephan 1996, pp. 48–50).

3. "The thesis is that our identity is partly shaped by recognition or its absence, often by the misrecognition of others, and so a person or group of people can suffer real damage, real distortion, if the people or society around them mirror back a confining or demeaning or contemptible picture of themselves. Nonrecognition or misrecognition can inflict harm, can be a form of oppression, imprisoning someone in a false, distorted, and reduced mode of being" (Taylor 1997, p. 225).

WORKS CITED

Dewey, J. 1930. *Human Nature and Conduct: An Introduction to Social Psychology.* New York: Modem Library.

———. 1954. *The Public and Its Problems.* Athens: Ohio University Press.

Eck, D. 2001. *A New Religious America: How a "Christian Country" Has Become the World's Most Diverse Nation.* New York: HarperCollins.

Eoyang, E. 1995. *Coat of Many Colors: Reflections on Diversity by a Minority of One.* Boston: Beacon.

Green, Judith M. 1999. *Deep Democracy: Community, Diversity and Transformation.* New York: Rowman & Littlefield.

Higham, J. 1984. *Send These to Me: Immigrants in Urban America.* Revised ed. Baltimore: Johns Hopkins University Press.

Lim, T.-S. 1994. "Facework and Interpersonal Relationships." In S. Ting-Toomey, ed., *The Challenge of Facework: Cross-cultural and Interpersonal Challenge.* Albany: State University of New York Press.

Littlejohn, S. W. 1999. *Theories of Human Communication.* 6th ed. New York: Wadsworth.

Merton, R. K. 1949. "Discrimination and the American Creed." In R. H. MacIver, ed., *Discrimination and National Welfare.* New York: Harper & Row.

Nash, G. B. *First City: Philadelphia and the Forging of Historical Memory.* Philadelphia: University of Pennsylvania Press, 2001.

Stephan, W. G., and C. W. Stephan. 1996. *Intergroup Relations.* New York: HarperCollins.

Taylor, C. 1997. *Philosophical Arguments.* Cambridge, Mass.: Harvard University Press.

Ting-Toomey, S. 1999. *Communicating across Cultures.* New York: Guilford.

West, C. 1989. *The American Evasion of Philosophy: A Genealogy of Pragmatism.* Madison: University of Wisconsin Press.

Wolf, A. 2001. *Moral Freedom: The Search for Virtue in a World of Choice.* New York: Norton.

11 Race, Education, and Democracy

Scott L. Pratt

At the center of what it means to be democratic is the commitment to equality. This commitment emerges in our talk about public policies, in our talk about careers and economic opportunity, and in our talk about education. In light of equality, we say, we must overlook differences among individuals in order to treat everyone as the same. When the so-called playing field is not "level," we think it undermines equality and ought to be changed so that the ideal of equality can be more nearly achieved. At the same time, democracy seems to call for a parallel commitment to maintaining the distinctiveness of individuals. In this case, public policies, economic processes, education, and so on are thought about in a way that supports individual development and opportunity. Difference, in this case, is a goal, not a hindrance, and is what makes the level playing field worth having. This tension within the context of a democratic society is manifest as well in its institutions, including those most central to the education of a democratic citizenry—public universities. Such institutions capture their democratic commitments in a variety of policy statements and programs and make the tension most clear in their overall mission statements. My own institution, the University of Oregon, makes the commitments to equality and distinctive individuals central to the education we provide when we say in our mission that the university is dedicated to "the principles of equality of opportunity and freedom from unfair discrimination for all members of the university community and an acceptance of true diversity as an affirmation of individual identity within a welcoming community."[1]

The mission statement, however, complicates the matter. Not only does it affirm the commitment to equality and the importance of individuals, but it also asks for an acceptance of "true diversity." At one level, this is to say no more than I have said—democracy and, by extension education in a democracy, ought to foster individual distinctiveness, "true diversity." But the moment one starts to talk about individual distinctiveness in relation to differences of gender or race there is a problem. Doesn't recognition of race difference, for example, undermine equality by highlighting an aspect of individuals that cannot be shared by all? Not everyone, of course, is white nor is everyone black, and, given our usual understanding of being white or black, they can never be. At the same time, the recognition of race difference seems to undermine the commitment to individuals as well. To emphasize individuality is to emphasize what makes a person different from everyone else, but to recognize that someone is African American or that someone is white is to fail to recognize them as individuals—as Peter or Patricia—and instead to recognize them for the groups to which their skin color connects them. In fact, if racism is understood as practices which violate our commitments to equality and individuality because of race, then it seems that recognizing race is itself a form of racism. In light of this sort of argument, some people, black and white, are ready to set aside the notion of race because it is an obstacle to ending racism.[2]

At the same time, others argue that the only way to solve the problem of racism and other forms of oppression based on difference is to address the problem on its own terms. The response to discrimination against blacks in hiring or college admissions is something that calls for the identification of people's races in order to change the practices of discrimination. One cannot argue that there are no black faculty members in a philosophy department or black students in an entering class unless one is willing to identify the racial backgrounds of the faculty and students. We cannot even get a sense of whether or not things are changing without systematically recognizing racial difference. To do so from the perspective of democracy, however, is to be in tension with the commitments to equality and individuality. Again, the recognition of race runs the risk of becoming identified with racism.

Individuality and Diversity

Once race and racism are taken together, it becomes hard to see how race difference can fit in the context of education in a democracy. For students of color, the identification of race and racism devalues and excludes a crucial aspect of experience—because it connects racial identity with the acknowledged evil of racism. For white students, the connection amounts to permission to disregard the role and construction of race and so to unwittingly perpetuate the oppression that we are otherwise quick to acknowledge in the process and institutions of education.

For most of us, however, the "reasoned" argument does not persuade. Even if our commitments to equality and individuality seem necessarily at odds with our commitment that race matters, we nevertheless remain committed to each. The problem, I want to suggest, is not that any of these commitments ought to be suspended, but that they need to be rejoined with a different conception of identity and humanity.[3] Rather than viewing human beings as individuals accidentally born into various circumstances with bodies that aren't relevant to our humanity, we need to reconceptualize human beings as fundamentally embodied, and so gendered, racial, and historical beings. To deny the importance or relevance of race in our social relations, or to think that by acknowledging race we have only racism, is to misconceive humanity.

The source of the alternative view I will propose is found in the work of W. E. B. Du Bois. When, in 1903, Du Bois declared that the "problem of the

20th century is the problem of the color-line," he did not also declare that the solution was its elimination. Rather, Du Bois argued for the conservation of races and, in that sense, the preservation of the color line, reconstructed in a way that recognized that talk of race, thinking about race, identifying by race, is not fundamentally racist but fundamentally a source of enrichment, insight, and growth for individuals and for the wider community. This approach, grounded in pragmatic pluralist commitments like those of William James, Jane Addams, and John Dewey, aimed at transformation of American society by offering an alternative to the "melting pot" on one hand, and racial apartheid on the other.[4]

In his controversial 1897 paper "The Conservation of Races," Du Bois argued that races be conserved on the grounds that each race had a contribution to make to humanity as a whole. In this light, he argued that African Americans, as part of the African or black race, had a responsibility to help maintain racial distinctiveness even in the oppressive world of American apartheid. On this view, to talk about race is not to be racist in the usual sense, but rather to participate in a dialogue that helps to develop a kind of distinctiveness indispensable to the character and development of human beings. Rather than undermining democratic commitments, Du Bois aimed to provide a means by which democracy would actually be supported by the recognition of race. Under this reconstructed notion of race, democracy itself is transformed from a society that emphasizes the priority of individuals of the sort presented by J. S. Mill and classical liberal thinkers, to a society in which individuals share priority with groups. Du Bois says, "the history of the world is the history, not of individuals, but of groups, not of nations, but of races, and he who ignores or seeks to override the race idea in human history ignores and overrides the central thought of all history" (Du Bois 1897, p. 817).

In order to make sense of this transformed notion of democracy, we must understand the relationship between individuals and races. Du Bois defines a race as "a vast family of human beings, generally of common blood and language, always of common history, traditions and impulses, who are both voluntarily and involuntarily striving together for the accomplishment of certain more or less vividly conceived ideals of life" (Du Bois 1897, p. 817). The definition points out three important features of Du Bois's notion of race. First, the notion that race is "a vast family . . . generally of common blood and language" suggests that race depends in part on aspects of ourselves that come to mind when we talk about family resemblance. From one angle, it means that a similarity of look and speech more or less places individuals in relation to each other. From another angle the idea of a vast family makes the connection among people depend upon our most intimate physical and emotional connections—our bodies, our earliest memories, our expected inheritances. In effect, race is physically in the bodies of individuals, an inheritance of the most direct kind. Second, the idea that race is a matter of a shared or common history suggests that race depends not just on the connection between members of the "family," but also upon the shared story of its own development and its struggles, misfortunes, failures, and successes in interactions with other groups. Third, the idea that a common "voluntary and involuntary striving" asserts that races are not only inherited bodies and histories, but are also in part joined by visions of a shared but distinctive future.

Some current theorists of race try to reduce race to questions of morphological differences. From this perspective, the lack of a definitive biological basis for the differences then supports arguments that race is a meaningless category.[5] Other race theorists, especially in light of the problems that follow from reliance on morphological differences, reduce the idea of race to a matter of culture or ethnicity, preserving racial distinctiveness but converting it to a set of beliefs and practices that can be shared by all.[6] Du Bois will not permit either a reduction of race to physical difference or a reduction of race to ethnicity. He says, "But while race differences have followed mainly physical race lines, yet no mere physical distinctions would really define or explain the deeper differences—the cohesiveness and continuity of these groups. The deeper differences are spiritual, psychical, differences—undoubtedly based on the physical, but infinitely transcending them" (Du Bois 1897, p. 818).

From this perspective, races as groups are not sharply defined genetic (or ancestral) groups, or communities of individuals who share only a particular set of established customs and beliefs, or even more or less random groups joined in the face of particular political or economic need. They are ongoing, distinctive groups of individuals who have a richly shared past—in physical inheritance, cultural practices, and remembered history. Since Du Bois, like James and Dewey, believes that what we can do depends upon what we bring to the process, racial distinctiveness understood in this complex way has a direct bearing on the things that people produce, the ideas they have and share, their art, literature, ambitions, and constraints. Taken together these distinctive productions dependent on a racial past, present, and future are what Du Bois calls racial "gifts." Viewed from the standpoint of human community, these gifts amount to the means by which human beings grow as individuals and by which human groups develop, innovate, and enrich each other. To lose such "gifts" reduces the potential for human flourishing; to conserve them is to foster growth. Racial "gifts," then, justify the conservation of races. Du Bois concludes, "We believe that the Negro people, as a race, have a contribution to make to civilization and humanity, which no other race can make. . . . We believe it the duty of Americans of Negro descent, as a body, to maintain their race identity until [the] mission of the Negro people is accomplished, and the ideal of human brotherhood has become a practical possibility" (Du Bois 1897, p. 825).[7]

For Du Bois, the features that define race—embodiment, social history, aspirations for the future—also define individual identity. In this sense the broad characteristics of racial difference are in fact only manifested in the lives of individuals. Du Bois suggests this notion of individual identity in his famous description of African American identity in his collection of essays *The Souls of Black Folk:*

After the Egyptian and Indian, the Greek and Roman, the Teuton and Mongolian, the Negro is a sort of seventh son, born with a veil, and gifted with second-sight in this American world—a world which yields him no true self-consciousness, but only lets him see through the revelation of the other world. It is a peculiar sensation, this double-consciousness, this sense of always looking at one's self through the eyes of others, of measuring one's soul by the tape of a world that looks on in amused contempt and pity. One ever feels his two-ness—an American, a Negro; two souls, two thoughts, two unreconciled strivings; two warring ideals in one dark body, whose dogged strength alone keeps it from being torn asunder. (Du Bois 1903, pp. 364–65)

Notice the elements of the description. The body serves as the necessary ground in terms of which one must understand oneself. The body is also what is seen by others so that one is not only what one sees from one's own eyes, but one is in crucial ways almost literally what others see. Beyond the body and the self as seen by others, one is also a self of "strivings" and ideals which take one beyond one's present physical moment to a moment of self-definition. This definition of one's self is constrained by the physical and social, but is not fully determined by it. Du Bois continues (bracketing his gendered terms):

The history of the American Negro is the history of this strife,—this longing to attain self-conscious manhood, to merge his double self into a better and truer self. In this merging he wishes neither of the older selves to be lost. He would not Africanize America, for America has too much to teach the world and Africa. He would not bleach his Negro soul in a flood of white Americanism, for he knows that Negro blood has a message for the world. He simply wishes to make it possible for a man to be both a Negro and an American, without being cursed and spit upon by his fellows, without having the doors of Opportunity closed roughly in his face. (365)

Identity is to be understood as an embodied consciousness where individuals are a complex of perspectives, histories, and aspirations joined together in a living and active—that is, a striving—body.

If I ask who I am, I cannot properly answer "a thinking thing" in the manner of Descartes, nor "a material thing" in the manner of contemporary materialists like Paul Churchland, or even "a biological thing" in the manner of some "naturalists." For Du Bois, I am this body and material location in relation to characteristic material things (looking a certain way, wearing certain clothes, living in a certain place, and so on). I am also this social creature—with a set of roles and social relations (a teacher, a father, and a white man). And I am someone with certain dispositions and aspirations as well. I cannot be reduced to any of these things, nor can any of these be set aside as mere epiphenomena irrelevant to who I "really" am. This body constrains and enables social relations; these social relations constrain and enable these aspirations; these aspirations constrain and enable this body and material location. William James, with whom Du Bois studied at Harvard, had a similar conception of the self, and, in a response to those who would define selves as "separate souls" free of embodied constraints, James writes, "Unless our consciousness were something more than cognitive, unless it experienced partiality for certain of the objects, which, in succession occupy its ken, it could not long maintain itself in existence; for, by an inscrutable necessity, each human mind's appearance on this earth is conditioned upon the integrity of the body with which it belongs, upon the treatment which that body gets from others, and upon the spiritual dispositions which use it as their tool, and lead it either towards longevity or to destruction" (James 1892, p. 194).[8]

Du Bois complicates the self that James proposes by recognizing that embodied selves come to be in a historical moment such that distinctive morphological differences play an overt role in how people sort themselves and others. The resulting groupings that at first depend upon overt physical differences become the contexts in which individuals develop other features (such as social practices and future aspirations) which eventually are labeled as racial differences. Races, as a result, are natural but contingent historical developments, and although physical difference plays a role in this development, it is by no means a sufficient condition for race identity nor a wholly determinant element in human lives. In "The Conservation of Races" he gives a genealogy of race that emphasizes this point:

> Although the wonderful developments of human history teach that the grosser physical differences of color, hair, and bone go but a short way toward explaining the different roles which groups of men have played in Human Progress, yet there are differences—subtle, delicate and elusive, though they may be—which have silently but definitely separated men into groups. While these subtle forces have generally followed the natural cleavage of common blood, descent and physical peculiarities, they have at other times swept across and ignored these. (Du Bois 1897, pp. 816–17)

When we consider "real history," as Du Bois says, we find the "widespread, nay, universal, prevalence of the race idea, the race spirit, the race ideal" (817). It is not, however, a prevalence that has in general blocked human progress and development, but has been a way in which diversity has flourished to the benefit of the widest human community.

This is not to say that the conception of race in general or of what it means to be black or white has not changed over time, but it does suggest that race and races are not just the product of prejudice and exclusion. Rather, race emerges first as an aspect of life in a physically diverse world in which bodily differences become connected with differences of intimate relations, interests, dress, ceremonial forms, beliefs, aspirations, and so on. That race has come to be associated with virulent prejudice, violence, and dehumanization has as much to do with the attempt to eliminate race and its associated diversity in favor of a single way of looking, thinking, and acting. Given the close connection between racial differences and the ways in which people see themselves and others, the attempt to overlook race does not enhance the individual as an individual, but rather undermines her. To set aside race is really only to suppress distinctiveness in favor of some other ways of thinking and being which, from Du Bois's naturalistic perspective, can only have been the product of some particular racial history. The result is that the body, social location, and aspirations of individuals not of the dominant race are seen as deficiencies and failings that must be overcome. To live in such an environment and attempt to respond to the demands to not be African American or Native American or Asian or Latin American is itself a form of physical and psychological violence. As Du Bois puts it, under such circumstances "The price of culture is a Lie" (Du Bois 1903, p. 504).

The idea of individual identity Du Bois proposes initially focuses on conceptions of race, but the general approach which identifies the importance of one's physical and material place, one's social relations, and one's aspirations provides a general way to respond to other sorts of difference. Du Bois himself recognized that gender and economic class mark two other important kinds of "family resemblance" that are, in part, constitutive of one's self in the context of twentieth-century America. Despite the real and distinctive perspectives possible from different gender and class "locations," the dominant thinking advocates that the same process of elimination demanded for race is demanded for these perspectives. Even though women, on this view, have distinctive embodied perspectives that connect with contributions to the wider community, knowledge and insight classified as "women's" can only be ignored. Even though the evils of poverty are best understood from the perspective of those suffering, such perspectives must, from the dominant point of view, be set aside in favor of the perspective imposed by those most distant from a life of poverty. In each case Du Bois argues that the distinctiveness of these embodied lives must be promoted rather than overlooked and suppressed in a way that will ameliorate suffering and lead to growth.[9]

Race, then, for Du Bois becomes a transformative notion. By focusing on the history and experience of race, he transforms James's notion of individual identity largely formed from the perspective of a privileged white academic to a broader notion of identity that recognizes the categories that people in racialized societies actually use to organize their own lives. In this way Du Bois is able to avoid arguing that race is an a priori category in which humanity must be understood, and instead argue for its status as a kind of organizing ideal. This ideal, he argues in the celebrated first chapter of *The Souls of Black Folk*, emerges in particular as one of the gifts of "Black Folk" to humanity. He says:

> Work, culture, liberty—all these we need, not singly but together, not successively but together, each growing and aiding each, and all striving toward that vaster ideal that swims before the Negro people, the ideal of human brotherhood, gained through the unifying ideal of Race; the ideal of fostering and developing traits and talents of the Negro, not in opposition to or contempt for other races, but rather in large conformity to the greater ideals of the American Republic, in order that some day on American soil two world-races may give each to each those characteristics both so sadly lack. (Du Bois 1903, p. 370)

Equality and Difference

I began this paper by proposing that education in a democracy is faced with a problem about the role of race in learning. It seemed that if we systematically recognize race we apparently undermine our democratic commitments to equality and individuality. Du Bois, I think, gives us another perspective. If we take up his perspective, then it appears that our identities are only human but depend as well on how we look, our material circumstances, our histories, and our dreams. Race as a term captures the aspect of our selves—developed historically—that identifies the importance of certain physical, material, social, and cultural characteristics. If this is so, then the recognition of race does not undermine our commitment to individuality at all, but rather is necessary to it. That such recognition locates individuals as members of groups not only does not make them less individual, but grants standing to groups as well. When we recall the university commitment to "true diversity," Du Bois gives us a conceptual standpoint from which such diversity can be promoted.

Equality is another matter. It appears that our commitment to the recognition of racial difference is bound to undermine the notion of equality at every turn. Yet, by reconstructing the notion of individual identity, Du Bois also reconstructs the notion of equality. In a 1929 debate on whether or not African Americans should be "encouraged to seek cultural equality," Du Bois argues against understanding equality as "absolute identity or similarity" among cultures, but rather to understand equality as an expectation that each culture has the potential to make an equally valuable "gift" to the wider community (Du Bois 1929, pp. 47–50). Following this approach, equality among individuals is not a comparison between the circumstances of individuals, but rather an assessment of the circumstances of individuals with respect to their potential to develop their particular "gift" to the community.

An example might be useful. Suppose a person is a talented musician but has no opportunity to develop that talent. Perhaps through some community organization, the musician is provided with music lessons and a tuned piano. From one perspective, some in the community will argue that since another person, a talented painter, is not given music lessons, they are being treated unequally. From Du Bois's perspective, if the painter is in a position to develop her talents and the musician his, then they are equally treated regardless of whether they have "the same" opportunities. Equality is defined with respect to the growth of individuals, not by antecedent or independent standards.

Consider a second example. One objection to bilingual education is that it produces inequality in the learning environment by privileging bilingual students with extra resources and opportunities and denying the same to those who speak English only. Given the approach suggested by Du Bois, bilingual education would be better understood as a response to the particular circumstances and the "gifts" of bilingual students. Contrary to the criticism, Du Bois would find that failure to provide bilingual education or some appropriate alternative would undermine equality by failing to respect the distinctive gifts of those students whose language needs are different from the majority. Similar arguments could be made about affirmative action programs and educational opportunity programs. In general, Du Bois reconstructs the notion of equality by shifting the standard from blind comparison to relative comparisons within particular circumstances.[10]

On this approach, a democratic commitment to equality cannot ignore race but, on the contrary, must recognize it as an aspect of the individuals who are to be treated equally. Since one's race negatively and positively supports and constrains what one does, if we are interested in an equality of gifts, we must also be interested in promoting those aspects of life which enable these gifts. Again, from Du Bois's perspective, individuality and now equality in our present time and place demand that we recognize race.

But what are the implications of this approach for the place of race in learning? It is interesting to see that in 1955, shortly after the *Brown* v. *Board of Education* Supreme Court decision that reversed the *Plessy* v. *Ferguson* decision and established the legal requirement for integrated schools, Du Bois gave a talk in which he made two important observations. First, the *Brown* v. *Board of Education* decision was long sought and much needed but would come at a high price. "With successfully mixed schools," he said, African Americans "know what their children must suffer for years from southern white teachers, from white hoodlums who sit beside them and under school authorities from janitor to superintendents, who hate and despise them." These new circumstances will also change how race is conceived: African Americans "must eventually surrender race 'solidarity' and the idea of American Negro culture to the concept of world humanity, above race and nation. This is the price of liberty. This is the cost of oppression" (1955, p. 283). Despite this surrender, however, Du Bois observed that, second, African American culture will persist and must. "It's just one more long battle," he concluded, "but we are ready to fight it" (284). From a vantage point nearly fifty years later we may be able to heed the implicit warning and address the issue of race and learning in a more careful way than through uniform integration, now informed by Du Bois's conceptions of race and identity.

If we follow Du Bois's thinking, it seems clear that race and learning must not be separated, but rather they must be brought together. If we are in part constituted by the contingent developments of racial inheritance and our view of ourselves and others is framed by how we are seen by others in racial terms, then it seems clear that whatever our gifts as teachers and students, they will be realized only in an environment where race plays a role. This conclusion is perhaps not easy for anyone. Taken seriously, it means that the university, for example, ought to take an active role in making itself an environment that promotes "true diversity" in general and racial diversity in particular. For the university, this means a transformation from every perspective: the student population would become more diverse, as would the faculty and the administration. It also means that the university curriculum would change, not only by incorporating an ethnic studies program, but by incorporating opportunities to understand racial difference, history, and possibilities across all departments and courses.

The impact of such a change in approach would be most striking, I think, for those of us who are white. The usual fear on everyone's part is that attention to whiteness can lead only to claims of supremacy on one hand and guilt on the other. Both conclusions, I think, extend from a notion of race that Du Bois would have us set aside. In fact, Du Bois was one of the first to theorize publicly and at length about whiteness. His essay in *Darkwater*, "The Souls of White Folk" (1920), and the chapter of his autobiography *Dusk of Dawn*, entitled "The White World" (1940), show how his conception of individual identity can make race an issue even for those of us who assume that only other people are racial. From Du Bois's perspective, whiteness, like blackness or brownness or Indianness, combines a range of bodily features, a history of social relations, and aspirations for the future for purposes of conservation as well as criticism and reconstruction.

If race is taken personally, white people would be immediately aware that at least part of who they are is how they—or rather we—are seen by those who understand themselves to be racially different. While we may think that such views of ourselves do not matter, they do, both in what is possible for those of us with "white" bodies and in what is not possible. That we have overlooked these opportunities and constraints is not proof that they do not exist, but rather that we have been so possessed of overconfidence and single-mindedness —perhaps overpossessed of Western philosophy—that we have failed to see what African American, Native American, and Latino and Latina authors have long been saying. In the context of learning, attending to the distinctiveness of our bodies, the histories that have produced them, and their implications for our future is a way to attend to how we are heard and how we listen.

By consciously placing race into the context and process of learning, white people will also come to notice the ways in which they have been advantaged by social and economic history and how these same relations though transformed in various ways still play an important role in what we teach and what we learn. Once we recognize our whiteness, we recognize as well the way in which we speak with authority and are heard, often without challenge, and sometimes with rage. When we speak in class, we are not speaking as disembodied "human beings" who are defined only by what we have in common with those who are racially different; we are also embodied white people who are what we are because of a history of white prejudice, economic exploitation, and genocide. When a student of color speaks with anger or refuses to speak, it is not just a matter of so-called academic ability, as some would say, but something connected in part to a long history of what we—the student and the teacher—bring to the classroom. When a student of color speaks with rage, it is not, on this view, mere bad behavior, but something grounded in a larger circumstance and must be dealt with, not dismissed.

Finally, the aspirations which make us in part who we are are not separate from how we are viewed by others, from our histories, and from our bodies.

Aspirations are about what we think possible and, at least as importantly, what we think valuable. We set goals for ourselves in light of what we have come to value and in light of what we believe to be possible for ourselves. One of Du Bois's charges against African Americans is that they had come to value the gifts of white folk but not their own. The problem from the white perspective is that many of us have come to value gifts and futures that are consistent with what we take to be a line of development of what Du Bois called the "childish idea of progress" (Du Bois 1971, p. 64). To value progress is to value "bigger better results always and forever" regardless of the cost. At first glance, in the context of education it may seem that the distinctive aspirations associated with racial difference are best seen as motivating ideas whose only real consequence is in whether one moves forward in a course or toward a degree. Perhaps this is right, but to notice that one's values also structure one's thinking about subject matters and even whether teachers think that a student is successful merits further consideration. When aspirations become dominant and are imposed without regard to the persons on whom they are imposed, even the most "noble" values and aspirations become oppressive. As white teachers, for example, some of us become convinced that the standards of success that we adopt based on our own history are the only standards and are also the ones we ought to instantiate in our students. At times, I would say, such unthinking impositions result only in tragedy. There is, I think, no solace in thinking that such a tragedy is for the best since the unfortunate student was not up to the challenge.

By bringing race and learning together Du Bois would have white educators realize that aspirations and values are as much a part of one's identity as social location and skin color. From the perspective of an educator, this realization should compel us to pay careful attention to the role our aspirations play in the classroom and the extent to which the aspirations that are part of each student's life can come into play.

One might argue that while we are recognizing difference, it appears that we are also losing the possibility of a critical perspective. I think that this is mistaken. Du Bois is the last to accept an uncritical stance. From his view, awareness of issues is the first step to assessing the circumstances and taking seriously a commitment to the gifts each person has to offer. For whites to critically assess the role of whiteness in learning is not some process of guilt assignment, but rather a genuine effort to see the ways in which race affects one's self and the process of teaching and learning. To adopt the sort of position advocated by Du Bois is to come to focus on the possibility of individual growth, the equality and value of individual gifts. To critically assess the role of racial identity in general and the role of "whiteness" in particular with respect to gifts is to discover ways in which some gifts are suppressed and undermined and, in so doing, find ways of changing the situation. To critically engage the general theory of race and conceptions of blackness, brownness, and American Indianness is to find ways to enrich the process of learning for all students. When issues of race are attended to, faculty and students can more directly avoid the behaviors that block the development of gifts and actively (and even at times passively) structure relations in a way that respects individual identities and their gifts to come.

The place of race in learning is complex, but in light of Du Bois's approach several concluding observations can be made. First, if race, at least race of the sort understood by Du Bois, is taken seriously, then it will conserve distinctiveness, not as strictly individual distinctiveness, but as shared difference informed by a history and place, one always growing and transforming. Second, if taken seriously, what we learn from attention to race is how it is to see the world from other perspectives—for those interested in the pursuit of truth, it is to see the world more truly. Third, race in the context of education provides a context in which to understand the moments of human flourishing and the moments of human suffering. To listen to one another across racial difference is to see problems as they are experienced and so to be able to address them. Fourth, making race an integral part of learning is to have a context for self-discovery and critique. To see the ways in which being white in early-twenty-first-century America affects the qualities and possibilities of my life will lead me to better understand the ways in which my identity is formed and undermined by racial oppression.

The University of Oregon mission statement calls for equality and individuality in a context of diversity. What we can learn from Du Bois is that equality amounts to equality of recognition of difference of individuals both as they are located in the world and as they embody race. If we are obliged to do anything with respect to race, it is to recognize its pervasive character, its consequences, for good and evil, and its transformative possibilities. In the end, democracy depends upon such education. In the conclusion of his 1946 assessment of the place of Africa in the developing postwar world, Du Bois concludes with this "message":

> Reader of dead words who would live deeds, this is the flowering of my logic: I
> dream of a world of infinite and invaluable variety; not in the laws of gravity or
> atomic weights, but in human variety in height and weight, color and skin, hair
> and nose and lip. But more especially and far above and beyond this, in a realm of
> true freedom: in thought and dream, fantasy and imagination; in gift, aptitude,
> and genius—all possible manner of difference, topped with freedom of the soul to
> do and be; and freedom of thought to give to a world and build into it, all wealth
> of inborn individuality. Each effort to stop this freedom of being is a blow at
> democracy—that real democracy which is reservoir and opportunity. . . . There
> can be no perfect democracy curtailed by color, race, or poverty. But with all we
> accomplish all, even Peace. (1946, p. 261)

NOTES

An earlier version of this essay, entitled "Race and Learning," was given as a Black History Month address at the University of Oregon, 23 February 1998.

1. From the University of Oregon Bulletin, 2002–3,
    http://darkwing.uoregon.edu/~uopubs/bulletin/welcome_index.shtml.
2. See Appiah (1990a), for example. Also see Zack (1998) for an excellent survey of the various theoretical approaches to understanding and responding to race.
3. When Cornel West spoke at the University of Oregon, he told the story of Casper Weinberger's comment on Colin Powell: "When I look at Powell," Weinberger said, "I see a man." West asked: "What do you think that Colin saw?" African Americans, West stated, have developed the ability to see race without losing track of humanity. "What Colin saw," West concluded, "was a man who is white."
4. The classification of Du Bois's work is controversial. Some claim that he adopts an existentialist framework (Lewis Gordon 1997); others argue that he should be seen as Hegelian (Zamir 1995). Of course, Du Bois's work is large and complex enough to sustain a variety of interpretations. Nevertheless, a strong case can be made for Du Bois as part of the pragmatist movement that began in the late 1890s with the work of William James. Du Bois was a student of James at Harvard at the time James was completing *The Principles of Psychology* (1890). Du Bois mentions James's influence many times in his published work including his final autobiography written in the 1950s. Here he writes that his initial study of philosophy at Fisk University "eventually landed me squarely in the arms of William James of Harvard, for which God be praised" (1968, p. 127). And it was James, Du Bois says, who "guided [him] out of the sterilities of scholastic philosophy to realist pragmatism" (133). Du Bois's earliest work appears to be influenced by historians such as Albert Bushnell Hart, black activists and theorists such as Alexander Crummell, and social researcher/reformers such as Jane Addams. Du Bois's early study of the black community in Philadelphia, *The Philadelphia Negro* (1899), in fact, was modeled on a pragmatist-framed study by Addams and her colleagues entitled *Hull House Maps and Papers: A Presentation of Nationalities and Wages in a Congested District of Chicago, Together with Comments and Essays on Problems Growing out of the Social Conditions* (Addams et al. 1895). Most importantly, his work over his long career is focused on the reconstruction of American society in ways that parallel the efforts of Addams and Dewey and are compatible with the kind of transformative pragmatism recently discussed by Michael Eldridge (1998) and Erin McKenna (2001). His work is also consistent with what I have argued are the central commitments of classical pragmatism (Pratt 2002, chap. 2).
5. See Zack (1994) for a good example of this argument.
6. This view is implicit in the work of Appiah (1990b), and long a part of anthropological views of race of the sort made prominent by Franz Boas in the early twentieth century. See Boas (1940).
7. Here the "ideal" marks the end of the need for the active conservation of races, but not the end of difference, since the ideal of "brotherhood" involves the expectation of both continued diversity among peoples and their mutual support as members of a wider "family."
8. James introduces the idea that selves as known are complexes made up of what he calls a material self, a social self, and a spiritual self. The view roughly anticipates Du Bois's notion of the self in *The Souls of Black*

Folk. Much of the social theory of George Herbert Mead, Josiah Royce, Jane Addams, and John Dewey can be seen as predicated on adopting a version of James's notion of the self. See James (1890, chap. X; 1892, chap. XII).

9. See Du Bois's essays "The Damnation of Women" and "Of the Ruling of Men" in *Darkwater* (1920), as well as *The World and Africa* (1946), and many of his essays in *Du Bois Speaks* (1970a, 1970b).

10. His approach is not unlike Dewey's idea that education needs to be framed around the particular needs and circumstances of students and their communities. See Dewey (1938).

WORKS CITED

Addams, Jane, and other residents of Hull House. 1895. *Hull House Maps and Papers: A Presentation of Nationalities and Wages in a Congested District of Chicago, Together with Comments and Essays on Problems Growing out of the Social Conditions.* New York: Crowell.

Appiah, Anthony. 1990a. "Racisms." In *Anatomy of Racism,* ed. David Theo Goldberg, pp. 3–17. Minneapolis: University of Minnesota Press.

———. 1990b. " 'But Would That Still Be Me?' Notes on Gender, 'Race,' Ethnicity, as Sources of 'Identity.' " *Journal of Philosophy* 87, no. 10: 493–99.

Boas, Franz. 1940. *Race, Language, and Culture.* New York: Macmillan.

Dewey, John. 1938. *Experience and Education.* In Jo Ann Boydston, ed., *The Later Works, 1925–1953,* vol. 13. Carbondale: Southern Illinois University Press, 1981–90.

Du Bois, W. E. B. 1897. "The Conservation of Races." In *Writings,* ed. Nathan Huggins, pp. 815–26. New York: Library of America, 1986.

———. 1899. *The Philadelphia Negro: A Social Study.* With an introduction by E. Digby Baltzell together with a special report on domestic service by Isabel Eaton (New York: Schocken Books, 1967).

———. 1903. *The Souls of Black Folk.* In *Writings,* pp. 357–547. New York: Library of America, 1986.

———. 1920. *Darkwater: Voices from within the Veil.* New York: Dover, 1999.

———. 1929. "Shall the Negro Be Encouraged to Seek Cultural Equality?" In Du Bois (1970b), pp. 47–54.

———. 1940. *Dusk of Dawn: An Essay toward an Autobiography of a Race Concept.* In *Writings,* pp. 549–793. New York: Library of America, 1986.

———. 1946. *The World and Africa.* New York: International Publishers, 1965.

———. 1955. "Two Hundred Years of Segregated Schools." In Du Bois (1970b), pp. 278–84.

———. 1968. *The Autobiography of W. E. B. Du Bois.* New York: International Publishers.

———. 1970a. *Du Bois Speaks: Speeches and Addresses, 1890–1919.* Edited by Philip S. Foner with a tribute by Martin Luther King, Jr. New York: Pathfinder.

———. 1970b. *Du Bois Speaks: Speeches and Addresses, 1920–1963.* Edited by Philip S. Foner with a tribute by Kwame Nkrumah. New York: Pathfinder.

———. 1971. *W. E. B. Du Bois: A Reader.* Edited by Andrew Paschal with an introduction by Arna Bontemps. New York: Collier Books.

Eldridge, Michael. 1998. *Transforming Experience: John Dewey's Cultural Instrumentalism*. Nashville: Vanderbilt University Press.

Gordon, Lewis R. 1997. "Introduction: Black Existential Philosophy." In *Existence in Black: An Anthology of Black Existential Philosophy*, ed. Lewis R. Gordon (New York: Routledge, 1996).

James, William. 1890. *The Principles of Psychology*. 2 vols. New York: Dover, 1950.

———. 1892. *Psychology: The Briefer Course*. New York: Henry Holt.

McKenna, Erin. 2001. *The Task of Utopia: A Pragmatist and Feminist Perspective*. Lanham, Md.: Rowman and Littlefield.

Pratt, Scott L. 2002. *Native Pragmatism: Rethinking the Roots of American Philosophy*. Bloomington: Indiana University Press.

Zack, Naomi. 1994. "Race and Philosophical Meaning," *The American Philosophical Association Newsletter on Philosophy and the Black Experience* 94, no. 1: 14–20.

———. 1998. *Thinking about Race*. Belmont, Calif.: Wadsworth Publishing Company.

Zamir, Shamoon. 1995. *Dark Voices: W. E. B. Du Bois and American Thought, 1888–1903*. Chicago: University of Chicago Press.

12 Building a Cosmopolitan World Community through Mutual Hospitality

Judith M. Green

When you see me, what do you see?
A tall "white" woman with a Ph.D.?
Or do you see me in my lived reality?
I am a member of a
Multicultural Community!

Introduction

Although great philosophy somehow exceeds its context of origin, as the great pragmatists have pointed out, all philosophy is at first the expression of a time, a place, a problem, as well as the memories, the deep values, and the hopes of a particular human being, addressing fellow human beings for a particular purpose. I write as an American woman of Irish descent, entrusted with the teaching of philosophy at New York City's Jesuit university, to invite others now present on the planet and those still to be born to join me in celebrating "an Irish wake" for all those lost on that awful day of terror, September 11, 2001, for all the good things that died with them, and also for the "terrible beauty," as William Butler Yeats put it, now being born among those of us who remain, and remain committed to the best for which the best have always stood. I am emboldened by an African American friend who challenges me to write in my own voice, and by an Italian American friend who admires the Irish tradition of meeting tragedy with a full heart, expressing grief in song and dance as well as story, of rebinding the wounds of a community of meaning in the face of gaping mystery, and of linking loss with laughter at the wonder of life. Of course, the latter friend is a romantic about this. We don't always get it right—sometimes we just stuff down our feelings—sometimes we're just angry with God—and we are not the only tradition that has found expressive ways of marking the death of our own and the lives that exceed them. Nonetheless, September 11th needs "an Irish wake," a celebratory reframing of grief and loss through the transformative powers of memory, love, and hope, to which all "the neighbors" and the traditions that made them are cordially invited—in fact, in which their active presence in a spirit of mutual hospitality is urgently needed—since nothing less will do justice to the day, to the dead, and to all of our traditions' great gifts and hopes for the future.

Please note the complex "racial" history and the pragmatist cosmopolitan vision that underlies this invitation: an Irish American is already something more culturally complex than an Irish-unmodified; and an Irish-unmodified is a peculiar descendant agglomeration of the "pagan" Celtic culture of people who migrated west from the Vltava River in that Central European area that is now Praha/Prague several thousand years before Jesus of Nazareth was ever heard of, turning up in western France with their Druid practices in the pages of Julius Caesar's *Gallic Commentaries,* perhaps crossing a land bridge that once may have linked the so-called British Isles with the main body of Europe, certainly encountering the Romans as embodied in our patron saint, Patrick, who (as everyone knows) drove the snakes out of Ireland and taught us trinitarian Christian theology by using the shamrock as his example of a three-in-one. The ancient Irish certainly were overcome militarily by Scandinavia's Vikings, who probably shared their gene pool with us, as well. Moreover, the Spanish Armada that was wrecked off Ireland's western shores almost certainly had survivors, who would have been taken in by the local people, leading to the sharing of both their composite culture (indigenous Spanish, Roman, Christian, Jewish, Moorish-Islamic, Native American) and their own complex gene pool. In any case, if the anthropologists are right, we're all Africans anyway, if we trace our lineages back far enough. My point is this: we Irish-Americans are a sufficiently "mixed race" outfit to be related to all of our global neighbors at some degree of separation, whether we always acknowledge it or not; and in times like these, families and neighbors need to come together. So please bring your memories and your voices and your culture-specific instruments, and let's tune up and tell stories and dream and dance together in celebration of the power and the beauty of all we have lost that binds us together in seeking the possibility of a more cosmopolitan, more deeply democratic world future.

What I bring to the party is a parcel with three parts. The first part is double-sided: a reminder that many of our ancient traditions concur in stressing a duty of hospitality, even to those one has met in strife, conjoined with a suggestion that we need to reactivate this duty of hospitality mutually and transactionally as a cosmopolitan virtue for our times. The second part of my parcel is some thoughts on the transformative practice of mutual hospitality inspired by the hospitality metaphor itself, by memories of real hospitality and the difference it makes, and by imaginatively projecting mutual hospitality as a necessary element of the democratic ideal. The third part is a concluding riff on what we might all gain as fruit of the practice of mutual hospitality: sustainable and enlivening cosmopolitan hopes that we may all become fully who we are and more than we are and better than we are, while giving birth to a genuinely "religious" spirit of democratic community amidst valued diversity. In tapping out this project, many great American pragmatists from earlier generations—Charles

Sanders Peirce, William James, Josiah Royce, W. E. B. Du Bois, John Dewey, Jane Addams, George Herbert Mead, Alain Leroy Locke, and Martin Luther King, Jr.—can guide our growth in understanding of the cosmopolitan spirit and of mutual hospitality. At the same time, a pragmatist piety toward the sources of our being and our thinking, in concert with sober realism about the enormous changes recent events have wrought in our world that includes recognition that some of these changes represent new possibilities for deepening democracy, should show us that we, the generations now living and soon to be born, must critically and creatively transform the dream of the Beloved Community we have inherited from these ancestor generations in order to realize it now, adding new and even more inclusive "racial" rhythms that are distinctively our own.

The Traditional Duty of Hospitality as a Cosmopolitan Virtue for Our Times

In the powerful and still resonant concluding argument of his last monograph, *Where Do We Go from Here: Chaos or Community?* (1967), Martin Luther King, Jr., argued that we now live in a "World House" in which an unduly separated family must learn to live together peacefully in order to inherit the shared legacy that will allow us each and all to live fully, richly human lives. After demonstrating that the scientific-technological revolution and the freedom revolution that had already occurred worldwide had made the old conceptual, legal, and military structures for maintaining oppressive relationships of inequality and indifference at national and global levels no longer effective, King argued that only a third revolution, "a revolution of values," could save the future inhabitants of the World House from a life of chaos, grief, and despair. Instead of racism and other forms of antigroup hatred and fear, combined with unquestioning acceptance of the inevitability of poverty, the entitlement of the fortunate, and militarism as an effective way of maintaining dominance and settling ancient grievances, King called for a new framework of values that we might sum up as neighborliness, including sharing the wealth to meet everyone's needs and planning together to include all in sustainable development, as part of a collaborative pursuit of peace and what makes for peace. The motive transformative power to fuel and guide this revolution of values, King concluded, can and must be agapeistic love:

> This call for a world-wide fellowship that lifts neighborly concern beyond one's tribe, race, class and nation is in reality a call for an all-embracing and unconditional love for all men. This often misunderstood and misinterpreted concept has now become an absolute necessity for the survival of man. When I speak of love, I am speaking of that force which all the great religions have seen as the supreme unifying principle of life. Love is the key that unlocks the door which leads to ultimate reality. This Hindu-Moslem-Christian-Jewish-Buddhist belief about ultimate reality is beautifully summed up in the First Epistle of Saint John: "Let us love one another: for love is of God: and every one that loveth is born of God and knoweth God."[1]

In an illuminating discussion of what King means by "love" and how its transformative power might be understood to work within what I have characterized as a pragmatist transformative politics, Greg Moses has drawn on some of King's philosophical influences that are cited and woven into his texts, especially Mohandas Gandhi and Howard Thurman, in order to show that King's appeal to us to nurture this crucially important moral emotion and world-ideal is grounded in a processive metaphysical vision within which love is one of the great cosmic forces that humans can access and multiply, and that we need for our sustenance and flourishing.[2] This is the kind of love King and countless ordinary people practiced within America's Civil Rights movement, which not only changed laws and at least some hearts and minds in America, but also offered an inspiring example to the leaders of South Africa's effective struggle against apartheid, to the student activists who overthrew the antidemocratic Milosevic regime in Yugoslavia, and to citizen groups in cities around the world who have collectively protested in recent years the great harms wrought by the World Trade Association and other mismanagers of economic globalization. This is also the kind of love that sustained the Huguenot French villagers of Chambon-sur-Lignon whom Philip Hallie has memorialized and analyzed in their capacity to make good happen through lives of dangerous service to desperate Jewish refugees fleeing the Nazis during the Holocaust, which allowed them to face arrest and imprisonment with determined hope, and which enabled them to save more than three thousand children from the death camps over a period of four intense, seemingly interminable years.[3]

We who mourn our enormous losses today need to know three particular things that require us to go beyond King's splendid words and Moses's remarkable insights: first, how this transformative, agapeistic love King and the French villagers practiced is supposed to work; second, how can we access it; and third, whether doing so is a good thing, especially given the importance of group-linked "racial" differences as sources both of deep meaning in our lives and of some of history's greatest harms. After all, in earlier stages of America's continuing struggle for democracy, great thinkers like W. E. B. Du Bois and Malcolm Shabazz emphasized both of these kinds of impacts of "racial" differences in their efforts to promote self-help and collective empowerment among African Americans, both of them envisioning the path to a preferable future as one that requires cultivating to a level of excellence and efficacy the unique gifts of African Americans as a people on the world stage, and then collaborating as an equal "race" with other well-developed peoples in building a humane international order that is just and respectful of the excellences of distinctive cultures as well as of the rights of their individual members. I frame my own suggestions about how agapeistic love-power can work within and between "racial" groups and their individual members in light of all of these great thinkers' insights and concerns.

Beyond a volitional focus, or an "instinctual drive" of parent animals to succor and protect their children, this love-power seems to be deeply coded into our life processes as guiding information—as deeply and powerfully encoded as the bits of our DNA. It is expressed in action and substantially embodied in the good things of the Earth on which our organic living depends, as well as in the faces, arms, and voices of our fellows on which our becoming fully human depends. Just as we can fight our DNA for the better by attempting to compensate for its undesirable elements and also for the worse by actively perverting some of its greatest gifts, we can fight to pervert love-power, or we can accept it gratefully while attempting to correct imperfections in its embodiments and to expand its articulations as we have received these from our ancestors.

Clearly, this love-power is a life-affirming relational force of the kind the first American pragmatists, Charles Sanders Peirce and William James, speculated about in their final works.[4] It is not "contained" within individuals, but rather shapes individuals into its generative multipliers and transmitters, after first working within them primarily as recipients. Even in their earliest moments of living, however, individuals must be more than recipients of love; they must also be responders to caring, or no mutually sustaining (even if unequally sustaining) relational energy is built up, and the "love generator" experiences burnout, as Nel Nodding and Rita Manning have noted, while the beloved one fails to flourish.[5] Because of its necessarily relational character, love in its various manifestations always has a ground and an antecedent history. At the same time, inequalities and imperfections in love-power of various kinds among participants in most kinds of love networks mean that love-bonded individuals need the interactive support of larger communities, and their communities need interactive support that goes beyond the nonhostility of still wider communities, so that they can draw upon as wide a network of support as the challenges within their functionally relevant natural-social ecosystem in its geographically and historically located specificity require.

This regrettably abstract analysis of the nature and needs of love-power may help to explain the central importance ancient peoples in various parts of our planet placed on the duty of hospitality, understanding it as the ground both for justice and for the fragile, always vulnerable possibility of the various kinds of love that sustain life and make it worth living. Echoing King's insight that the cosmic power of love has been coequally acknowledged by many of the world's various great wisdom traditions, we must note that the central importance of hospitality as creating the preconditions for initiating and sustaining love has been emphasized by ancient Greek, Roman, African, Native American, Taoist, Confucian, Buddhist, Hebrew, Christian, and Islamic traditions. In ancient Greek epic poems and cycles of tragedies like the Oresteia, failures of hospitality are the source of future woes; one owed those who came peacefully into one's camp, household, or kingdom food, shelter, and civility for as long as they stayed, even if all involved feared that taking up arms against one another at some future time might be inevitable. Similarly, the ancient Hebrew tradition of welcoming the stranger and the wayfarer, as well as the Torah's requirements to leave the margins of the fields for the widow and the orphan to glean, to let the land lie fallow in a sabbatical year, and to forgive debts and to redistribute land holdings during every fiftieth, "jubilee," year are traditions of hospitality.

Roman Stoics like the Greek slave Epictetus and the emperor Marcus Aurelius emphasized the duty to humanity that is grounded in our shared participation in the *logos,* the "mind-fire" that unites all humanity into one substance with its Source. In the same vein, the greatest moments of teaching and of transformation recorded in the life of the Roman-era Hebrew rabbi, Jesus of Nazareth, remembered by his followers as the Christ, are all associated with loving fulfillment of the hospitality tradition: how he produced a "miracle vintage" of wine to meet the needs of guests at a wedding celebration at Cana; how he fed miraculously multiplied loaves and fishes to an enormous crowd that followed him to a low mount, where they settled down to listen to him explain the ways of living that make life most deeply meaningful and transformatively powerful; a story he told of a good Samaritan, a member of a group traditionally scorned by his Jewish listeners as an "inferior race," who rescued a Jew from a ditch where he was dumped after being mugged and badly beaten, and who paid for his care at the nearest lodging before departing without seeking thanks or reward; how Jesus washed his friends' feet and then shared love-transformed bread and wine with them at a Seder in remembrance of the Passover—a meal since known as The Last Supper—as a necessary hospitable preparation for his greatest act of self-sacrifice as their teacher and friend, a symbolic moment that has since become a communal memory and interpretive key for breaking open his life's meaning and for continuously multiplying its love-power. Likewise, Islam's prophet, Muhammad, drew on the Hebrew-Christian Bible in teaching that Allah requires believers to practice certain kinds of hospitality to all, including Muslims, non-Muslim people of "The Book," and unbelievers; this hospitality requires tolerance of differing beliefs and practices of non-Muslims within communities governed by the Qur'an, as long as these people do not seek to lead believers astray from its prescribed path of living.[6]

African, Taoist, Confucian, Buddhist, and Native American traditions connect this ideal and practical duty of hospitality to one's fellow humans with a sense of gratitude for the processes and life-sustaining produce of the living Earth and its cosmic Sources, understood as "holy" and as ultimately "mysterious," in the sense that the more one knows, as one rightly seeks to know, the more one is struck with awe and wonder at its terrible beauty. This responsive and responsible gratitude is expressed in the Native American Lakota phrase *mitakuye oyasin* ("we are all related"), which functions as a greeting, a prayer, a formal expression of commitment, and a simple statement of a deep metaphysical-aesthetic-ethical truth that grounds a complex set of habit-guiding social practices, rituals, and philosophical reflections that aim to embody the ideal of "respect." The traditional Taoist, Confucian, and Buddhist emphasis on "softness" and "responsiveness" expresses a similar relational awareness and openness to receive the other, and perhaps to be beneficially altered in one's way of being thereby. African and African American traditions give this receptive spirit flesh through celebratory traditions of feasting, music, and dance, as well as through practical networks of collaboratively yet very personally caring for the poor, the outcast, the sick, the old, the young, the lonely, and those with troubled hearts, all the while honoring the Ancestors, the fertile Earth, and the Powers that sustain and transform this Life as it flows into future generations.

The postbiological, culture-focused insight about a unitive meaning of "race" that the great African American pragmatist philosopher and sociologist W. E. B. Du Bois hopefully articulated early in his long life of transformative leadership, and continually tried to operationalize in successive formulations across dangerous eras of dispiriting struggle, is still important for guiding human development and interracial reconciliation today—if we understand it correctly as a call to intragroup and intergroup mutual hospitality, rather than as an essentialist drawing of racial-cultural boundaries. In 1897, the year after the U.S. Supreme Court decided *Plessy v. Ferguson* and therein reinscribed American lines of color-based racial segregation in the guise of equality, the twenty-seven-year-old Du Bois was invited by Alexander Crummell to present a theoretical paper at the founding meeting of the American Negro Academy, a think tank of the "brightest and best" of the rising generation of African Americans whom Crummell brought together to provide collective intellectual leadership concerning the future direction of struggle. The paper Du Bois presented at this meeting, "The Conservation of Races," expresses his own visionary hopes about how these difficult, hope-damaging times might be transformed, as well as his responses to a complex set of formative influences, including his philosophical studies of psychology, of the growth of experience, and of the ideals of community and loyalty with William James and Josiah Royce at Harvard, his postgraduate studies in Germany of Herder's historicist approach to analyzing folk cultures, and his voluntary self-identification with the African American struggle during and after his years as an undergraduate at Fisk College. In "Conservation," Du Bois argued that "race" is not biologically real, but it is socially real nonetheless.[7] "Race," Du Bois suggested, is a set of characteristic commonalities of outlook and spirit, as well as a set of common social practices, which produce distinctive cultural gifts and goods that are shared by a broad group of people who come out of a common history and, to some extent, a shared biological genealogy. Although skin color and hair-focused "looks" are commonly associated with "race" in America, these do not pick out unique clusters of genetic characteristics, Du Bois argued; this claim, supported then by the best science of Du Bois's time, was resoundingly confirmed by the Human Genome Project a century later. Rather, the social, behavioral, linguistic, aesthetic, and spiritual signals of affinity and outlook we read as "race" are the real basis of a shared community life over the course of an oppositional history. Du Bois argued that these real, affinity-based "racial" communities, which were requisite for basic survival in the past, have the potential to turn their collaborative energies and their developed institutions toward the building up of remarkable individuals and toward the shared pursuit of excellence and insight that will allow them to fulfill the highest levels of human potentials, to meet other "races" as equals on the world stage, and to contribute there the highly developed cultural gifts and goods that can help to shape a new, cosmopolitan world civilization that celebrates both common humanity and the distinctive contributions of diverse racial-cultural groups. To reframe Du Bois's argument in "Conservation" in slightly different terms, the key to African American survival in the past and to civilization's progress in the future is the same: the tradition of intragroup hospitality, understood as having the transformative potential to be turned outward and extended to others in conditions of mutual respect and benefit.

Du Bois might have felt heartened to know that Americans as a whole have responded differently and better in an important respect to the shock of September 11th than we have in past times of crisis: with rare exceptions, we have not scapegoated a particular "race" or culture as responsible for our grief and fear, as we did after World War I, when mobs of "white" Americans panicked by economic adversity destroyed prospering African American businesses in many cities and drove out or killed their owners, and as we did again after Pearl Harbor, when the American government seized the businesses and homes of Japanese Americans, incarcerating them in concentration camps for the duration of World War II. Instead, we have pulled closer together as Americans without losing our sense that, as a people, we encompass many important racial, cultural, and religious differences.[8] Many memorable leaders in this process of grieving together, reflecting together, and rededicating ourselves to cooperatively building an even deeper democracy have been African Americans, speaking the language of "We, the People of the United States" and sharing with others the gifts of story, song, eloquent oratory, and hope-based capacity to endure through struggle expressed in the words "We shall overcome." I will never forget the powerful "we-ness" of these sentiments at an interracial, interfaith ceremony of candlelit prayer and song as night fell on Roosevelt Plaza in front of City Hall in my suburban city, Mount Vernon, New York, at which our civic Interfaith Choir sang, a rabbi blew the shofar, pastors of diverse communities prayed for us all, and a young girl asked me if war would ever end. Nor will I ever forget hearing the gifted African American jazz quartet Bleu Orleans, performing a few weeks later at the National Park Service's Jazz Heritage Center in the old French Market in New Orleans, as their spokesman reflected on how far we have come as an American people, and how deeply committed we all are to sustaining and expanding our mutual gains in liberty, security, and quality of living, as his way of introducing a powerful performance of Donnie Hathaway's anthem "Someday We Shall All Be Free." As Du Bois might have hoped, such powerful experiences of "we" also carried within them a sense of renewed commitment to preserve those differences among us that are special and precious gifts that allow various groups to contribute in their own ways to the energy we gained from touching one another amidst them.

Those "postcultural" thinkers who argued even a few years ago that globalization processes have created a world of cosmopolitan individuals who have shucked off the mediating influence of diverse historically, linguistically, and religiously based indigenous cultures, and who deal with one another directly on common terms within a broadly shared worldview,[9] have been shown to be wrong by September 11th and its aftermath. America's president George W.

Bush seems to have assumed such a cosmopolitan core commitment among the world's modern peoples, and thus, that their ethnic differences are merely ornamental and their historical antagonisms are unimportant relative to current financial and political advantages, in his assumption of unilateral leadership in a "war on terrorism," in which he demanded that all the world's nations choose sides. However, above and beyond the arrogance of such unilateral employments of diplomatic, economic, and military power, this reductionist cosmopolitan claim itself has been shown to be an irritant to those whose nations and cultures have been subordinated and left out in the process of negotiating or imposing the new terms of global engagement. The manifest willingness of many powerful nations to resist, and of some less powerful peoples to pay whatever price may be necessary to ensure that they are included on terms of respect and mutual benefit at the tables where future-shaping decisions are made, has clearly demonstrated that the only sustainable conditions of future peace will be intercultural rather than postcultural.[10] Moreover, a more insightful philosophical anthropology than that of the "postculturalists" suggests both a widely felt human existential necessity of participating in a shared people's history whose future one can help to shape, and also the desirability for all cultures and the intercultural civilizations of which they are dynamic elements to preserve and strengthen diverse, semi-autonomous social units, both as centers of adaptation to localized conditions and as experiments in alternative approaches to framing institutional structures and shared values whose fruitfulness will have significance for other cultures within a shared system of global transactions. Thus, the focal problem of peacemaking at the beginning of the twenty-first century is how to bring these diverse peoples together into a post–September 11th, postwar, postjihad, postdominance, culture-acknowledging process of negotiating sustainable, cooperative processes of mutual benefit.

If properly evoked and employed, the deeply embedded, overlapping, and converging traditions of hospitality of so many diverse cultures may offer the common ground for such a global peace-making process. Hospitality seems to be a "common humane value" of the kind that Du Bois's younger colleague in struggle, the African American critical pragmatist Alain Leroy Locke, theorized must exist, and called for an "anthropology in the broadest sense" to verify, to clarify, and to experimentally expand in its active influence. By "common humane values," Locke meant those already instantiated, functional variants of closely related cultural valuations that can become the practical ground for cultivating the kind of "cosmopolitan unity amidst valued diversity" that must be characteristic of the kind of democratic world civilization that Locke regarded as the highest and best potential mode of social organization for globally linked modern peoples—a civilization-type he believed was already coming into being, though in a birth of blood, grief, and loss, as he wrote during the final chaotic years of World War II and its uncertain aftermath.[11] During those years, Locke participated in annual cross-disciplinary conferences of researchers in the natural and social sciences, philosophy, and world religions, to which he contributed still-timely papers on how the victors and the vanquished who had been so recently destroying the most precious and beautiful elements of each others' worlds could sit down at the same table to plan for a deep and lasting peace. In essays like "Pluralism and Intellectual Democracy," "Cultural Relativism and Ideological Peace," and "The Need for a New Organon in Education," Locke argued that this common dream of peace could be realized through stagewise processes of cooperation and trust-building grounded in common humane values and in a self-validating process of practical demonstrations of trustworthiness, as collaborating parties would fulfill their vital commitments to help devastated nations to rebuild, to help poor nations to develop, and to help all nations to reform their educational processes in order to adjust their exclusive and adversarial cultural habits and the one-sided tellings of history that support these.

Locke's intellectual and moral touchstone for this process of readjusting values and habits was his teacher Josiah Royce's metaprinciple of "loyalty to loyalty," whose negotiated adoption and gradual, practical expansion would ensure that all nations might realistically hope for preferable, nonadversarial, more deeply democratic futures guided by common humane values. Understanding "races" as ethnic groups with highly permeable boundaries through which they express their own views and share their own "culture goods" with others, and likewise receive and find themselves influenced by others' cultural values and products (desirable and undesirable), Locke imagined a future in which critical and creative filters within this global communication process of fluid exchanges through cultural "skins" would allow diverse peoples worldwide to establish semiautonomous cultural trajectories of mutually beneficial kinds while building up a fund of shared democratic values and practices that would constitute a cosmopolitan world civilization, of which they would be diverse and valued member-cultures, and in which their individual citizens would find sources of liberation, inspiration, and practical protection and support for their development and flourishing.

An insight about connections between hospitality and democracy from the transformative practice of another great twentieth-century pragmatist, Jane Addams, can help us to appreciate the realistic efficacy and cross-difference desirability of the kind of process of mutual adjustment that Alain Locke saw as so necessary to a sustainable peace, yet that many today seem to fear requires disloyalty to one's own national or "racial" culture and its religious roots. In *Democracy and Social Ethics* (1902), her masterful collection of essays that arose within her practical efforts to give democracy actuality through charitable work, Addams wrote about experiences of undemocratic realities that revealed the need for a shared process of progressive, mutual transformation in many of the structures, processes, values, and putative "virtues" that guide American living, including our nominal commitment to equality:

> All those hints and glimpses of a larger and more satisfying democracy, which literature and our own hopes supply, have a tendency to slip away from us and to leave us sadly unguided and perplexed when we attempt to act upon them. Our

conceptions of morality, as all our other ideas, pass through a course of development; the difficulty comes in adjusting our conduct, which has become hardened into customs and habits, to these changing moral conceptions. . . . Probably there is no relation in life in which our democracy is changing more rapidly than the charitable relation . . . ; at the same time there is no point of contact in our modern experience which reveals so clearly the lack of that equality which democracy implies.[12]

As the cofounder with a community of educated, transformatively committed, middle-class "white" women of Chicago's Hull House, one of America's first "settlement houses," Addams sought to empower poor, greatly disadvantaged immigrants who were newly arrived from other embattled national cultures in their efforts to cope with the complex and often inequitable economic, political, and cultural systems of their newly adopted country. The initial motivations of the women of Hull House seem to have been framed in terms of pity, religious piety, and a sense of the democratic responsibility of the more fortunate to supplement the woeful inadequacies of America's educational and social welfare systems in ways that would transform the characters as well as the daily habits, the practical skills, and the self-expectations of the less fortunate, and thereby allow them to be successfully absorbed into the mainstream. That is, the Hull House women's initial purpose was to practice a one-sided hospitality of *noblesse oblige* that assumes the cultural and personal superiority of the more-fortunate to the less-fortunate, and that suggests that all the former can and should learn from the latter is the specific needs that must be met and the attitudes and habits that must be overcome for the latter to become replicas of the former.

However, Addams's charitable workers soon learned the humility that made a genuinely mutual hospitality possible, and with it, real advances in the situation of the disadvantaged, as well as real growth of learning and much-needed transformations of heart and mind among the advantaged:

> The young woman who has succeeded in expressing her social compunction through charitable effort finds that the wider social activity, and the contact with the larger experience, not only increases her sense of social obligation but at the same time recasts her social ideals. She is chagrined to discover that in the actual task of reducing her social scruples to action, her humble beneficiaries are far in advance of her, not in charity or singleness of purpose, but in self-sacrificing action. She reaches the old-time virtue of humility by a social process. . . . She has socialized her virtues not only through a social aim but by a social process.[13]

What Addams and the other women of Hull House learned is that hospitality that can fulfill its aim of meeting the needs of its intended recipients at the same time positively transforms the would-be benefactor in important ways through a growth of knowledge-based respect for the other that sheds light on her own assumptions and habits, as these interactively influence a now shared situation.

Taken together, the experience-based pragmatist suggestions of Alaine Locke and Jane Addams suggest that the kind of hospitality that can make a transactional ground for the desirable and effective readjustment of individuals, their cultures, and their cross-cultural relations toward a preferable cosmopolitan future of justice and agapeistic love must be mutual and mutually transformative. It suggests that such mutual hospitality requires a deeper self-knowledge reframed by a fuller understanding of diverse groups' relational history and by shared, potentially sustainable hopes. If Locke and Addams are right about these matters, as I believe them to be, then understanding the meaning of mutual hospitality in transformative practice must become a focal concern for the grieving people of the world in these early days of the twenty-first century, when we are again so freshly learning the heart-breaking cost and the hope-destroying futility of an equally ancient, alternative stream of cross-cultural value traditions about which Martin Luther King warned us, including the multiplicity of antigroup hatreds, the widespread willingness of the fortunate to tolerate others' poverty and experiences of injustice, and the all-too-common efforts of the dominant and the desperate to assert control or at least their own "somebodiness" through violence. To rebind our communal wounds and to reenergize the only kinds of social hopes that are realistic and sustainable in this global context, we must celebrate and cultivate mutual hospitality as a crucially important cosmopolitan virtue for our times, one that can only be developed and sustained by building effective, self-transformative, hospitable habits.

The Self-Transformative Practice of Mutual Hospitality

At the most literal level expressed by the ancient traditions of many cultures, hospitality is opening one's "home" to the other: "Mi casa es su casa." This means providing safety, protection from the elements, warmth or coolness as the season may make desirable, food and drink, medical care if it is needed, the receptive presence of a host family, and expansive relational activities associated with leisure, such as wide-ranging conversation, storytelling, music, and dancing. In this context of an "open home," guest and host open their hearts and minds to one another, developing a relationship of trust that carries future expectations and responsibilities. By ancient custom, no harm may come to the guest in the host's home. Moreover, those who have "broken bread together" are responsible to care about one another, to tell the truth to each other, to give consideration to each other's future needs and requests.

These ancient traditions still carry weight today, though the expectations and responsibilities associated with opening one's "home" to another are imperfectly understood and not reliably fulfilled. International diplomacy still places great weight on these hospitality traditions, and they do in fact make a difference in humanizing antagonists to one another and in deepening the bonds among national leaders who are already friends. Interfaith worship ceremonies are grounded in and gain their efficacy through these same traditions of hospitality. The peacemaking and humanitarian relief efforts of nongovernmental organizations and people-to-people programs rely on these traditions, as do the very personal, one-by-one processes of breaking down racial, cultural, and religious barriers in diverse societies like America's through the development of friendships and ties of neighborliness.

Thus, these ancient and still effective practices of building ties of mutual understanding and solidarity through the traditions of hospitality suggest a moral and epistemological approach for intentionally guiding authentic, mutually transformative, cross-difference encounters grounded in loyalty to loyalty that can give rise to specific processes of progressive understanding, emergent solidarity, and respectful, mutually beneficial cooperation. Some theorists have suggested that we can and should adopt the other's worldview as our own as a strategy for making peace.[14] This seems to me both impossible as an antecedent requirement for relationship because of our own ignorance, and also inauthentic and thus not credible if we are genuinely committed to and operating within our own cultural framework. Seeing others' films, reading their books, listening to their music, and trying their cuisine are good ways to prepare for authentic cross-difference encounters, but we must recognize that these do not take us inside the others' "home" or separate us from our own "home world," no matter how eclectically it may be furnished. However, when we are invited into the others' "home" or honored by their acceptance of an invitation into our own, and both parties take the traditions of hospitality seriously, we have the opportunity to be welcomed "inside" to a place where breaking bread, communicative sharing, and a progressive evolution of trust make it possible to open our worlds to one another's entry and influence. By inviting someone into one's "home," I mean to suggest both literally bringing another into the place where one lives securely away from the public eye, and more expansively, allowing that someone into one's inner life, so that one shares one's beliefs, one's feelings, and one's stories of important experiences honestly and in a relatively unguarded way, while listening with respect and an openness to learn from the other, though not with the kind of commitment-free determination to have no impact on the other's life and circumstances that is attributed to Emmanuel Levinas; such an attitude, I believe, is impossible to maintain, and also frustrates the point of hospitality. "Entertaining" the other's telling of history, values, customs, rituals, meanings, and hopes does not require fully understanding them, let alone fully agreeing with them, but it does require respecting them, acknowledging them, and taking up responsibilities of trust in our handling of them and of the beginnings of solidarity and cooperation that may flow from them so far as we find mutuality—not identity—between our "world" and that of our host or guest. Thus, hospitality in this contemporary, intentionally guided application of the tradition must be mutual, active, forward-looking, and transactional in John Dewey's sense of the term, both a doing and an undergoing.[15]

Initiating such mutual hospitality in modern settings of everyday living is sometimes very easy. "Where do you come from?" opens up a very different line of conversation than the more typical American conversational move, "What do you do for a living?" It asks for roots: a place and time, a community, a formative nexus that continues to be important to the person one thus freshly encounters and seeks to engage. It asks not just for facts, but for a perspective, an experience of becoming as considered and presented by a more mature version of the person. It offers many points of contact and difference between two persons' streams of experience. Likewise, sharing answers to the question "Why are you here today?" can, in many circumstances in which diverse people have come to a common place for a common event, be the beginning of opening up a conversation about shared and differing values, needs, and hopes.

Offering hospitality deepened and expanded by such simple questions was the guiding theme for those of us who prepared to welcome five thousand New Yorkers on July 20, 2002, into an interactive, "Listening to the City" conversation about the future of Lower Manhattan, focusing on new developments radiating out from memorial ground at the site of the now empty grave of the World Trade Center. At a training the previous day for the nearly five hundred discussion facilitators from every state in our country and several other countries, our leaders reminded us of the importance of making our roundtables safe havens for shared expression of our ten guests' painful memories, passionate hopes, and creative ideas about how to actualize them. This was to be a powerfully symbolic occasion for public participation in future-shaping by bereaved citizens of one of the most cosmopolitan cities on Earth, embracing all of the world's languages and cultures, and facilitated by host-witnesses representing America's great diversity and the wider world's caring. That it came on the heels of various political leaders' announcements that the future shape of this memory-charged place would be determined by "experts" responding to a narrow set of persisting private interests that had been expressed in a set of alternative site design concepts that were released with great fanfare the week before, on which "Listening to the City" participants were asked to focus their comments, made this great symbolic gathering all the more painful, volatile, and in need of the love-power of mutual hospitality. Because this spirit of mutual hospitality ruled the day, this enormous, diverse body of citizen participants, many of whom lost loved ones on September 11th, and all of whom directly experienced the shock and grief of a world undemocratically transformed by it, were able to bear with one another through a long series of guided conversations and, eventually, to speak in one voice on behalf of the people's right to democratically determine the future meaning of this hallowed place—their place—a world-shared place of symbolic future-making. Because of the power of this unified citizens' voice, the original design concepts were withdrawn, a fast rethinking by political leaders began, and the necessity of allowing others— including school children and international architects—into the future-planning process became an operative principle.[16]

Many other experiences—including in my classes at Fordham University, in contexts of making and sharing music for larger purposes, and at international conferences framed by a shared love of philosophy or by a common cross-disciplinary concern—have shown me both the transformative power of an inclusive, cross-difference, mutual hospitality and the importance of consciously cultivating the currently rare skills that ground and multiply its power. In my classes in African American Philosophy and Native American Philosophies at Fordham University, many of the students experience their first "mixed race" textual and personal encounters in a conversational setting grounded in mutual hospitality, for which I am the teacher-facilitator. Although New York City is enormously diverse, many of its residents live in "racial," ethnic, and religious enclaves, as do the suburban students from the surrounding metropolitan region who make up a significant portion of Fordham's enrollment. Thus, although our students know one another's racial "faces" from television and from countless brief encounters in public settings, they typically know very little about one another's group histories, contemporary situations, and personal aspirations. Most of the canonical works of philosophy they have encountered previously at Fordham were written by European men in very different times and places, motivated by often unmentioned particular purposes, based on now outdated science, expressing their own specifically contextualized hopes; moreover, the words of these great thinkers are too often read as timeless and placeless, and as if they spoke more universally than any thinker does or can. Thus, my pragmatist classroom is a very different kind of academic experience for my students: they read a pluralistic set of texts and relevant current information in which the canon is sometimes critically challenged and sometimes reaffirmed though with a different framing; and they discuss them, both in reference to their contexts of origin and in terms of their potential for illuminating and guiding our own very different times, in a classroom conversation that emphasizes hospitably wrestling together with the texts while making learning about one another's lives and future visions part of the appreciative, critical, and reconstructive work of the course. These are life-expanding, ear-tuning, voice-strengthening experiences that affirm the reality of a complex, dangerous, forward-looking past in which still stirring cosmopolitan ideals were imperfectly realized; that display the reality by our mutual presence that the best of our ancestors' hopes and struggles were not in vain—and thus, that stir students' hopes in the possibility of a more humane, more mutually beneficial, more deeply democratic cosmopolitan future that they together can help to bring into being through their active, loving unity amidst their valued diversity.

That this possibility of a beloved cosmopolitan future is real, though very difficult to actualize, is part of what I learn every week though participating in the Mount Vernon Interfaith Choir, also known as "The Mayor's Choir" because it was brought into being through the personal vision and the commitment of staff time by Mayor Ernest D. Davis as part of a project to revitalize the poorest areas of our ethnically and economically diverse suburban city through creation of an arts district, to be launched at what would become the First Annual Third Street Arts Festival. One of America's first planned cities, Mount Vernon developed more than a hundred years ago around and between commuter rail corridors that connect this dense city of 75,000, speaking more than one hundred languages, to New York City, other cities, and rural towns and villages in upstate New York and nearby Connecticut. Unfortunately, one of these railroad cuts divides the city "racially" and economically, as perhaps it once was in-tended to do. Thus, Mount Vernon's citizens who live on "the other side of the tracks" are likely to be poorer, more at risk from drugs and violence, and more predominantly African American or Afro-Caribbean than are residents who live in other parts of the city. Third Street is the main east-west business corridor through this south side of town, and many of its shops are boarded up while others struggle to stay in business, even though their rents are very low. How-ever, Mount Vernon is also a highly "churched" city, including a diverse set of churches, temples, and synagogues, some of them very large and active, on the south side of town. Many of these churches, especially those with large African American congregations, are deeply involved in the Gospel music tradition, a hope lifting music born of the dual marriage of the spirituals that once inspired the struggle for liberation from chattel slavery with two other distinctively American musical forms, the blues and jazz—both of which W. E. B. Du Bois and Alain Locke once regarded as bad social influences, though they were even-tually reconciled with them and even came to find them inspiring cosmopolitan models and sites for cross-cultural communication. This Gospel music tradition is one of Mount Vernon's distinctive cultural heritages and continuing areas of active arts contribution, as is the poetry of social criticism and inspiration, and as are their rambunctious offspring, hip hop music and its sibling dance and visual arts forms. The mayor's concept was to make Third Street a center for infusion of civic pride and public funding in support of these distinctive art forms, including a Hip Hop Museum, while at the same time employing more typical economic redevelopment remedies, such as luring a national grocery store chain, PathMark, to build a "big box" store in the target area, as well as planning to "bridge the gap" with a plaza that would connect a new hotel and conference center, to be funded with help from China.[17]

To stimulate shared civic pride in Mount Vernon's distinctive cultural contri-butions, the mayor asked his Third Street Task Force to form an Interfaith Choir that would draw members from all of the city's churches, as well as all of its "races," generations, cultural backgrounds, and income levels, for the purpose of singing Gospel music together in inaugural celebration of this hopeful, ex-tremely difficult, visionary project of revitalizing the area's economy by empha-sizing its special connection with the arts. Such a diverse choir, made up of some of the city's best singers, musicians, composers, and directors, immediately as-sembled and began to rehearse under the gifted leadership of Maureen Wilson, a city employee whose other full-time professional commitment is to direct-ing, writing, and performing Gospel music. It was a powerful success, a site for mutual hospitality in which deep cross-difference communication and heal-ing amidst shared purpose began and continues to occur, three years, several awards, and countless performances around the New York metropolitan region later. We perform where we are asked and needed to come, including as partici-pants in an early morning ministry to "street people" and gang members that the city's churches have cooperatively begun. Funds from a CD soon to be recorded that will share the Mount Vernon Interfaith Choir's particular modes of hospitable, hopeful, cross-difference musical communication with a wider audience are expected to flow back into our city's project of economic revitalization, with a special focus on arts education and celebration in our Third Street Arts District.

Experiences at international philosophy conferences have also shown me that mutual hospitality has the love-power to allow participants to express, to hear, and to interactively reflect on how to transform some of the great contemporary tensions among the world's nations and cultures. The periodic World Congresses of Philosophy are, as one might expect, wonderful opportunities for scholars from enormously diverse "racial" and cultural backgrounds as well as tensely linked geopolitical locations to come together through the hard work of host countries on the hospitable ground of their common commitment to the work of philosophy, and both in formal sessions and in conversations in corridors that may continue over dinner to share both common and startlingly different perceptions of the world and of the values and ideas that should guide its becoming. I have found that interdisciplinary conferences with international participants drawn by their interest in the common theme can be even richer opportunities for cross-difference exchange, provided that a commitment to inclusive, mutual hospitality is maintained by those playing the various "host" roles in spite of all provocations. I was playing such a "host" role as chair of a session at a conference on democracy in August 1999 that was organized through the hard work of gifted scholars at the Jagiellonian University in Krakow, Poland, and cosponsored by the Friedrich Naumann Foundation, during the days when American planes were bombing areas of Yugoslavia as part of a futile international attempt to force out the Serbian dictator, Slobodan Milosevic.[18] One of the participants who sought my recognition to speak from the floor was a scholar from Serbia; and even though I had expressed in my own earlier paper certain criticisms of the incompleteness of America's realization of democracy and the impact on other nations of these shortcomings, this Serbian colleague treated me as the symbolic embodiment of America in denouncing the bombing, refusing to cut off his remarks until he was finished, after perhaps twenty minutes. Perhaps because I listened calmly, others waited for him to have his say, and later in the conference, we were able to converse warmly together over breakfast about the particular difficulties of multicultural cooperation in the Balkans and in other parts of Europe, as contrasted with related challenges in America; I think he found our exchange as memorable and as illuminating as I did. We may never meet again, but we know many other people to whom we may tell this story. Such an experience made it easier for me to converse in cosmopolitan mutual hospitality with colleagues from other nations at a recent Summer Institute in American Philosophy, at which they shared with me both their compassionate concern for America on September 11th and their fears about President Bush's determination to make a seemingly unlimited, functionally unilateral "war on terrorism." They reminded me once again that in the twenty-first century, grief and fear are globally shared, and thus, that our hopes and our collaborative strategies for realizing them must be democratic, inclusive, and diversely cosmopolitan.

The Fruits of the Practice of Mutual Hospitality: Cosmopolitan Hopes

In learning to transform ourselves and others through the love-powered practices of mutual hospitality, we can benefit from the guidance of the life examples and the still living words of earlier American pragmatists who wrestled with how to transform the meaning of "race" from an adverse limit of exclusive social valuation into a more open term affirming a shared heritage and a practical group unity within a larger ideal project of building a diverse, cosmopolitan world community. In this sense of the term, W. E. B. Du Bois, Alain Leroy Locke, and Martin Luther King, Jr., exemplify the possibility of being both a "race man" and a cosmopolitan visionary, though what this would mean in our times of grief and sorrow is a story for the now-living to write. Likewise, William James, Josiah Royce, Jane Addams, George Herbert Mead, and John Dewey exemplify the growth in wisdom, character, and meaningful experience that is the much-needed benefit to the "racially" and economically more powerful that comes from recognizing and acting from their own need to engage in mutually hospitable cross-difference cooperation with the less powerful. We who proudly call ourselves "Americans" today across the old "racial" lines that once divided us must learn a similar open-hearted humility toward the world's less fortunate nations, if we are to save ourselves from a future of chaos and despair by learning from the many peoples who have lived with these vulnerabilities for a much longer time, and who may have much to teach us about how to transform their causes and how to live in the meantime with their costs. In respectfully seeking the blessings of such individual and cultural "fusions" of experience and insight through sharing and cooperatively creating "culture goods" for wider, world audiences, as these earlier pragmatists hoped we would in the cosmopolitan future they envisioned for us, we would be acting with pragmatist piety within the hospitable traditions that many of the world's ancient and still living cultural traditions share. That is, we would be acting with deep appreciation for the heritage they and our other forebears have bequeathed us, and for their struggles that made it possible, while loyally recognizing that their times are not our times, and that narrow loyalties must be abandoned or reframed in light of a wider "loyalty to loyalty" if all of the great hopes for us and for our shared future that animated their lives in the past are to come to fruition.

Such a course of mutually transformative action on such a common ground gives us our best reasons for hoping that the terrible "burnt offering" of September 11th, with all its sad sweetness of remembering particular, wonderful people who died blamelessly that day, will leave a lasting, empowering deposit of agapeistic love in our characters and in our action-guiding worldviews, helping us to "think with our hearts," in the wise words of Native American Skagit elder Vi Hilbert. Through such a course of self-transformative and world-transformative action, each of us may hope to become more fully who I am and more than I am and better than I am, exemplifying the process of selective individuation in response to others' needs in times of crisis that John Dewey traced in Abraham Lincoln's growth of heart and mind from "racially" narrow to world-encompassing over the course of his career.[19] At the same time, our interlinked, mutual self-transformations may give rise to what Dewey called a genuinely "religious" spirit in the old Stoic sense of this Latinate term: a love-powered, respect-based "rebinding" of our lives together as neighbors, nations, and world citizens guided by shared cosmopolitan hopes that our spirit of unity amidst valued diversity will make possible a more inclusive, more just, and thus more peaceful future for our children's children. So let the hospitable sharing of food and drink, of story and song, of active help for the needy and cosmopolitan hopes for us all continue in a determination that, as King said, love may have the final word.

NOTES

1. Quoted in James Melvin Washington, ed., *A Testament of Hope: The Essential Writings of Martin Luther King, Jr.* (San Francisco: Harper and Row, 1986), p. 632.

2. See Greg Moses, *Revolution of Conscience: Martin Luther King, Jr., and the Philosophy of Nonviolence* (New York: Guillford, 1997), which explores connections of influence on love-power and nonviolence between Gandhi, Thurman, and King; see also Howard Thurman's *Jesus and the Disinherited* (originally published 1949; Richmond, Ind.: Friends United Press, 1981), which King read and began to borrow from as soon as it was published, and a posthumously published collection of Thurman's shorter writings, sermons, and speeches, *A Strange Freedom: The Best of Howard Thurman on Religious Experience and Public Life,* ed. Walter Earl Fluker and Catherine Tumber (Boston: Beacon Press, 1998).

3. See Philip Hallie, *Lest Innocent Blood Be Shed: The Story of the Village of Le Chambon and How Goodness Happened There* (New York: HarperPerennial, 1994).

4. See Peirce's 1893 essay "Evolutionary Love," in *Chance, Love, and Logic: Philosophical Essays* (New York: Harcourt, Brace and World, 1923), and James's *Varieties of Religious Experience* (1902), *A Pluralistic Universe* (1909), and *Essays in Radical Empiricism* (1912), all in *The Works of William James,* ed. Frederick H. Burkhardt (Cambridge, Mass.: Harvard University Press, 1975–88).

5. See Nel Noddings, *Caring: A Feminine Approach to Ethics & Moral Education* (Berkeley: University of California Press, 1984), and Rita Manning, "Just

Caring," in *Voices of Wisdom: A Multicultural Philosophy Reader,* 2nd ed., ed. Gary E. Kessler (Belmont, Calif.: Wadsworth, 1995).

6. See Abu'l A'la Mawdudi, "Political Theory of Islam," in *Voices of Wisdom: A Multicultural Philosophy Reader,* 2nd ed., ed. Gary E. Kessler (Belmont, Calif.: Wadsworth, 1995), an influential speech by an early-twentieth-century Sunni theorist and activist who also argued that Islam requires a form of participatory theo-democracy that includes women and that locates ultimate sovereignty in Allah. See also Abdullahi Ahmed An-Na'im, "Islam, Islamic Law, and the Dilemma of Cultural Legitimacy for Universal Human Rights," in *Applied Ethics: A Multicultural Approach,* 3rd ed., ed. Larry May et al. (Upper Saddle River, N.J.: Prentice Hall, 2002), for a contemporary discussion of Islam's way of framing the golden rule as a group difference-recognizing principle of reciprocity that can lead to a helpful reconceptualization of universal human rights, as well as to a loyally critical reconstruction of aspects of Shari'a that discriminate against women and non-Muslims.

7. I am indebted to Lucius Outlaw for his illuminating sessions on "Conservation" and related essays at the Third Annual Summer Institute in American Philosophy at the University of Vermont (Burlington), July 2000.

8. See "9/11 Bridged the Racial Divide, New Yorkers Say, Gingerly," *New York Times,* 16 June 2002, p. 25, which reports that in a *New York Times*/CBS News Poll, "a growing number of New Yorkers say that they have seen a remarkable change in race relations since the September 11th terror attacks at the World Trade Center," and that "for the first time in 14 years, a majority of respondents of all races to the poll said racial relations were generally good in the city."

9. Jason Hill's *Becoming a Cosmopolitan* (Lanham, Md.: Rowman & Littlefield, 2000) celebrates a postcultural cosmopolitanism's potentials while overlooking its dangerous misuses, about which Richard Rorty warned in *Achieving Our Country* (Cambridge, Mass.: Harvard University Press, 1998), as had Christopher Lasch some years earlier.

10. Leaders of Europe and Iran have all denounced the Bush administration's unilateral dictation of the lines and modes of struggle in an international "war on terrorism," as well as the multifaceted pressure it has placed on its presumed allies to exempt Americans from prosecution for war crimes in international courts that are just coming into being. See "European Union Urges Aspirants to Rebuff U.S. on World Court," *New York Times,* 14 August 2002, p. A11. Clearly certain factions of the Palestinian resistance to Israeli occupation have been hardened in their determination to use terrorist attacks against civilian targets by their sense that the Bush administration acts alone, without regard to their interests and without heeding others who plead their cause. See "Iranian President Says U.S. Leaders 'Misused' Sept. 11," *New York Times,* 14 August 2002, p. A1.

11. I am greatly indebted to Leonard Harris for my awareness and appreciation of Alain Locke's important legacy to current and future processes of intercultural peacemaking and world-shaping. See Leonard Harris, ed., *The Philosophy of Alain Locke: Harlem Renaissance and Beyond* (Philadelphia: Temple University Press, 1989) and *The Critical Pragmatism of Alain Locke: A Reader on Value Theory, Aesthetics, Community, Culture, Race, and Education* (Lanham, Md.: Rowman & Littlefield, 1999), as well as the central chap-

ter on Locke's contribution in my own *Deep Democracy: Community, Diversity, and Transformation* (Lanham, Md.: Rowman & Littlefield, 1999).

12. Quoted in John J. Stuhr, *Pragmatism and Classical American Philosophy* (New York: Oxford University Press, 2000), p. 631.

13. Ibid., p. 644.

14. I am indebted to Jim Garrison for bringing this suggestion to my attention.

15. For his most detailed explanation of what Dewey meant by the two-sided process of "doing" and "undergoing" that, in combination with reflection, makes up experience, see his *Experience and Nature* (originally published in 1925; Carbondale: Southern Illinois University Press, 1981). In his final works, including *Knowing and the Known* (originally published in 1949; Carbondale: Southern Illinois University Press, 1989), Dewey adopted the term "transaction" to express the mutual, transformative impact on all parties of sharing in an experience. For an insightful explanation and application by a contemporary pragmatist feminist of these conceptual tools that also draws on Du Bois and Locke, see Shannon Sullivan's *Living Across and Through Skins: Transactional Bodies, Pragmatism, and Feminism* (Bloomington: Indiana University Press, 2001).

16. See Edward Wyatt's series of articles on the struggle over who will design the future of Lower Manhattan, including (with Charles V. Bagli) "Officials Rethink Building Proposal for Ground Zero—Criticism during Forum—After Public Meeting, Planners to Give Process More Time and Look at Land's Use," *New York Times*, 21 July 2002, p. A1; "Slowing Down, at a Cost—Clamor for Fresh Visions of Ground Zero Could Delay Lower Manhattan's Recovery," *New York Times*, 22 July 2002, p. A1; "Even Critics Say Some Designs for Downtown Aren't So Bad," *New York Times*, 23 July 2002, p. B1; and "Further Designs Are Sought in Rebuilding of Downtown," *New York Times*, 15 August 2002, p. B1.

17. The story of how Mayor Davis succeeded in interesting the Chinese in this project is fascinating, yet simply told: during the darkest days of the Clinton administration, when very few American civic officials wanted to be seen with the president, Mayor Davis was one of the few who responded to an invitation to help President Clinton welcome China's vice premier to the United States. He pitched; they said yes. Planning is ongoing.

18. See the very interesting collection of essays presented at this conference, *Democracy in Central Europe, 1989–1999: Comparative and Historical Perspectives*, ed. Justyna Miklaszewska (Kraków: Meritum, 1999).

19. See Dewey's "Time and Individuality" (1940), in *John Dewey: The Later Works*, vol. 14, ed. Jo Ann Boydston (Carbondale: Southern Illinois University Press, 1988).

Afterword: A Conversation between Cornel West and Bill E. Lawson

Lawson: Now that the niceties are done, let's get to the issue of pragmatism and the problem of race.

West: Let's do it!

Lawson: Does the pragmatic approach have value in responding to the contemporary problem of race?

West: Well, pragmatism, in addition to its volunteerism, its fallibilism, and its experimentalism, is a philosophical orientation that highlights history, context, and problem solving. You can't talk about race unless you talk about history; you can't talk about race unless you talk about changing context and history; and you can't talk about race unless you are really trying to wrestle with it and, I believe, trying to ameliorate the conditions that white supremacy produces. So that pragmatism in many ways is, I think, the most ideal philosophical view. Now, of course one needs social analytical tools. You really need an analysis of capitalist economy; you need an analysis of the relation of the economy to the state; you need an analysis of the relation of state to the educational system and its relationship to civil society in general. But as a philosophical orientation, pragmatism is ideal; it's just so sad that for the most part pragmatist philosophers have evaded race.

Lawson: Why do you think that is the case?

West: I think that it is just quintessentially American. America in general has evaded the vicious legacy of white supremacy in its past and present. And most pragmatic philosophers tended to go hand and hand with the dominant orientation of that American evasion of wrestling with race. If a Martian were to come down to America and look at the American pragmatist tradition, they would never know that there was slavery, Jim Crow, lynching, discrimination, segregation in the history of America. This is a major indictment. This is one of the reasons that I am so excited about this book, in that you really do dig deep into the resources of pragmatism. You bring to bear some of its methods, its orientation, its preoccupation with inquiry in wrestling with America's rawest nerve, America's most difficult dilemma, namely, the vicious legacy of white supremacy.

Recorded November 20, 2003, MSU School of Communications. We would like to thank Dean James D. Spaniolo and Rich Tibbals, MSU College of Communication Arts and Sciences, for their assistance.

Lawson: But has not American philosophy in general evaded the question of race? Why should we expect more from pragmatism?

West: I think that evasion is certainly true. But pragmatism is a tradition that we expect more from. Because it really talks about wrestling with concrete realities in various historical contexts and trying to keep track of a certain kind of experimental improvisational nondogmatic orientation, but also producing some very discernible consequences. So we expect more out of pragmatism in a way, in American philosophy, than we do from logical positivism, analytical empiricism, phenomenology, existentialism, post-structuralism, deconstruction, and so forth.

Lawson: Do you think that is the reason some people are disappointed with Dewey's engagement with the problem of race?

West: I think so! We all know that Dewey is the great giant of American philosophy. We all know that as a person Dewey was an anti-racist. We all know that he played an important role in the founding of the NAACP. And yet, when it comes to his philosophic wrestling with various issues, he does not hit race head on. Here I think the Michael Eldridge essay that talks about the three moments and reflects on racial prejudice, as well as the piece by Gregory Pappas, validates what I am saying. I think the brilliant essay by Eddie Glaude is a powerful wrestling, because it shows that Dewey actually had resources that remained untapped. Eddie puts him in conversation with one of the greatest writers alive, Toni Morrison, which I think is quite useful in terms of a defense of the resources of Dewey as opposed to the practice of Dewey in relation to race. That's why I think Glaude's piece is a brilliant piece.

Lawson: You feel that Dewey could have addressed the problems of race more forthrightly.

West: That's right!

Lawson: Isn't his failure partly because of his being in America and an American?

West: Absolutely. I think that the great John Dewey never saw white supremacy as a major priority in his wrestling with philosophy and democracy. I think that is sad. Anybody who wrestles with democracy in the United States knows that white supremacy has contributed greatly to the arrested development of American democracy. So you can't really be wrestling with American democracy unless you also come to terms with its legacy rooted in slavery, Jim Crow, and so on. So in that regard I think, despite his greatness and his genius, it is a major silence, and I think that this text really shatters that silence. That is one of the things that make this text a major contribution to not just American philosophy but American thought in general.

Lawson: One important aspect of the Dewey tradition is the role of education. Some claim that the most important element in the fight against racism is education.

West: I deeply appreciate the wonderful essay by your co-editor Donald Koch and Scott Pratt's essay on education. I think they have much to say. I do not think that education is at the center of the problem of race in America. I think that it is a crucial component. But the fundamental problem of race in America is that most fellow citizens of European descent have a weak will when it comes to pursuing racial justice. It is an issue of will, and when you talk about structures and institutions in America it is an issue of power. So that the issue of will and power cuts much deeper than education. Education can make a significant contribution, but it still can't get at the will. We know that some of the most educated and sophisticated Americans have had a weak will toward racial justice anyway. They were masters of Homer, they knew Shakespeare backward and forward, they lived with Goethe, they carried Nietzsche around in their back pockets, and they still had a weak will toward racial justice. So we know that education can't be the key even though it is very important. I don't want to downplay it.

Lawson: This is in part a carryover of the Enlightenment understanding of reasoning.

West: That right!

Lawson: It is the belief that people reason wrongly because they lack knowledge.

West: I do not believe that for one minute. That's like believing that if the Nazis had listened more closely to Beethoven's Ninth Symphony, which is an indictment of European authoritarianism, if they had listened more closely, they would not have been Nazis. They loved the Ninth Symphony, but they went on and mistreated their fellow citizens and threw Jews in concentration camps anyway. Education does not cut that deep when it comes to will and power. You need something else. You need some serious organized pressure and power, and you need some leadership that can appeal not just to people's cognitive faculties but also to their hearts, minds, and souls in light of that organized power and pressure. This has been, of course, my critique of pragmatism.

Pragmatism has not come to terms with the existential dimensions of life, death, dread, despair, and disappointment; nor has it come to terms with the structural and institutional dimensions of life, which is where Marxism, Weber, Du Bois, Simone de Beauvoir, and other social theorists have been quite insightful.

Lawson: This leads us to a discussion of the role of race and in particular the concept of race. Does the concept of race have any contemporary value?

West: The text has a fascinating discussion between David McClean and Paul Taylor. I am so glad to read both essays. I think that David McClean has a very subtle argument to do away with race, but in the end it is not persuasive. I think that Paul Taylor has written the finest defense of still using race that we have. It is that good of an essay. It sidesteps all of the traps of essentialism; it sidesteps all of the traps of the old classical racial scholarship that argued that race actually existed. He responds to McClean, and while he recognizes the insights of McClean, he goes on to argue that the use of race, the deployment of race as a way of keeping track of certain realities of race, while socially constructed, is still lived and still experienced. Paul Taylor actually provides the kind of very refined understanding of social construction of race that I resonate with deeply.

Lawson: One of the things I do in the text is to discuss Booker T. Washington. I know that in the *American Evasion of Philosophy* you do not cite Washington. What are your thoughts on Washington and pragmatic thought?

West: I think that your defense of Booker T. just as a leader is the most powerful thing that I have read on him. I have always been very critical of him. I tended to highlight his conservatism. You acknowledge his conservatism, so you are able to embrace my criticism and still defend him. That is always the best kind of defense. Your essay is subtle in that it acknowledges the critique of him by Du Bois and others, but by building on Harold Cruse you are able to show what it means to pursue vital options under dire situations. And with Booker T. Washington, both in his life but also in his writings, not enough people really come to terms with his writing. I like your treatment of his writings in the essay; it shows that he was very clear about what his ends and aim were. He was not the kind of crass opportunist that he is often portrayed to be. I agree that he had a pragmatic sensibility.

I do want to make the distinction between being a leader with a subtle pragmatic sensibility versus being a pragmatic philosopher. I think that you would agree that he would not be a pragmatic philosopher in the sense that he does not write in relation to the tradition: James, Peirce, and Dewey, explicitly. Implicitly, that pragmatic sensibility is at work, and so one can still argue that he is a pragmatist without his being a pragmatic philosopher.

Lawson: That is my reading of Washington. He often said that he was a man of action, not words—and thank you for your kind comments on my essay.

West: To me it is the best piece I have seen. I think the reason why I did not include him in my *American Evasion of Philosophy* is because I do think that Dubois's relation to James and his relation to the world of ideas is much more intense and sustained than Booker T. Washington. I was really just looking at pragmatic philosophers as opposed to those leaders who had pragmatic sensibilities.

Lawson: Judith Green discusses the concept of hospitality, and Al Prettyman discusses the notion of civil smothering. Do you have any comments on these essays?

West: Those are fascinating pieces. Al, of course, goes back almost thirty years and is one of the founding fathers of black philosophy. That's important to say.

Lawson: He has allowed black philosophers to use his home for discussions for over twenty years.

West: That is right! In his essay he shows the persistence of white supremacist sensibilities—how deep it cuts and how it has always been a problem. That's one of the reasons why Dewey, and we should mention James as well, wrote his little letter to the Springfield newspaper against lynching and so forth, but it was only Josiah Royce who wrote a whole book on race in the American pragmatic tradition. One reason is that they believed in problem solving, but it seems as if they had hit a problem that could not be solved in America. Once they hit that limit, then that tragic dimension comes in, what Plato in the *Timaeus* calls *ananke*, the constraint that cannot be escaped; and when you are in a problem-solving tradition and you think you have a problem that cannot be solved, you are not going to spend a lot of time on it.

Lawson: We see that with our white colleagues when they come to the issue of race in their own writings.

West: Even our dear friend Richard Rorty, who I love dearly and respect deeply. And you ask, has there been sustained writing on race by Rorty? We know that he is an anti-racist—I know that personally, just as a friend, but I also know it from his history, his close relation to A. Phillip Randolph through his father, James Rorty, who was a public intellectual in his own right. But it is true also with Rorty; there is no sustained wrestling with the legacy of white supremacy as an object of serious reflection and investigation.

And yet we know the problem of race cuts so deep, and this is what Al Prettyman is able to show in his wonderful essay. I think that the call for the kind of love generated, love centered, mutual hospitality in Judith Green's work—I found it actually quite insightful and inspiring; of course, in my own tradition as a Jacobean Christian with a pragmatic sensibility, I resonated with it deeply. It is just that we must ensure that it does not remain at the level of moralism or simply spiritual edification. We've got to be politically, historically, and socially engaged in very concrete analysis of our historical moment. This is my Gramsci influence here. And we have to be organized and mobilized with different forces in the society so that the spiritual edification and the moralism may play a role in how we organize, how we try to galvanize forces in our society. But we have to have very sharp analytical tools. We have to have that historical, contextual, nondogmatic orientation to the problem; and we have to be also very aware of the operations of power.

Lawson: Can you say elaborate a little more on the concept of *ananke*?

West: Remember in the *Timaeus,* in his cosmology, where the demi-God has to work pre-existing material. That is the *ananke.* So the gods themselves have limits that they have to come to terms with, whereas the Christian God creates out of nothing. Plato's God creates over against that pre-existing material, that limit, that constraint, that *ananke.*

Lawson: How does this relate to the problem of race and racism?

West: There is a sense in which race functions as a kind of *ananke* in American society. It is so difficult to deal with, and it cuts so deep, that people just assume it's always already there. And people who want to go on as if they are actually solving problems focus on other problems rather than this one. Of course, as people who are morally committed to wrestling against all forms of unjustified suffering and evil, as well as black folk who have to live it, we have to begin with the *ananke.* That's where you get the kind of movement that is presented in this book. This book is the most important representation of the movement in American philosophy, of the most indigenous philosophical tradition, dealing with the most difficult problem in American civilization: pragmatism in relation to race. That's why I am blessed to be part of the conversation.

Lawson: Thank you! Let me conclude with a question I think some people have about your "public" activities. How do you situate your "rap CD," the movie, and other public appearances in your work as a pragmatic philosopher? What do you see these practices doing?

West: That's a very interesting question. There is the very nice quote by Al Prettyman at the beginning of his essay that sums up my feelings about democracy.

Lawson: Let me find the quote.

West: For me democracy is a mode of being in the world; it is not just a form of governance. Democracy is a form of being in the world. At the center of that form of being is the free and enriching communion that is wedded to the art of full and moving communication. And my passion to communicate leads me to be multi-contextual. The academy is one context, television is another, the church, the mosque, and the synagogue another, radio is another, the streets another, the labor movement another. I am honorary chair of the Democratic Socialists of America, that's another. I move from one context to the next because of my passion to communicate. But I attempt to do it in such a way that I always deploy the deliberation experiment mode of inquiry that pragmatism highlights. For me the most democratic thing to do is to pursue the passion of communicating from text, from CDs, from whatever, to make the message known, and to try to convince and persuade persons.

Lawson: You see all of the activities as part of the commutative element of pragmatism?

West: Absolutely! For me it is profoundly Deweyan in terms of my own witness. Now of course in the end my Jacobean Christian view cuts much deeper than my pragmatism; that is to say in the end, when it comes to where I stand, what my bedrock is, it is the tragic comedic sensibilities that you get out of Chekhov, and it is a very threadbare notion of hope connected to loving one's way through the darkness that I get out of the Christian narrative.

Lawson: I have the quote from Prettyman's chapter: "Democracy . . . a name for a life of free and enriching communion . . . will have its consummation when social inquiry is indissolubly wedded to the art of full and moving communication."[1]

West: That is the story of my life right there, brother!

Lawson: That statement should be the last line of this interview.

West: Absolutely.

Lawson: That's a great note to end on! Thank you!

Note

1.   John Dewey, *The Public and Its Problems;* see p. 177 of this volume.

Contributors

Michael Eldridge teaches at the University of North Carolina, Charlotte. He is the author of *Transforming Experience: John Dewey's Cultural Instrumentalism.*

Eddie S. Glaude, Jr., is Associate Professor of Religion at Princeton University. He is the author of *Exodus! Religion, Race, and Nation in Early Nineteenth Century Black America,* editor of *Is It Nation Time? Contemporary Essay on Black Power and Black Nationalism,* and co-editor of *African American Religious Thought.*

Judith M. Green is Associate Professor of Philosophy and Faculty Associate in the Department of African and African American Studies at Fordham University. She is the author of *Deep Democracy: Community, Diversity, and Transformation* and *Pragmatism and Social Hope: Deepening Democracy in Global Contexts.*

D. Micah Hester is Assistant Professor of Biomedical Ethics and Humanities at Mercer University School of Medicine. He is the author of *Community: Pragmatist Ethics in Medical Encounters* and co-editor of *Computer and Ethics in the Cyberage* and *Dewey's Logical Theory.*

Donald F. Koch is Emeritus Professor of Philosophy at Michigan State University. He is editor of three volumes of John Dewey's previously unpublished lectures: *Principles of Instrumental Logic: John Dewey's Lectures in Ethics and Political Ethics: 1895–1896; Lectures on Psychological and Political Ethics: 1898;* and *Lectures on Ethics: 1900–1901.*

Bill E. Lawson is Professor of Philosophy at Michigan State University. He is co-author of *Between Slavery and Freedom,* editor of *The Underclass Question,* and co-editor of *Frederick Douglass: A Critical Reader* and *Faces of Environmental Racism.*

David E. McClean is president of the Society for the Study of Africana Philosophy and president of Polinitics, a consultancy specializing in business and organizational ethics.

Gregory Fernando Pappas is Associate Professor of Philosophy at Texas A&M University. He has presented numerous papers and written articles on topics in

American philosophy and racial questions. He is working on a book on John Dewey's ethics and moral experience.

Scott L. Pratt is Associate Professor and Head of the Philosophy Department at the University of Oregon. He is the author of *Native Pragmatism: Rethinking the Roots of American Philosophy* and co-editor of *The Philosophical Writings of Cadwallader Colden*.

Alfred E. Prettyman teaches at Ramapo College of New Jersey. He is the editor of *U.S.: The Intercultural Nation* and is a contributor to *The Encyclopedia of African-American Culture and History*.

John R. Shook is Associate Professor of Philosophy and Director of the Pragmatism Archive at Oklahoma State University. He is the author of *Dewey's Empirical Theory of Knowledge and Reality* and is co-editor of the forthcoming *Blackwell Companion to Pragmatism*. He is webmaster for the Pragmatism Cybrary.

Paul C. Taylor teaches in the Departments of Philosophy and American Ethnic Studies at the University of Washington. He is the author of *Race: A Philosophical Introduction*.

Cornel West is Class of 1943 University Professor of Religion at Princeton University. He is the author of many books including *The American Evasion of Philosophy; The Future of the Race* (with Henry Louis Gates, Jr.); and the best-selling *Race Matters*. He won an American Book Award in 1993 for his two-volume work *Beyond Eurocentrism and Multiculturalism*.

Index

community, 11, 79–81, 87n5, 104–105, 207
conflict resolution, 52
Confucianism, 207
consensus, 54
"Conservation of Races, The" (Du Bois), 144, 190, 193, 209–10
conservatism and conservatives, 63, 146
context, 25, 26, 167
contingency, 90, 91, 97, 104, 114, 166
control, race and, 82–83
Coon, Carleton Stevens, 143
Correspondence of John Dewey, The, 11
cosmopolitanism, 151, 172, 205–14
"Creative Democracy—The Task before Us" (Dewey), 11
Crisis magazine, 13, 19
Crummell, Alexander, 209
Cruse, Harold, 126, 137
culture, 76, 81–83, 155, 157, 172

Darkwater (Du Bois), 197
Darwin, Charles, 96
Davis, Ernest D., 217, 223n17
death, 106, 108–109
decision making, 53, 99–100
deliberation, 16, 17; context and, 98; group, 53, 54; moral conflict and, 101; republicanism and, 55; values and, 58
demands, 42–44
democracy, 4, 24, 206; communication and, 44, 185; Dewey's philosophy of, 89–90, 109–10; education and, 48–49, 188, 195; hospitality and, 212–13; integration of minorities and, 50–51; justice and, 60; problem of evil and, 106, 115. *See also* citizenship
Democracy and Social Ethics (Addams), 212
Descartes, René, 192
"Development of American Pragmatism, The" (Dewey), 96–97
Dewey, John, 1, 4, 19–20, 30–31, 205, 220; on action, 97, 115, 116n20; on the American nation, 61–62; approach to inquiry, 5; attitudes toward race and racism, 12–15, 24, 32n4, 109–10; on deliberation, 101; on democracy, 44, 57, 177, 184; on education, 48, 51, 60–61, 68; on experience, 27, 59, 81; as a founder of NAACP, 22, 50, 69n6, 89; Gifford lectures, 97; on human agency, 96–97; on human nature, 34, 57, 94; on humility, 89; on knowledge, 164; lectures on ethics, 6, 40; on morality and moral conflict, 36, 81, 93, 95–96, 98, 99; on philosophy, 25, 27–28; political theory of, 55; problem of evil and, 102–109; relation of thought to ac-

tion and, 39; role of philosophy against racism and, 22–24; science and, 33, 166; on social change, 15–19; social philosophy, 49–50; tragic vision and, 114
Dewey, Roberta Grant, 12, 13
Dewey, Sabino, 12
difference, 80
disease, 106, 108–109, 142, 156
dogma, 58, 59, 62, 93, 145, 157
Douglass, Frederick, 139
D'Souza, Dinesh, 33
Du Bois, W. E. B., 6, 28, 69n3, 140, 174, 205; as ally of Dewey, 12–13; attitude toward racist policies, 128; on blues and jazz, 218; conservation of race and, 189–94, 209–10; contrasted with Booker T. Washington, 126; cosmopolitanism and, 220; critique of Booker T. Washington, 138; on democracy, 199; on equality, 195; influence of James, 200n4; on progress, 198; "vindication" concept of race, 143, 144–46
dualities, 99
Dusk of Dawn (Du Bois), 168, 197

Eames, Samuel, 28
Eck, Diana L., 185
economics, 15, 26, 44, 139
education, 4, 13, 198; coercive action and, 17; competition and, 37, 38, 64; equal opportunity and, 51–62; formal ("schooling"), 51, 62–68; industrial, 128–29, 134; reform of, 48; totalitarianism and, 49; Tuskegee Institute, 125; universal, 34, 45
Eldridge, Michael, 4, 6
eliminativist position, 74, 76, 83, 87; "ethnic cleansing" and, 155, 157; rejection of, 163, 168–69, 172, 173
Emerson, Ralph Waldo, 90, 102, 104
Engel, Michael, 65
Enlightenment, 152, 153, 154, 155
environment, transformation of, 38, 86
Epictetus, 208
epistemology, 30
equal opportunity, 44, 49, 51, 62–68
equality, difference and, 195–99
essentialism, 83, 168, 173, 175, 209; persistence of, 150; "racialism" as, 74
ethnicity, 74, 80, 143, 152; cult of Reason and, 154; eroticism and, 173; "ethnic identities," 153, 156; genealogy of concept of, 170
ethnocentrism, 3, 139, 161n15, 179, 180
eugenics, 144
Eurocentrism, 153
evil, problem of, 102–109

ontology, 83–86, 164
opportunity, freedom of, 49, 60
optimism, 103
Otten, Terry, 111, 112
out-groups, 179, 180
Outlaw, Lucius, 74, 86, 150–59, 172
Outlawry of War campaign, 17, 18

Pappas, Gregory F., 4
Peirce, Charles S., 1, 118n43, 145, 204–205; on anomalies, 2; on beliefs, 167; scientific community and, 39
pessimism, 102, 103, 105, 118n43
philosophy and philosophers, 22, 25, 31, 44, 103, 166; blindness to racism, 50; communal role of, 30; "distance" and "closeness" of, 27–31; public tasks and, 177; racism as subject matter of, 28; World Congresses of, 219
Plato, 44, 53, 177
"playas," 136–37
Plessy, Homer, 127
Plessy v. Board of Education, 196
Plessy v. Ferguson, 209
pluralism, 51, 54, 60, 62, 143; concept of race and, 158; context of inquiry and, 164–65; "school choice" argument and, 66
political technology, 17, 18
positivism, 153
postculturalists, 211
postmodernism, 152
poverty, 53, 205
power, 82–83
pragmatism, 30, 126, 162–63; American democracy and, 89–90; cultural conservatism and, 146; as general approach to race problem, 3–4; holism of, 154; meaning of, 163–67; means and, 4–7; nonfoundationalism of, 11; origin and character of, 1–4; pluralism and, 80; racialism and, 167–68; theory and, 24–25
"Pragmatism and the Sense of Tragic" (West), 91
Pragmatism and the Tragic Sense of Life (Hook), 92
Pratt, Scott L., 6
Prettyman, Alfred E., 6
primitive cultures, 38, 43
Principles of Psychology, The (James), 77
private schooling, 63–64, 65
problem solving, 52
problematic, 5
Protestants, 64
Psychology (James), 2

public services, 44
Putnam, Hilary, 91, 99–101, 120n64

Quest for Certainty, The (Dewey), 93

race, 41, 80, 190–94; arguments for and against, 171–75; color-blind metaphor, 184; conservation of, 144–46, 150–59; cosmopolitanism of New York and, 217; as culturally conditioned term, 14; culture and, 81–83; ethnicity and, 155, 157, 170, 191; as fixed category, 15; history of idea of, 73; positive meaning of, 168–71; "race problem," 1, 131, 134; sexuality and, 170; social class and, 138, 169, 171; social constructivist view of, 147–50; theory of, 28; typologies of, 143–47; unreality of, 142–43
racial prejudice, 23, 33, 127; as acquired social characteristic, 19; Dewey's attitudes toward, 13–15; elimination of, 50; in employment, 85; remnants of, 45; "scientific" treatment of, 14–15; toleration of, 58. *See also* racism
"Racial Prejudice and Friction" (Dewey), 22, 89
racial profiling, 169
racialism, 73, 74, 171
racism, 1, 14, 16; aversive, 186n2; black accommodation to, 125; contextualism and, 24, 26; Dewey's concept of democracy and, 109–10; economics and, 26; "facts" and, 34, 35; as family inheritance, 65; general inquiry about, 31; individualism and, 168; methods of inquiry and, 26–27; pluralistic nature of, 27; pragmatic-empirical method and, 22; racial conservation and, 150–51; recognition of race as, 189; social difficulties of African Americans and, 36. *See also* racial prejudice
Randall, John Herman, Jr., 17–18
rationalism, 154
Ratner, Joseph, 17
Rawls, John, 53, 54, 76, 83, 143
Reagan administration, 65
Reconstruction period, 110, 132
reductionism, 23, 26, 147, 164
relativism, 105, 108
religion, 64, 185, 205, 207
Renewing Philosophy (Putnam), 91, 120n64
republicanism, 52, 53, 55, 57, 66
Rescher, Nicholas, 164
rights, 59–60
Roediger, David, 173
Romans, ancient, 43–44
Rorty, Richard, 108, 119n63, 147, 159n1

Index 237